Asymmetric Warfare

DATE DUE

	MAY 2 4 2012
	FEB 1 0 2016

To the memory of Dobrila Koliba,
who took my advice, and died because of it.

ASYMMETRIC WARFARE

THREAT AND RESPONSE IN THE TWENTY-FIRST CENTURY

ROD THORNTON

polity

Copyright © Rod Thornton 2007

The right of Rod Thornton to be identified as Author of this Work has
been asserted in accordance with the UK Copyright, Designs and Patents
Act 1988.

First published in 2007 by Polity Press
Reprinted in 2008

Polity Press
65 Bridge Street
Cambridge CB2 1UR, UK.

Polity Press
350 Main Street
Malden, MA 02148, USA

ISBN-10: 0-7456-3364-1
ISBN-13: 978-07456-3364-0
ISBN-10: 0-7456-3365-X (pb)
ISBN-13: 978-07456-3365-7 (pb)

A catalogue record for this book is available from the British Library.

Typeset in 10.5 on 12 pt Times NR
by SNP Best-set Typesetter Ltd, Hong Kong
Printed and bound the United States by Odyssey Press Inc., Gonic,
New Hampshire

The publisher has used its best endeavours to ensure that the URLs for
external websites referred to in this book are correct and active at the time
of going to press. However, the publisher has no responsibility for the
websites and can make no guarantee that a site will remain live or that the
content is or will remain appropriate.

Every effort has been made to trace all copyright holders, but if any have
been inadvertently overlooked the publishers will be pleased to include
any necessary credits in any subsequent reprint or edition.

For further information on Polity, visit our website: www.polity.co.uk

CONTENTS

PREFACE

This book is concerned with describing today's threats posed by the weak against the strong. It seeks to look at ways in which, in the twenty-first century, the powerful Western states can still, despite the vigour of their liberal democracies and the preponderance of their military forces, become subject to the will of much smaller and weaker opponents. These opponents will practise 'asymmetric warfare'. In any discussion of contemporary security and defence issues the term 'asymmetric warfare' rarely fails to make an entrance. Its ubiquity, however, seems to stand in some contrast to how much it is understood. Asymmetric warfare is, as one analyst puts it, a term 'shrouded in mystery'. The aim of this book is to attempt to de-mystify the concept and to show how asymmetric warfare manifests itself. *It seeks to answer the question, 'What does asymmetric warfare look like today?'* The point is that asymmetric warfare means something different in different realms of security and defence analysis. Those concerned with tackling terrorism may consider the terrorist to be an asymmetric foe practising asymmetric techniques. Those who work in the field of information warfare have their own ideas as to what an asymmetric opponent looks like and what practices they indulge in. Others who look at threats to Western air, naval and land forces likewise know their asymmetric enemy – from terrorist group to state actor – and their respective *modus operandi*. Thus asymmetric warfare is a broad church; it consists of a range of activities carried out by different actors in different spheres employing different means. The link that binds all these together is the element of the West being challenged in a *new* way by significantly smaller and less powerful entities. Its democracies and its military organizations are being threatened by the weak, using methods that were not possible to apply before or which did not work as well up until the very recent past. This threat from the asymmetric 'warrior' is new, and it is profound.

And because the threat is new and profound, then so must be the methods utilized to deal with it. Wherever an asymmetric threat is posed, then counters must be made. The new threat requires new responses by Western anti-terrorist forces and by Western air forces, navies and armies. During the Cold War the threats came from terrorists who had limited political aims and from a Soviet Union which offered a known quantity in terms of a 'symmetrical' opponent. Those days of quiet certainty are gone. Nowadays, and for the foreseeable future, the most pronounced threat to Western states and their militaries will come, in large part, from unknown quantities: from weak adversaries who make up for such weakness in their skill, dexterity, nimbleness, intelligence and, above all, in their zeal, their will to win. The challenge is for those charged with defending Western interests in a variety of fields and in a variety of battle spaces to introduce effective responses. It is a challenge specifically because there is always some robbing of Peter to pay Paul. Responses to the new terrorist threat can impinge on civil liberties and on international law. Responses to the asymmetric adversary in the military realm must not mean that capabilities are not maintained that can deal with some future 'symmetrical' adversary of the future. The balance has to be right. This book seeks to find where that balance should be. The Bibliography is select and contains only the most important and relevant sources. These items are cited by author's last name and short title in the notes; items not listed in the Bibliography are given in full at first mention.

ACKNOWLEDGEMENTS

Thanks go to the students and staff at the Joint Services Command and Staff College at Watchfield, Wiltshire. They supplied inspiration whilst keeping my feet firmly on the ground. Appreciation also goes to Chris Hobson and his staff in the JSCSC library for their helpfulness and their patience as I hung around among their shelves and stacks for far too long. Specific thanks, most notably, go to Dr Bettina Renz and to Dr Bertie Trevor; also to Dr Terry Terriff at the University of Birmingham, and to Professors Wyn Bowen, Geoff Till and Matt Uttley at the JSCSC. Their abilities to support, to direct, to give me time to work, and to keep me on the right track were invaluable. Professor Greg Kennedy did his invaluable bit on the golf course when it all became too much. Thanks also to the helpful advice provided by Louise Knight, Emma Hutchinson and Jean van Altena at Polity. The administrative support I received from the likes of Marea Arries, Tricia Carr and Susie Oldnall should not be forgotten, and neither should the work, down the years, of Angela Jones, Emma Sale, Erica Richardson, Claire Greenalgh and Dawn McKen.

1 WHAT IS ASYMMETRIC WARFARE?

Introduction

When the terrorists of September 11 struck, they struck with box cutters. They brought down four aircraft, destroyed the twin icons of American economic power, damaged the nerve centre of American military might, and killed almost 3,000 people.[1] They did this, these men armed only with box cutters, in the most powerful state in the world possessed of the world's most sophisticated military machine. They did this with an outlay of perhaps $500,000, causing $18 bn worth of direct damage.[2] They brought the United States – the super-power – virtually to a halt for a few days as panic took hold. In response, the superpower lashed out and invaded Afghanistan and introduced draconian anti-terrorist legislation. Apart from the lives lost, at least $700 bn has been spent on the 'war on terror' since September 11.[3] These few men with their box cutters had an effect out of all proportion to their profile and status.

The September 11 attack was perhaps the supreme example of what has come to be known as 'asymmetric warfare'. This phrase is one that is now dominating the lexicons of military and security forces around the developed world. At its simplest, asymmetric warfare is violent action undertaken by the 'have-nots' against the 'haves' whereby the have-nots, be they state or sub-state actors, seek to generate profound effects – at all levels of warfare (however defined), from the tactical to the strategic – by employing their own specific relative advantages against the vulnerabilities of much stronger opponents. Often this will mean that the weak will use methods that lie outside the 'norms' of warfare, methods that are *radically different*. It is this element of difference that lies at the heart of asymmetric approaches. It was the difference – the surprise factor – that contributed so much to the shock of September 11. As the Chairman of the Joint Chiefs, US Air Force General Richard Myers, said of the September 11 attack, 'You hate to admit it, but we hadn't thought about this.'[4]

Asymmetric approaches, of course, are themselves nothing new. The history of human conflict is replete with examples of 'asymmetric' thinking. Even the oldest written works on warfare refer to the principles of targeting vulnerabilities and of doing the radically different. The Chinese strategist-philosopher Sun Tzu, writing in the fourth century BC, clearly understood this philosophy when penning his seminal work, *The Art of War*. Focusing in large part on how the weak can defeat the strong, he wrote: 'An army may be compared to water, for water in its natural flowing avoids the heights and hastens downwards. So in a war, an army should avoid strength and strike at weakness [where] the soldier works out his victory in relation to the foe with whom he is fighting.'[5] His compatriot Sun Bin, writing in the second century BC, pointed out that, having studied the enemy, the good strategist will look to generate surprise by acting differently: 'When conventional tactics are altered unexpectedly according to the situation, they take on the element of surprise and increase in strategic value.'[6] Much later, in 1513, the military thinker Niccolò Machiavelli agreed: 'Whosoever desires constant success must change his conduct with the times.'[7] So, of course, did the hijackers of September 11. Asymmetric warfare is as old as warfare itself and as recent as the last terrorist outrage.

The lesson, even from the time that military tactics and strategies were first being written down, is that those weak players who wish to emerge with the situational advantage will have to apply those tactics and strategies that will act most effectively against a certain opponent at a certain time. Often this will mean adopting tactics and strategies that are very different from those normally employed by the stronger opponent.

History serves up several examples of what are perceived to be asymmetric encounters, where the weaker protagonist has used unusual methods – often based on what were new technologies at the time – to challenge the stronger. Certain examples have come to exemplify the art of asymmetric warfare. In AD 9, for instance, the Germanic chieftain Arminius was able to completely destroy three Roman legions because he went about 'unlevelling' the battlefield in his favour. His methods of warfare were at odds with the norms as practised by the Romans. Through a combination of psychological warfare, treachery, deceit, thorough knowledge of his enemy, and sound tactical thinking, Arminius was able to create a situation whereby the strength of the legions, so reliant on correct troop formations, was dissipated in long columns of march in difficult terrain. His tribal warriors could then harass and totally destroy the Roman formations.[8] At the Battle of Agincourt in 1415 English infantry proved victorious because they generated surprise through the effective employment of a new weapon, the longbow, against a superior French force dominated by knights on horseback. The French were being killed by arrows long before they could get close enough to engage the English forces.[9] Much later, the invention of both the torpedo and the submarine created scope for smaller naval powers to create significant impact on much larger maritime foes.[10]

Closer to our own times, the effectiveness of the smaller, weaker protagonist – or what will henceforward be called the 'asymmetric adversary' – has been most evidently apparent in the actions of sub-state actors such as terrorist groups. Among sub-state asymmetric actors, though, we must also include guerrillas and insurgents. Warfare against such opponents has been occupying the militaries of many a large power since the time of Sun Tzu, and probably from long before. The aim of the mobile and flexible guerrilla/insurgent has always been to exploit their stronger enemy's immobility and inflexibility in terms of their tendency to rely on fixed positions, their organizational conservatism, and their desire to fight set-piece battles.[11] Such tactics were most evident in Europe in what is perhaps the most famous guerrilla campaign of all time as Spanish irregulars crippled an entire Napoleonic French army.[12] More recently, in Vietnam in the 1960s and 1970s, the asymmetry was more apparent, but the result much the same. And here it was not merely a question of superior tactical approaches employed by the Vietcong against US troops in Vietnam itself; it was also the way in which the Vietcong and their North Vietnamese allies exploited that most fundamental vulnerability of their opponent by targeting public opinion in America itself. Thus, the US 'defeat' came about not so much through battlefield reverses as through the way that domestic pressure came to be applied on US politicians to bring their troops home.[13] This aspect of attempting to undermine domestic support is one copied by the familiar asymmetric adversaries of today: the likes of Al Qaeda and the Iraqi insurgents. This particular approach will be apparent in many cases described in this book.

Of course, when weaker opponents employ radically different means of conducting warfare, a sense of unethical behaviour can be engendered. The side that does not initiate the change alludes to an 'unfairness', an infringement of the laws of war as they exist at the time. The French knights at Agincourt thought Henry V's use of the longbow 'despicable'.[14] The British, too, with their emphasis on the battleship as ruler of the waves, could not countenance the early German use of the submarine and thought it 'underhand'.[15] Even today, asymmetric approaches have been seen by one US military seat of learning as 'a version of "not fighting fair"'.[16] And few, it seems, in the West would apply the adjective 'fair' to the actions of terrorist groups.

In reviewing such examples of asymmetric warfare, it needs to be borne in mind that *asymmetric* does not mean *unequal*. 'Symmetrical' implies a mirror image; sometimes that image can be smaller, but nonetheless a likeness exists. 'Asymmetrical' implies a relationship that cannot be considered to be alike. If one side in a conflict, for example, has lots of tanks and its opponent far fewer, then the battle would still be symmetrical. As Christopher Bellamy notes, 'Whatever differences there may be in numbers and quality, conventional military forces are still designed, trained, and equipped to fight near mirror images of themselves; forces with broadly similar infrastructures. A true asymmetric conflict is where the means used are quite different.'[17] Roger Barnett confirms this aspect of difference: 'True asymmetry [involves] those actions that an adversary can exercise that you either cannot or will not.'[18] And here it is useful to point out that asymmetric techniques can also be applied by the *stronger* power. The US, for instance, dropped nuclear bombs on Japan in 1945 in a truly asymmetric exercise. It is the purpose in this book, however, to concentrate only on those aspects of asymmetry that are most pertinent to the current security situation: i.e. how the weak today will be challenging the strong. In this book 'the strong' are taken to be the Western liberal democracies – and specifically the United States – that emerged 'triumphant' from that most symmetrical of encounters, the Cold War.

Having considered some examples of asymmetric warfare in history we must be aware that it is only recently that the adjective 'asymmetric' has been retrospectively applied to them. Much of the process of looking back and then using the word 'asymmetric' to describe past military engagements has come about because of the emphasis today on the subject of 'asymmetric warfare'. This phrase has now become ubiquitous. It can be readily found, not only in the pages of books, journals and magazines devoted to military matters, but also in more mainstream media. In such circles it has been called the 'term du jour' and the 'new buzz phrase of the moment'.[19]

But why has it achieved such currency? Obviously, acts of international terrorism have brought the term to the attention of a larger audience; outrages such as that perpetrated on September 11 are new, and demand our attention. This is asymmetric warfare in the civilian realm. But the use of the phrase had already, for several years prior to 2001, been prevalent among a *military* audience. This was because by the 1990s it was obvious that there existed a variety of factors, more than at any time hitherto in the history of human conflict, that were creating unique conditions allowing small, weak players – the asymmetric adversaries – to have great effect on their stronger foes in distinctly new and profound ways. These effects could be felt both by military actors on battlefields and by civilians in their own homelands. These new factors that are crucial to the emergence and the importance of the asymmetric threat today – from both state and sub-state actors – can be seen to be the following: the current difference in military potential; the new missions being undertaken by Western forces; the new antagonisms that exist in the world; the pronounced sense of casualty aversion now extant; the increase in the power of media images; the vulnerability created by the current reliance on information; the greater availability of weapons, and the general increase in the West's sense of moral rectitude.

A new difference in military potential

There is now a huge disparity in the capabilities of the military arsenals of the world's 'haves' and 'have-nots,' be they state actors or non-state actors. For the 'haves' – the Western liberal states and, of course, the United States in particular – now possess extremely powerful military organizations. These organizations were shaped by a Cold War that set Western scientific know-how against that of the Soviets to create a dynamic that pushed forward the boundaries of military technology. The constant drive for the next cutting-edge weapons system helped the Soviet Union down a road to economic collapse and left the United States with an unrivalled lead in military power. The US now looks to high-tech systems to provide its forces with information dominance, unparalleled command and control networks, unrivalled weapons accuracy and unmatched firepower. Currently, such technologies as Unmanned Aerial Vehicles (UAVs) and Precision Guided Munitions (PGMs) provide supreme war-winning potential, something shown to great effect in the wars in Iraq. If these recent conflicts have taught the world anything, it is that the US cannot be challenged on an open battlefield. In a symmetrical conflict where tank faces tank, aircraft faces aircraft, and ship faces ship, it is no contest; the US and its close allies will win every time. Thus any state or sub-state actor who wishes to stand in military opposition to the US must adopt strategies and tactics radically different from those employed by the superpower.[20] As the former US Secretary of Defense, William Cohen, pointed out, the post-Cold War world which promised so much in terms of peace in the end produced a 'paradox [whereby] American military superiority actually increases the threat of . . . attack against us by creating incentives for adversaries to challenge us asymmetrically'.[21] And the concomitant, of course, of the fact that there is this new thinking abroad among those who are militarily weak is that the militarily strong then have to think – and think hard – about new ways to defend themselves. They have to be able to respond to the asymmetric adversary.

New missions

There is undoubtedly a disparity in military potential across the world. However, the disparity has been somewhat nullified by the fact that the powerful armed forces of the Western liberal democracies are being used more than ever before on expeditionary operations. Such operations are taking the West's armed forces where they were never really designed to go. The troops and armoured vehicles, for instance, of the United States and its allies are now having to operate in what is known as 'complex terrain', such as urban areas and mountainous regions. In such environments their combat power is markedly reduced (see chapter 6). Western warships, built to undertake missions out in the open oceans, are now being asked to operate more in littoral regions, and thus in areas where they are far more vulnerable (see chapter 5). Top-of-the-range Western fighter aircraft, designed for the most part to deal with high-level bombers and other fighters, are now increasingly being tasked to support ground troops. In doing so, they must fly lower and thus expose themselves to weapons they were never meant to cope with: anti-aircraft artillery and shoulder-launched missiles (see chapter 4). Military systems designed in the Cold War to function in distinct areas or on distinct terrain find themselves exposed and vulnerable in new battle spaces that actually suit the weaker, asymmetric adversaries who themselves lack warships, aircraft and heavy land forces.

New antagonisms

In today's world, overarching global antagonisms have a different hue. The Cold War's painful dichotomy between Soviet Bloc and 'Free World' has been replaced by less defined animosities, but ones that are often very powerful nonetheless. These have led to, and will yet spawn, an increased level of asymmetric thinking by possible foes of the West. At the top of the conflict spectrum, certain states may develop as threats to the US and its closest allies. These, seeing how powerful the US is, will be forced to think along asymmetric lines. China, for instance, is a rising power, but also one which will need to apply something other than symmetrical approaches if it is to emerge, as it patently seeks to do, as a credible future military challenge to the US. As Robert Kaplan puts it, 'In Iraq the insurgents have shown us the low end of asymmetry . . . but the Chinese are poised to show us the high end of the art.'[22]

The most pronounced sense of antagonism, however, and the one which brings asymmetric warfare truly to the forefront of analysts' consciousness, is that existing now between extremist elements within the Muslim realm and the West. This has led in large part to the current wave of international terrorism. A sentiment now seemingly exists within parts of the Islamic world (or *ummah*) that the West is impinging more and more on Islamic values. Through the process of globalization (or McDonaldization/Coca-Cola-ization, as some would see it), the feeling is growing that Western mores and culture – and in particular those of the United States – are advancing in a pseudo-imperialistic enterprise that is supplanting indigenous mores and culture.[23] And, as with any such imperial expansion, hatreds are naturally engendered. As Eliot Cohen elegantly puts it, the antipathy that the American 'empire' brings upon itself 'stems from the swirl of hostility to the colossus'.[24]

This hostility is stoked also by several specific factors beyond the supposed iniquities of globalization. There is the West's support for Israel.[25] There is the presence of Western troops in many parts of the Middle East, troops that are seen in some quarters as the vanguard of a latter-day crusade. Al Qaeda, for instance, first came to prominence as an anti-American organization in its moves to rid Saudi Arabia of 'infidel' US troops. For after the First Gulf War (1990–1)

US troops remained behind in Saudi Arabia in order to deter any further Iraqi aggression. Having Christian soldiers based on 'holy' Saudi soil was anathema to many in that country who felt it their religious duty to take action to correct the insult. Among them was one Osama bin Laden. He took the view that the dishonour to his country and to Islam in general meant that it became 'the duty of every good Muslim to wage Jihad' against the US.[26] This was Al Qaeda's principle *raison d'être* in the 1990s – to try and force US troops to leave Saudi Arabia.[27] As part of its campaign in Saudi Al Qaeda operatives bombed a US barracks at Khobar Towers in Dharan in 1996, and later struck the US embassies in East Africa in 1998.[28] Such actions *appeared* to work: US forces had left Saudi Arabia by 2003.[29] They still remain, though, in other parts of the Middle East, and their presence continues to generate considerable enmity among many Arabs and Muslims in general.

This hostility has more recently manifested itself in an increased desire amongst radical Muslims – or, more correctly, Islamists[30] – to kill US citizens in particular and Westerners in general, *wherever* they happen to be. This desire to strike is driven by a sense of supreme *will* among Islamists – exemplified by the number of suicide bombers – that seems never to have been present before on such a scale. Thus, besides September 11, Western interests, from Bali to Baghdad, from Morocco to Madrid, and from Istanbul to London, have been the target of Islamist bombers. Many of them have been willing to commit suicide in the process.

The level of will apparent now in many Muslim communities to commit outrages against Westerners not only allows for the execution of violent *action*; it also allows for considerable *inaction*: Islamists can be seen to display great patience. The patience is there for the planning of terrorist operations that can take years to bring to fruition, and the patience is there to allow time for the West to drop its guard and with it its sense of vigilance. In contrast, patience is a quality considerably lacking now in the Western world. The powers want all conflict to be a matter of the swift, clinical use of force. We lack the *will* to create the patience to prosecute lengthy campaigns. There is seemingly a new and profound difference in the mental approach to conflict between Islamists and Westerners. The psychological fortitude of the 'strong' powers, with their desire to have the duration of wars measured in hours rather than years, stands in sharp contrast to that of their newly prominent Islamist adversaries, who expect their 'wars' to last decades, or, indeed, however long it takes (see chapter 2).

Casualty aversion

The Western powers have no patience for long wars. Neither can they abide the casualties that long wars generate. There is the general sense that, over recent years, the West has become 'soft'.[31] At one and the same time as the US and its allies have become supremely militarily preponderant, there has appeared what perhaps can be seen as an 'End of History' malaise.[32] The American academic Francis Fukuyama, in his famous article written at the end of the Cold War, was of the opinion that, because the liberal democracies had triumphed over communism in that Cold War, then the world must have reached the broad, sunlight uplands of peace and prosperity such that nothing significant should ever happen again in world history. Wars and major political disputes should be things of the past. And thus, if the liberal democracies have triumphed, what is there left to fight for? If 'freedom' has emerged victorious, then what is there left to die for? In the post-Cold War years it became apparent that it was becoming difficult to generate, among the governments and peoples of the liberal democracies, the resolve to conduct military operations and to accept the damage, destruction and death that went with them. Not only was this a question of 'friendly' casualty aversion – whereby states become reluctant to sacrifice their sons and daughters in conflicts[33] – but it was also a question of the need to avoid the 'collateral damage' of non-combatant deaths, and even to avoid inflicting casualties among the 'enemy' as well. We now, supposedly, fight only 'wars of choice' – where true national interests are only peripherally at stake – and so we strive to have them 'bloodless'. In the USA, for instance, there was created what Thomas Weiss once called 'a zero casualty foreign policy'.[34] It is a policy, moreover, enhanced by the increasing availability of air power and its technological promise to make war a clinical, sanitary exercise in which the number of deaths would be severely circumscribed and the risky commitment of ground forces need not occur. Tremendously accurate PGMs would be available to reduce the chance of collateral damage, and there would be UAVs on hand to keep even pilots out of harm's way (see chapter 4). A situation had been reached wherein death and destruction were seemingly no longer central to conflict; they had no place in an era where there should be no 'history'.

It appears then, to many an enemy of the liberal democracies, that they lack resolve. Here is a vulnerability to target. In appearing 'soft', the countries of the West are probably attracting a greater use of violence by their much smaller opponents of whatever ilk – terrorists or insurgents (or possibly state actors in the near future). The asymmetric adversary will seek to home in on this weakness that sets such store by human life, and will engineer scenarios that put lives at risk: both on the battlefield and off it. For we are now plainly shocked by the pain of death, and are more shocked the closer such pain is to our homes and hearths. It is this *shock* that asymmetric adversaries will be continually trying to generate. They will always be working to the formula that for many years terrorists have been applying: *impact = shock × damage × visibility*. Impact is thus related to shock: the more shocking, the more impact. To this end, there has been, and there will be, more targeting of non-combatants by asymmetric adversaries. In the case of sub-state actors this will occur especially in the homelands of the liberal democracies as *international* – as distinct from indigenous – terrorism becomes more of an issue. This targeting policy establishes them as something new and different (see chapter 2).

The *impact* created by asymmetric adversaries in their mission to inflict casualties can result in two specific effects. First, it can maintain the status quo. When it comes to issues where the strong Western powers wish to make changes that suit their strategic interests, they can be *deterred* from doing so by the threat of casualties. Secondly, weak actors can bring about strategic change – they can *coerce*.[35] Small states and even sub-state groups such as terrorist organizations can, with only a small outlay, create inordinate advantage against much larger foes simply because of the fear of casualties. They will be hoping to do what all asymmetric warriors seek to do: create strategic effect from actions at the lowest tactical level. The prime example of such coercion was seen in Somalia in 1993. Here the United States, in the wake of the loss of eighteen of its soldiers in the 'Black Hawk Down' incident, was forced to abandon its original mission and not only leave Somalia, but actually also to abjure involvement in the affairs of the continent of Africa for several years afterwards.[36] The decision, according to Osama bin Laden, showed 'the weakness, feebleness and cowardliness of the US soldier who fled in the dark of night'.[37] And when the Somalia episode is allied to the fact that, seemingly, a few Al Qaeda operatives were able to force the United States to abandon its bases in Saudi Arabia, then there seems to be a clear message to disaffected but weak players in the Muslim world: 'kill a few Americans and strategic consequences can result'. Whatever the actuality, a few casualties *appeared* to create profound strategic *impact*.

Care, of course, needs to be taken in assessing just how pronounced this idea of casualty aversion is. We have come quite a way since

Fukuyama in 1989. Saddam Hussein, for instance, thought that the fear of casualties would prevent the US invasions in both 1991 and 2003. It did not.[38] Moreover, the further away we move from the Cold War's end, the weaker seemingly becomes the sense of casualty aversion. There is a general feeling now that the US is not as casualty conscious as it once was, and that missions such as the current one in Iraq are a cause worth dying for. As Jonathan Foreman writes in 'The Casualty Myth': 'when important interests and principles have been at stake, the public has been willing to tolerate rather high casualties. In short, when we take into account the importance of the perceived benefits, the evidence of a recent decline in the willingness of the public to tolerate casualties appears rather thin.'[39] That said, however, it is not always the case that politicians can convince their publics that 'important interests and principles' are at stake.[40] The fact is that Slobodan Milošević was right in 1999 when he 'assessed that America's intolerance of casualties [is] one of [its] major weaknesses'.[41] He was convinced that the US would not commit ground troops for an invasion of Kosovo in 1999. To a large degree, he was right. US chariness over possible casualties was noteworthy.[42] Even in the most recent war and subsequent counter-insurgency operation in Iraq there is a sense that the public must be denied knowledge of the deaths that are occurring, both military and civilian. The Bush administration plays down the incidence of casualties in Iraq because it is clearly aware that 'political support is highly sensitive to . . . fatalities'.[43] US authorities, for instance, have taken radical and operationally debilitating force protection measures in places like Iraq and Afghanistan to keep their soldiers from harm.[44] The media have been kept out of places like Fallujah (see chapter 5) so that civilian suffering is not recorded. Additionally, Pentagon officials have 'objected strenuously to the release of photographs of the coffins of American service members returning home' from Iraq and elsewhere.[45] Indeed, since March 2003, a new US regulation has forbidden the taking or distributing of images of coffins of soldiers who have died overseas.[46] A similar, though not quite so draconian, situation exists in the UK. The number of injured servicemen from Iraq to have passed through the UK's military hospital could only be revealed when the Freedom of Information Act was employed. Senior politicians, in supposed efforts to avoid drawing attention to the number of British wounded, have been markedly remiss in visiting the injured.[47]

So it is still possible to recognize casualty aversion among the US and its allies. And the longer any operation continues, and the longer the list of casualties becomes, both friendly and civilian, in places like

Iraq, the more it contributes to the general lack of *patience*. Soon the call to 'bring our troops home' may become clearer and more compelling. The casualty aversion weakness may be less pronounced than it was, but it still exists. And it will remain a vulnerability that asymmetric adversaries can and will focus on.

The power of media images

There is an irony in that as Western states appear to be more conscious of casualties, modern technology has conspired to ensure that, at the same time, images of such casualties are being made ever more available. These images are becoming strategically crucial. As Bruce Hoffman notes, the weapons of the modern asymmetric warrior are 'not only the guns and bombs that they have long been, but also the mini-cam, videotape, television, and the Internet'.[48] This was clearly evident, for instance, in the way that the brief firefight in Somalia in 1993, nothing much in itself, actually led to policy changes in large part because the images of naked, dead Americans being dragged through the streets of Mogadishu appeared on television screens in the United States. According to the 'impact' formula, any increase in 'visibility' will naturally increase the impact. In Somalia, casualties *and* images meant much greater impact. Any sensible asymmetric player will ensure that any minor tactical actions against much superior foes are committed to film. In Somalia it was one man with a cheap video camera who produced enduring strategic results. The US military casualties were probably acceptable; the images of dead Americans were not.

One man or woman with a camera can show today what has never really been shown before: 'our' people dead and dying in full colour in far-flung and fly-blown corners of the world. Whether it is soldiers being blown up or hostages being beheaded, such images are designed, and designed very well, to undermine the resolution of their enemies. The trauma generated has caused Coalition partners – such as the Philippines – to pull their forces out of Iraq.[49] Weak state players, such as Yugoslavia and pre-invasion Iraq, likewise latched on to the power of images. Both regimes employed television pictures in many ways; showing, for instance, the results of misplaced NATO or Coalition bombing raids in attempts to give pause to the attacks of their enemy (see chapter 3).

The power of the image can be used not only to undermine the strong, but also to encourage the weak. The effects of any small attack carried out by asymmetric players can be leveraged into something with far greater propaganda impact through the help of media outlets, notably Internet sites. Whereas once all media organizations would be under the control of governments to some degree or other, nowadays they are not. Thus every bomb attack against US forces in places such as Iraq tends to be filmed and then put on the Internet or sent to a host of media outlets that are not government-controlled – Al Jazeera, for instance. The impact produced by such images in terms of showing how the powerful are capable of being humbled can be enormously successful both as a recruiting tool and as a means of gaining more general support across a broad constituency of latent support (see chapter 3).[50]

A new vulnerability

Any of the enemies of the Western powers who wish to create profound impact have had, over recent years, a plethora of opportunities opened to them. This is because the world, and the West in particular, is now experiencing an information 'revolution'. We have become reliant to a great extent on the unhindered passage of information as our societies have become beholden to the power of Information Technology (IT). Computers have come to occupy the central space in our lives. They manage the passage of information and generate control of everything from the electricity in people's homes to the world's financial markets. In the military realm, the current preponderance of the West's armed forces can be sourced to the efficiencies provided by the quality of today's IT capabilities. Without IT the Western way of life could possibly grind to a very quick halt, and the Western way of warfare would likewise be severely circumscribed. But the problem with the use of IT, of course, is that we have perhaps become *too* reliant on it. The irony is that what we in the West perceive to be great strengths appear to others as great vulnerabilities. As Pfaltzgraf and Schultz note, 'It is important to draw a distinction between weakness and vulnerability. Actors are vulnerable where they are weak. However, they may also be vulnerable at points that are indispensable to the maximization of their strengths. What is perceived by the superior power to be a strength may in fact become a weakness.'[51] This turning of strengths into vulnerabilities forms one of the fundamental bases of the thinking of the asymmetric warrior. And in this sense any important IT capability will stand proud as a tempting target for weak actors bent on creating impact *vis-à-vis* stronger opponents.

Many non-state actors with a grievance against the West have noted the reliance on IT as being a weakness. Those small organizations, including Islamist ones, intent on causing severe damage to Western interests have only to look to the capabilities of a laptop, a modem, and some fairly common hacking skills to realize considerable effect. Al Qaeda, for instance, seeing the possibilities on offer, created 'schools for hackers' in Pakistan in the 1990s (see chapter 2). Beyond groups, legion are the stories of young computer hackers creating mayhem in supposedly secure sites. In previous generations, no one single individual, let alone a spotty teenager in his bedroom or an Al Qaeda operative in the wilds of Waziristan, could hope to cause chaos in the higher echelons of governments, in financial institutions or in military organizations. Nowadays they can. Neither could they aspire to cause panic in societies through the targeting of the computer network of such Critical National Infrastructures as the banking, power transmission and transportation systems. Nowadays, they can. Be they unaffiliated teenager or Al Qaeda operative, the very weak, through the application of the requisite IT skills, today truly have the ability to damage the strong in very profound ways (see chapter 3).

Among the weak here we must also include state actors. They too will take advantage of the opportunities provided by many a Western power's reliance on IT. China, itself a weak actor in comparison to the US, is one state which has examined such opportunities. The Chinese military has been very open about the way it would conduct any future war with the US. Realizing that China can never hope to prevail in a traditional conflict, officers in the People's Liberation Army (PLA) have sought to explore asymmetric avenues of attack across the full spectrum of warfighting. This very much includes 'information warfare'. Two PLA colonels, indeed, wrote a book in 2002 laying out China's possible future strategy and tactics.[52] In particular, they criticized what they referred to as the American 'military technical' approach to warfare, and saw that this opened up the possibility of Chinese utilization of major cyber-warfare attacks (see chapter 3).

New access to weapons

The ability of asymmetric actors, be they state or sub-state, to generate impact against the powerful Western states has also been aided recently by the increasing availability of weapons systems of considerable potency. Among these are the dreaded weapons of mass destruction (WMD).[53] To the asymmetric adversary – in particular, terrorist groups – WMD offer to create the requisite effect from a reasonably small outlay, a greater 'bang for buck'. They offer the prospect of creating, at the very least, a climate of fear in powerful enemies and, at most, hugely significant impact.

The fact that WMD can now be more easily acquired is down to several factors. To start with, the world's security stasis has been removed by the ending of the Cold War. During that period, Moscow and Washington were anxious about any minor conflagration in the world leading to the involvement of the superpowers and to possible nuclear war. Both sides tried to keep the peace. The use of WMD – by anyone – was clearly a destabilizing factor, and the two superpowers kept a firm grip on their own stocks and closely watched their client states to make sure that they did not develop any themselves. The lid was kept on this particular Pandora's box. However, after the collapse of the Soviet Union, the world was left with one less policeman and a lot more unemployed or underpaid WMD scientists whose skills, given the chaos of the post-Soviet space, were available to the highest bidder, state or sub-state. Do-it-yourself weapons could then, with a bit of investment, theoretically be produced by those free agents skilled in nuclear physics or the production of biological and chemical agents. Moreover, the involvement of experienced scientists was not strictly required. One aspect of the explosion of information through the IT revolution is the fact that the Web now carries technical details about WMD which, when allied to a modicum of individual scientific knowledge, could be used to produce limited, but nonetheless effective, 'home-made' WMDs (see chapter 2).[54]

The problem of weapons availability is not restricted to WMD. There now exists also vastly increased access to more mundane conventional weapons. This is a case not only of the post-Cold War opening of many an East European armoury (such as that in Albania), but also of the East European arms plants that used to supply the Warsaw Pact still having to sell their wares and find markets somewhere.[55] They can, and will, sell quite sophisticated systems – such as man-portable surface-to-air missiles (MANPADS) – that any individual with an instruction manual can use. Much of the market for these weapons will be found among sub-state actors such as terrorist groups, rebels, guerrillas, etc. Small states, however, will also want to buy weapons. At one time client states of the superpowers would receive *gratis* 'symmetrical' military equipment in the form of tanks and aircraft and the training to go with them. Now, in the chill light of the post-Cold War order, small states have to stand on their own and will buy what they can afford.[56] And what they can afford on the open market tends to be not aircraft and tanks, but low-order, cheaper items such as machine guns, anti-tank rockets, mines, and anti-aircraft missiles. Weak states are thus being forced down the asymmetric road, in that they will have militaries that look less and less like those of the most powerful states.[57] Symmetry between powerful and weak state adversaries is being lost.

A new sense of moral rectitude

Roger Barnett, as we have seen, noted that 'True asymmetry [involves] those actions that an adversary can exercise that you either cannot or will not.'[58] His point mainly centres around the idea that the Western powers are hamstrung by the fact that they are 'powers'. Historically, it has been the world's great powers that created and formulated the international legal system. They liked being the powers, and so set up a system that kept the status quo. Thus, down the years, and utilizing the ideas of theologians and jurists such as Augustine, Aquinas and Grotius, the powers set out to establish – through the likes of the Hague and Geneva conventions, the League of Nations, and ultimately the United Nations – the standards of today's international law.[59] The problem with creating laws, of course, is that you then have to abide by them. You have to conform to the accepted criteria that, in terms of the legal use of military force, the following should be present before resorting to its use: just cause, right intention, proportionality, legitimate authority, probability of success, and last resort.[60] Thus the powers not only have to *go to* war in accordance with these legal norms (*jus ad bellum*), but they also have to *conduct* war in accordance with legal norms (*jus in bello*). In this latter case the most important criterion is that of proportionality: i.e. whatever force is used must be discriminate and commensurate with the reasons for, and object of, the war.[61]

The Western powers are today more hamstrung by the laws of war than they ever were. Where 'wars of choice' are concerned, great care needs to be taken in regard to the aspect of proportionality especially. If we have seen the 'triumph' of liberal democracy, and if there are no major enemies out there, the liberal democracies must act in a restrained manner that befits a world 'at peace'. The use of violence should be targeted, precise, and 'clinical,' and never inhumane.[62] Other, smaller players feel no such compunction. China, for instance, in the guise of the two colonels (writing a book that must reflect state policy), has pointed out that international law is a bourgeois invention of the West. As the colonels put it, when it comes to warfare, 'The first rule is that there are no rules. Nothing is forbidden.'[63] Terrorists take the same line. Today's asymmetric opponents, unhindered by legal encumbrances, can and will use violence in ways that are far less restrained than the violence employed by the status quo powers – the Western liberal democracies (see chapter 2).

Not only are many asymmetric adversaries unrestrained in the use of violence, there is actually a great incentive for them to use or threaten to use violence in a different, *illegal* way that stands outside the norms of accepted behaviour. For when violence stands outside norms, it is more shocking, and thus it has greater *impact*. September 11 – involving sub-state actors – is patently an example of this; but weak state actors will also resort to such tactics. Whereas the liberal democracies could never countenance the deliberate targeting of civilians or non-combatants, states such as Serbia and Iraq (in the First Gulf War) could resort to such actions as 'hugging': i.e. tying people to, or gathering them around, objects of tactical or operational worth to prevent their being attacked by NATO or Coalition forces (see chapter 4).

'Wars of choice' throw up other issues. These wars, be they against state actors, insurgents or terrorists, have been, and are being, conducted by states which have not themselves been exposed to a 'clear and present danger' in their homelands – apart from some terrorist actions which can be dealt with for the most part by enhanced domestic vigilance. If states are not themselves truly threatened, do they have a right to take military action – and kill people – abroad, as in Iraq and Afghanistan? The first problem here for the liberal democracies is that they need to convince their own populations that such 'wars' are *necessary*; that they are a last resort where diplomacy has been clearly seen to have failed. The second problem is to convince the international community that the 'war' is legal (that there is *jus ad bellum*).[64] The UN Charter, at its simplest, is a little grey in regard to what makes certain military interventions legal and others not. The Charter says that action can be taken if there is a 'threat to international peace and security'.[65] Defining such a threat is difficult, though, and the UN will often be wary of sanctioning offensive action by Western powers. The way to side-step UN niceties, and also to convince domestic audiences that interventions are legal, is to fight war as a coalition. Coalitions can be seen as representing the voice of the international community – as a 'small UN'[66] – even if few in that community are taking part. Coalitions also avoid the accusation that any one state is acting unilaterally in its own naked national self-interest. Thus acts become legitimate without being exactly legal.[67] Whether the legitimacy comes from the UN (as in Iraq, 1990–1, Afghanistan, 2001), from NATO (Kosovo, 1999) or from a limited coalition (Iraq, 2003), there must always be coalition partners for conflicts to be seen as at least approaching some measure of legality under international law. And once hostilities have begun, of course, and when legitimacy is replacing legality, then the states involved have to be very careful that their forces conduct themselves in a manner that befits the original point of the conflict – i.e. 'to do good' (that there is *jus in bello*).[68] Domestic support must be maintained. Thus, when taking military action, the shackles are always on for the liberal democracies. With power has to come responsibility.

Of course, the very fact that these powerful states need coalitions means that weaker adversaries can poke away at the differences in approach between coalition partners and possibly bring the whole edifice down. Thus the asymmetric adversary today has a new target. Slobodan Milosevic attempted to destroy the coalition created by NATO in the Kosovo War in 1999 in his strategy of dragging out the conflict so that coalition resolve would weaken. It very nearly succeeded (see chapter 4). Again, in Iraq, insurgent/terrorist groups have attempted to loosen the bonds of the Coalition by targeting such countries as Italy, the Philippines and, most notably, Spain.[69] If coalitions start to collapse, then legitimacy is lost, and campaigns may have to be wound up.

The current sense of Western moral rectitude is setting up points of attack for the asymmetric adversary. But this sense, it seems, is standing in marked contrast to many of the West's opponents, who appear to have lost any sense of moral behaviour. We have seen what the fervour of Islamists can generate. Indeed, weak *state* actors are also more likely to operate outside international law. They can no longer afford to fight on a level playing field. In the current era, such states are faced with Western enemies who have become so powerful that any advantage possible has to be employed to counter them, including tactics that may be deemed 'illegal'.

Given all the above factors, it is easy to see how, in the contemporary international security situation, the term 'asymmetric warfare' has become the 'term du jour'. At all levels of warfare, from the strategic to the tactical and involving both state and sub-state actors, new methods are being applied by weak protagonists that suit the conditions of the era. We have terrorists who now have increased zeal and a new ability to bring that zeal to bear in effective actions, and we have state actors who, while lacking power as traditionally understood, have new opportunities to create impact on much stronger foes. The 'have-nots' can nowadays influence the actions of the 'haves' more than at any other time hitherto in the history of conflict.

A definition of asymmetric warfare

Having discussed the threat from what appears to constitute 'asymmetric warfare' in the twenty-first century, it is essential that, before completing this introduction, a definition is agreed upon. Generating one, however, is not easy: 'asymmetric warfare is a theme shrouded in some mystery'.[70] The first and most pertinent point to include in such a definition is the sense of *difference*. David Grange, for instance, says simply that asymmetric warfare is 'conflict deviating from the norm, or an indirect approach to affect a counter-balancing of force'.[71] But there is rather more to it than this, and we need to be wary of oversimplifying the concept. If the evolution of the US military's definition of asymmetric warfare is considered, then some sense of the range of issues involved can emerge.

Asymmetry as a concept in modern warfighting made its first official entrance in print in the 1995 US doctrinal statement *Joint Warfare of the Armed Forces of the United States*. The basic definition offered talked merely about engagements between 'dissimilar forces'.[72] In 1997, the publication *US Military Strategy* had it that asymmetric challenges include 'unconventional or inexpensive approaches that circumvent our strengths, exploit our vulnerabilities, or confront us in ways we cannot match in kind'.[73] This is better, in that it appreciates the point (raised by Barnett earlier) that true asymmetry should involve actions which cannot be mirrored by the stronger opponent. By 1999, the *Joint Strategy Review* had added more rounding to the definition:

> Asymmetric approaches are attempts to circumvent or undermine US strengths while exploiting US weaknesses using methods that differ significantly from the United States' expected methods of operations . . . Asymmetric approaches often employ innovative, nontraditional tactics, weapons or technologies and can be applied at all levels of warfare – strategic, operational and tactical – and across the spectrum of military operations.[74]

Such a definition, of course, is very US-specific and tied to thinking along military lines, and it does not take account of the aspect of the inability to mirror.[75]

The British in their definitions have other stresses. They tend to put more emphasis on the variable of 'values'. They note the vulnerabilities of the democracies as compared to the general *Weltanschauung* of their less liberal asymmetric opponents. The *British Defence Doctrine* of 1996 says that asymmetric conflict is 'characterised, on the one hand, by a state with modern, powerful, well equipped forces, but limited national interest or public support and severe political and moral constraints. On the other hand, by a state or group of people with total commitment, and showing scant regard for life and property.'[76] In the UK's 1998 *Strategic Defence Review* there was some further discussion, taking into account attacks in the domestic realm. It talked of future potential adversaries who 'may choose to adopt alternative weapons and unconventional (or asymmetric) strategies, perhaps attacking us through vulnerabilities in our open civil societies'.[77]

These British definitions are more cognizant of the fact that while the military preponderance of the US and other Western powers is seemingly so absolute, it is set against a background of their being liberal democracies and having to act as such. The fact is that these militarily powerful states have a back door left open, in that they have different value sets when they take up arms in their 'wars of choice'.

Bearing the above points in mind, perhaps the most cogent definition comes from Steven Metz and Douglas Johnson. This is quite thorough. Asymmetric warfare, they say, is

acting, organizing and thinking differently than opponents in order to maximize one's own advantages, exploit an opponent's weaknesses, attain the initiative or gain greater freedom of action. It can be political-strategic, military-strategic, operational or a combination of these. It can entail different methods, technologies, values, organizations, time perspectives or some combination of these.[78]

Here there are elements such as the difference in values and in the degree of patience being displayed. It does not mention, however, that to be truly asymmetric in nature, there can be no 'matching in kind'. It also fails to note that asymmetric approaches can be adopted down at the tactical level.

The whole problem here with trying to find definitions of asymmetric warfare – this 'term du jour' – is that different parties want it to mean different things in order to apply some sort of nomenclature for their own particular benefit. It is so new and takes so many different forms in different spheres – in terms of terrorism, of information warfare, of land combat, of combat at sea, and of combat in the air – that definitions become almost pointless. The term is descriptive rather than definitive.[79] 'Asymmetric warfare' describes a threat, and the threat appears in different guises in different battlespaces and operational realms. It describes the ways in which new enemies are adopting different approaches in different areas of conflict. All that we truly know is that these threats are radically different from those that we had become used to. And the fact that there are these new threats 'out there' means that new responses must be engineered; and they, likewise, must be radically different. The old ways will not cut it with these new threats, and in each and every battle space and operational realm there must be a particular response to the particular asymmetric threat faced. But response is difficult. It is a problem in essence because Western security structures and military organizations were designed to deal with threats that were not quite so asymmetrical in nature.

We do not really need to define asymmetric warfare as much as to understand what it means. And here we come back to Grange again. Sometimes simple is good. 'Asymmetric warfare', he says, 'is best understood as a strategy, a tactic, or a method of warfare and conflict.'[80]

Conclusion

Since the dawn of warfare, protagonists have been adopting what today we would call asymmetric approaches. The weak have always had to think of methods that were different, out of the ordinary, if they were to defeat more powerful foes. Sun Tzu, of course, was writing about such methods many centuries ago. No protagonist engaged in conflict in Sun's time or in any other era up to our own, however, has had opened up to them the *range* of possibilities now on offer to practise techniques that differ from 'normal' warfare. Thus we are, today, at a point and time where the *idea* of asymmetric warfare has achieved unmatched prominence.

The new-found opportunities for the asymmetric warrior, both state and sub-state, are based on various factors that have emerged recently. The powerful states of the West, and in particular the US, have such preponderant military capabilities that they can no longer really be challenged symmetrically – at least for the foreseeable future. If they are to be challenged, then it must be by asymmetric means.

Much of the current threat to our military organizations and to Western societies in general is coming from Islamic extremists. For a deadly antagonism has developed in recent years between Islamists and the West. This has manifested itself in insurgent activity and terrorist attacks in a number of countries, including Western states. These attacks are having greater impact now because such asymmetric warriors have greater access to the countries they wish to attack, greater access to IT means to undermine their enemy, and greater access to a range of weapons, including WMD. They now have a vastly increased potential to create mass casualties and mass effect. Moreover, this ability to generate high-casualty scenarios appears in sharp relief against a background of general 'peace'; there are no *real* threats 'out there' to the United States and to the West in general.

Conflict was supposed to have been over after the Cold War's demise. Conflict, however, is still with us. Western states have found themselves intervening abroad in 'wars of choice', either for humanitarian purposes or to prevent terrorist actions. These new missions for the West's armed forces are taking them away from the types of battlespaces in which they were designed to operate. These new battlespaces are increasing these forces' vulnerability to asymmetric attack. Much of the vulnerability centres on the fact that if the 'wars' are merely to be those of choice, then they should be almost bloodless. Thus, when blood is spilt, and especially when it is caught in images by the plethora of media outlets that exist today, then the liberal democracies hesitate, wring their moralistic hands, lose patience, and can allow tactical setbacks to lead to strategic failure. The asymmetric opponent is thus handed a distinct advantage – a weakness to poke at.

The asymmetric player, indeed, will always be trying to leverage small actions into having huge, strategic effect. They will often conduct strikes at the lower, tactical level in the hope that they can produce enormous impact at the much higher, strategic level: bombs at one point designed to engineer a change of government policy at another, a hacker attack on one computer designed to shut down a whole economy, the downing of one aircraft to stop a whole bombing campaign, the disabling of one warship to stop a whole armada, the killing of a few troops to engineer a general 'pull-out', and the dragging out of wars so that interest in outcomes and the will to win are lost. We are vulnerable to such approaches.

At one and the same time the West is stronger than it ever was and yet weaker than it ever was. It is weaker because often the core competencies inherent in its great strengths – liberalism, information passage, powerful militaries – can be turned, seemingly so easily, into vulnerabilities. How they are turned into vulnerabilities depends on the skill of the asymmetric warrior. The level of skill displayed is in many ways a function of the fact that they *have* to think differently. They are forced to act adroitly and to apply nuance. The West is in many ways the architect of the asymmetric threats it now faces. There is an action–reaction model at work here: develop in one direction, and the opponent will develop counters. We cannot escape the laws of physics. As Newton's third law of motion puts it, 'For every action there is an equal and opposite reaction.' Often, though, the powerful think that iron laws do not apply to them. One of the problems for the strong powers throughout history has been their hubristic belief that power is a strength and can never be turned into a vulnerability. As Thucydides quotes the Athenian generals, 'The strong do what they will, the weak do what they must.'[81] Power has always bred an arrogance that can blind.

The powerful must not allow themselves to be blinded. The action–reaction model has to go further. The Western states must themselves respond to the actions of the asymmetric adversaries they now face. They must make changes that reduce their vulnerabilities. The experience of decades, if not generations, of being prepared to fight the 'symmetrical' wars that characterized the two world wars and the Cold War has, in the parlance of organization theory, to be 'unlearnt'. Governments and military organizations have to adopt new measures to deal with these new threats. For governments, this will involve new policies and new laws that can defeat terrorists and protect information. For militaries, it will involve new doctrinal thinking, force structures, equipment, and, above all, mind-sets.

Asymmetric warfare is a broad church. It can be practised by many actors in many different ways across a broad spectrum of civilian and military activity. The aim in this book is to point out where, and in what ways, the West can expect such warfare to manifest itself. It will concentrate on two Western states in particular – the United States and the United Kingdom – since these are the two states most threatened across the board by asymmetric opponents. Each chapter in this book considers one of the key areas of attack open to weaker players against the likes of the US and the UK. Chapter 2 ('The Terrorist Asymmetric Adversary') undertakes a review of the current threat from terrorism. It considers the increased danger that there is from the terrorist and how Western states should be developing counters that can ameliorate this threat without – and here's the rub – actually making the situation worse. Chapter 3 ('Asymmetry and Information Warfare') examines how the West's current reliance on information – in both civilian and military realms – is opening up opportunities for weak players to have considerable impact. Again, defensive responses are proposed which can go some way to nullifying attacks in the IT realm. Chapter 4 ('Asymmetry and Air Power') looks at how air power, the favoured tool today of Western military action, can be negated by the skills of weaker opponents. The latter are aided immeasurably here by the ready availability of weaponry that can bring down aircraft of great sophistication. The chapter makes clear that if the West's air power – designed as it was to oppose the long-gone Soviet threat – is to be truly successful in countering asymmetric threats, then changes have to be implemented that will make air power a far more adaptable and flexible instrument. Chapter 5 ('Asymmetry and Sea Power') considers how warships can come under attack asymmetrically. As with air power, the currently extant Western naval forces were designed for Cold War operations, and not to deal with the most obvious current threat: from opponents close inshore employing a variety of means to level the maritime battle space. The present structure of Western navies will be looked at, and an examination made of the level of response emanating from the naval powers. Chapter 6 ('Asymmetry and Land Power') examines the difficulties that the West's land forces have in countering asymmetric adversaries in 'complex terrain'. The fact that these forces are faring so poorly in such terrain gives scope to consider making numerous changes. Finally, chapter 7 ('The US Military and its Response to the Asymmetric Opponent') analyses how the United States military, the most powerful military on the planet, is dealing with the numerous asymmetric threats it is facing today in places like Iraq and Afghanistan. The fact is that, despite the degree of difficulty it is having in dealing with such threats, this organization seems to have little desire to change in order to better tackle this new and dangerous foe – the contemporary asymmetric warrior of the twenty-first century.

2 THE TERRORIST ASYMMETRIC ADVERSARY

Introduction

Terrorists are perhaps the archetypal asymmetric adversaries.[1] They are weak; they lack both numbers and resources. Despite this, however, they can on occasion generate devastating strategic effect by leveraging what numbers and resources they do have to great advantage. In this regard, the attack of September 11 stands as a prime example. Al Qaeda personnel made exceptional use of their assets of skill, patience, a certain degree of funding, and a whole-hearted willingness to die for a cause.[2] The impact they created was truly astonishing. It was an impact that came both from the trauma of having iconic buildings demolished and most decidedly from the sheer scale of the loss of life. This latter effect was an alarming and, indeed, a new feature of terrorism. For up to September 11 terrorist acts in the West had been characterized, on the whole, by their restraint.

The restraint came from the fact that terrorism, before the late 1990s, was seen as being purely 'political' in nature. The main aim of these 'old' terrorists, as we now have to call them, was not necessarily to kill people, but rather to make a statement. They wanted to gain some measure of political change through actions that were of a scale to gain notoriety, but not so egregious as to generate a high degree of public antagonism. In the old saying, terrorism was 'propaganda by deed'.[3] As Brian Jenkins once put it, 'The terrorists want a lot of people watching, not a lot of people dead . . . [Terrorism] is aimed at people watching, not the actual victims. Terrorism is theatre.'[4] It was theatre aimed at both people *and* governments. For these terrorists of yesteryear would carry out small acts of violence against the state to encourage the state to overreact by introducing draconian security measures. These would be unpopular with 'the people', and the people would thus be drawn, theoretically, away from the government and towards the agenda of the terrorists.

The well-known terrorist organizations of the past, such as the People's Will (*Narodnaya Volya*) in Tsarist Russia or the more modern varieties from the 1960s onwards, such as ETA (Spain), the IRA (Northern Ireland), the Red Brigade (Italy) and the Red Army Faction (West Germany), all acted in roughly the same way. They conducted small-scale 'propagandistic' attacks against symbols of the state – such as its security forces. If innocent bystanders were killed, it was usually unintentional.[5]

The West is now faced, however, by the 'new' terrorists. These no longer feel that they have to be limited in their actions.[6] The Islamist threat is far more dangerous than any previous manifestation of terrorism. These new, Islamist terrorists have, as one analyst put it even before September 11, 'modified Sun Tzu's edict from "kill one person, frighten a thousand" to "kill a thousand, frighten a million"'.[7] For with modern Islamist terrorism and, to a degree, with millenarian terrorism,[8] there is a religious fervour that defies moral boundaries: 'Religious terrorist violence inevitably assumes a transcendent purpose and therefore becomes a sacramental or divine duty . . . [it] arguably results in a significant loosening of the constraints on the commission of mass murder.'[9] Thus with Islamist-inspired terrorism there are strong elements of killing for the sake of killing, with no particular political purpose in mind. Such terrorists are 'on a divine mission to carry out acts of extreme violence that have been ordained and sanctioned by a higher deity'.[10] Often a fundamental aim of such terrorists is to achieve purification by eliminating the infidel, the non-believer. The added convenience of this religious motivation is that if, as sometimes happens, innocent Muslim bystanders are killed in attacks on infidels (usually Christian), then that is excusable: if they were devout Muslims, then they will go straight to heaven; if they were not devout, then they deserved to die anyway.[11] There seem to be no ethical boundaries delimiting Islamist terrorist outrages. Attacks are no longer confined to symbols of the state, but have broadened to include 'the whole enemy society'.[12] The goal is destruction, not propaganda.

September 11 was the first time in the West that an attack backed by such a philosophy occurred. We have now, though, come to expect the worst: bombs exploding with no warning, suicide bombers prepared to take the lives of many others as well as themselves, the use of airliners as guided missiles, and the threatened use of weapons of mass destruction (WMD).

The lack of restraint means that the 'new' terrorist presents major challenges to Western security services. Dealing with the 'old' terrorist was one thing; dealing with their 'new' brethren is something else entirely. Before coming on to discuss responses, however, we need first of all to understand adequately why this particular asymmetric threat exists and the degree of danger it actually poses. In this regard, there are three major characteristics of the 'new' terrorists that need to be considered: their increased *degree of fervour*, their increased *ability to implement attacks*, and their increased *ability to cause mass casualties*.

An increased fervour

The current acute terrorist threat to the powerful liberal democracies has developed from an increased level of anti-Western fervour in Islamic communities. This has emerged mostly as a backlash against certain dynamics that have been evident over the last few decades. These dynamics are concerned principally with the spread of Western influence into Islamic lands.

The French and British began the process with their post-First World War carve-up of the defeated Ottoman Empire. State boundaries were created in the Middle East (including Iraq) that suited these imperial powers and hardly anyone else.[13] There then followed, after the Balfour Declaration of 1919, the founding of the state of Israel – now perceived in the Muslim world as a ruse by the West to create a firm ally in the region. The plight of the Palestinian refugees that this move generated has acted as a further source of resentment. More recently, and perhaps more painfully, has come the supposed imposition of American cultural values via the process of globalization. The impinging of a foreign culture, in forms ranging from lewd TV channels, through the increasing number of fast-food golden arches, all the way up to having US troops on holy Saudi soil and Coalition forces in Iraq and Afghanistan, has created its own backlash in a falling back on, and a reinforcing of, indigenous values based on Islamic teachings. Such anti-Western angst, of course, is not universal across the Muslim world – or *ummah* – but it is deeply significant.[14]

More generally, there is a wealth distribution issue.[15] Relative poverty has grown in the *ummah* in a Malthusian dynamic that sees populations mushrooming but doing so in environments that lack a social infrastructure to adequately sustain them.[16] Even in relatively rich countries like Saudi Arabia there is social deprivation. A new underclass has emerged in the *ummah* as young, educated people find themselves without work and without a niche in their own societies. Such poverty does not, of itself, lead to terrorism. But such poverty is set in sharp relief as those lacking material possessions are able to observe, through the more widely available medium of television, how the rich, especially those in the West, live out their lives.[17] Disaffection has been seen to grow, and one outlet is found, again, in a turn towards religion and particularly towards the sharply anti-Western Islamist rhetoric of certain mullahs.[18]

Such background anti-Western sentiment has been reinforced by recent political developments. While the presence of Israel has been providing a thorn in Muslim flesh for many years, the latest Palestinian intifada has added considerable fuel to the flames. The actions of Israel are perceived badly enough in the *ummah*, but when pictures are being constantly beamed into Muslim homes around the world of US-supplied helicopter gunships and F-16s helping the Israelis crush opposition, then the US is seen as – visibly – culpable as well. And where Bosnia is concerned, the feeling exists that the US and Western intervention there was actually designed to act *against* the interests of the Bosnian Muslims.[19] Even the attack on September 11 is seen across the *ummah* as a Christian/Jewish plot.[20] With such standards having been set and such a background created, the likes of the US and the UK have difficulty saying to Muslims in general that their 'invasion' of Iraq was benign and had the sole aim of toppling Saddam. Across the *ummah* this does not ring true. And what is perhaps significant about the neutering of Iraq by Coalition troops in the 1990s and the utter defeat of Saddam's forces in 2003 is the fact that the Muslim – and in particular the Arab – world is now devoid of a powerful 'champion' state that can stand up to both the West and Israel. Since opposition cannot coalesce around any state actor, a broad swathe of Muslim opinion sees terrorism as now the only way of actually 'defending' themselves and of thwarting Western 'aggressive' designs.[21]

Many young men and women of the Muslim faith are thus drawn to extremist groups. The message these groups expound is that the hatred derived from feelings of pain and injustice needs to be channelled into action. Al Qaeda and other extremist groups such as, for instance, Jammah Islamiya in Indonesia and Abu Sayyaf in the Philippines (both with links to Al Qaeda) are most decidedly not short of recruits.[22] There is a fervour at large that begets a common purpose: these groups all 'aim at the punishment and if possible destruction of America and Western civilization'.[23]

And these sentiments that have underpinned the recent upsurge in terrorist acts by extremist Muslim actors are not going to be ameliorated soon. The fervour will not abate. The asymmetric threat from Islamist terrorism is predicted to worsen in the coming decades.[24] Globalization is not going to stop; in fact, the process will probably increase in pace. And poverty is not going to go away. Poverty, indeed, is storing up another problem for the future. Parents in many parts of the *ummah* are commonly having to send their children to the only schools they can afford: the madrassas funded by religious organizations. These, of course, put heavy emphasis on Koranic teachings, and many, though not all, place the blame for many of the woes of Muslims at the door of the West and on the US in particular. Madrassas can and sometimes do serve as a breeding ground for the type of discontent that may lead to the development of Islamist terrorists. Wary of the influence of the madrassas, countries like Pakistan and Indonesia have tried to close many of them down. But such actions are difficult given the madrassas' contributions to society in terms of providing free education and the fact that in both countries, even if the central government wanted to close the schools, their writ can be very weak in remote rural areas.[25]

Of course, under the rubric of today's dangerous terrorists we must extend our thinking beyond Islamist groups. There are others out there who have already, and will in the future, exhibit a high degree of fervour: Aum Shinrikyo[26] in Japan, for instance, and the occasional small group (such as the Oklahoma bombers[27]) or individual (Theodore Kaczinski, the Unabomber[28]). They, however, do not represent the degree and range of threat to Western states that the Islamist terrorists do. The latter, in terms of asymmetric warfare, are the far more dangerous opponent.

An increased ability to implement attacks

Those aggrieved fanatics in the Muslim world who would once have quietly and impotently chafed have now a much greater capacity to turn ire into action. For the process of globalization is at once both a bane and a boon. It might bring with it foreign and threatening influences, but it also provides the capabilities to violently counter those influences.

To begin with, globalization allows for greater freedom of move-ment. Once it was difficult for terrorists and potential terrorists to move freely around the world. Now, with the general drift to a smaller, more compact global society, those with nefarious designs – from the Middle East or from anywhere else – can move more easily from country to country. Increasingly liberal laws such as the Schengen Agreement in Europe (wherein arrivals in one European Union state then have free access to most of the others) also help in moving per-sonnel around.[29] Such movement can be financed by those Muslims who have become rich in the general worldwide spread of wealth and who have taken it upon themselves to back terrorist organizations (e.g. Osama bin Laden).

Globalization has also led to increased emigration. More people from Muslim lands are settling in the West, and they can provide from amongst their number, as some would see it, a terrorist 'fifth column' able to attack their host state from within. Moreover, many individu-als bent on terrorist acts who have remained in their own countries have an increased capacity nowadays to travel to the West and not arouse suspicion. For although globalization may not have helped the employment situation in over-populated Muslim countries, it has led to a spread of wealth enabling the financing of more efficient educa-tion systems. Such systems are producing a growing number of people who have the ability to understand the West, to adapt to life there, to speak the relevant languages, to operate more freely, and thus, if motivated and if required, to carry out terrorist acts with greater ease. The Islamist terrorist of today does not stand out as many of their counterparts in the past did; he or she can be merely part of the 'background noise'.[30]

The 'new' terrorists have also become 'more attuned to the . . . tech-nological imperatives of the information age'.[31] Most importantly, they have become comfortable with the use of computers, the Internet and the World Wide Web. They have easier access to information on everything from Mao's teachings on guerrilla activity to the making of improvised explosive devices (IEDs), i.e. bombs. They have access to information technology (IT) means that can bring people and resources together in a process that could never have been possible before and which enables activities to be undertaken that could never have been undertaken before.[32] The Web and the Internet also enhance the capability today to attract funds, to draw recruits, to spread propaganda, and to disseminate opinions on an uncensored means that avoids the message manipulation traditionally carried out by media outlets and by governments.

IT allows, too, for new terrorist structures to develop. Once terrorists, to avoid infiltration by security forces, had to have a rigid cell structure controlled by a strict hierarchy of command. They had 'bureaucracies' dedicated to tight control.[33] Now advances provided by the Internet and the Web mean that bureaucracies are less important. There can exist now *loose* associations of individual terrorists and groups with similar leanings that are 'lighter', more flexible and self-contained. They no longer need the 'centre'. They can learn their trade from information on the Web. Gatherings dedicated to instruction periods conducted by experienced hands are no longer required, and likewise clandestine meetings with 'leaders'. Terrorists need no longer consult and receive orders by phone, which often proved their downfall in years past. They can often work with their own financing and thus do not need to tap into an outside source. They can carry out independent missions under general strategic guidance or via the inspiration of a central figure or group (e.g. Al Qaeda).[34] Thus the information 'revolution' has given licence for terrorist organizations to operate with a dramatically reduced profile. As with any asymmetric warrior, the lower the profile that can be developed, the less likely terrorists are to show up on the 'radar' of their more powerful state opponents.

As well as facilitating the 'new' terrorists in their *own* actions and organizations, information also helps them in their endeavours to strike at their enemies. Terrorists can follow the activities and operations of their opponents often simply by looking at a few websites. As Donald Rumsfeld put it, they watch 'how you're behaving and then alter and adjust at relatively little cost'.[35] And the fact that the West has also adopted IT so assiduously opens up new avenues for *cyber attack* by terrorists. They now have the ability to engineer profound strategic effect on our societies with very little outlay. We are vulnerable. The West now has economies that are run, in essence, by the Internet. As Condoleezza Rice, when US National Security Adviser, put it, 'Today, the cyber economy is the economy.'[36] As well as the banking system, many critical infrastructures in the West, such as the energy industry, have moved to adopt Web-based systems that, while gaining from the interconnectedness provided, have become vulnerable to terrorist hackers. Osama bin Laden himself was aware of the capabilities provided by IT in respect of striking at the heart of the US: 'It is important', he said, 'to hit the economy of the United States, which is the base of its military power.' Thus it was no surprise when, in the post-September 11 Coalition intervention in Afghanistan, laptops were found in Al Qaeda camps that contained detailed information on the software used throughout many US critical infrastructures. Al Qaeda also at one time had a 'school for hackers' in Pakistan that even handed out certificates at the end of courses.[37] (See also chapter 3.)

An increased ability to cause mass casualties

The 'new' terrorists are aided in their endeavours to kill more people by the fact that there are now more instruments of death available to them. Acquisition of the tools of the terrorist trade was a constant and profound problem for the 'old' terrorist. Often weapons and explosives could only be obtained through theft from official sources or through supply by state sponsors. Both were problematic. Relying on the former carried considerable risks, while the latter left the terrorists in thrall to the state that supplied them. Now the Internet can provide the information that allows many terrorists to make their own explosives from household products.[38] There are also several dedicated individuals who were trained in Al Qaeda's camps in Taliban-administered Afghanistan in the 1990s and who now roam the world advising would-be terrorists about bomb-making and other terrorist techniques.[39] Moreover, the arms market is now awash with many products that the terrorist finds affordable. Included here are some weapons that are very sophisticated indeed. Surface-to-air missiles, for instance, are now widely available and have been used.[40] It also seems possible to have access to weapons of mass destruction (WMD) or, in the more accurate and less hyperbolic current terminology, Chemical, Biological, Radiological and Nuclear (CBRN) weapons.

WMD, indeed, *appear* to provide the perfect tool for the 'new' terrorist. They offer large impact from a small outlay. The impact comes from the fact that terrorists with WMD can seemingly not only kill lots of people, but can also generate the next best thing: panic on the streets of their opponents. The fear that WMD engender makes them ideal weapons for strategic effect. Moreover, the terrorist can use WMD without fear of retaliation. Whereas state adversaries will be wary of using WMD against the Western powers for fear of the retribution that would be visited upon them, the terrorist adversary has no real profile that would invite targeting from the WMDs of the US or anyone else.[41] In the true asymmetric sense, the weak can use certain weapons, but their stronger opponents, while they might have them in their arsenals, 'cannot or will not' use them.[42]

Access to WMD now seems to be a given. They can either be bought ready-made from ex-Soviet sources, or there are the do-it-yourself possibilities created both by the Internet and by the presence of many newly available ex-Eastern Bloc scientists. Having all the theoretical knowledge to hand, however, does not guarantee that WMD can be manufactured by terrorists. Although Osama bin Laden told his followers that it was their 'religious duty' to use WMD against the foes of Islam, Al Qaeda laboratories in Afghanistan dedicated to research into such weapons could not actually produce any usable agents.[43] These laboratories were destroyed when Coalition forces moved into Afghanistan in the post-September 11 *Operation Enduring Freedom*. WMD, though, have been used by terrorist groups (Aum Shinrikyo, for instance), and they will be used, however amateurishly, in the future.[44] As the head of the UK's security service, MI5, put it, 'it will only be a matter of time before a crude version of a WMD attack is launched against a major Western city.'[45]

WMD are the most feared tool in the hands of the terrorist. It is thus worthwhile here to take a moment to establish the actual nature of the threat from WMD. Each type of agent will be looked at here in a *tour d'horizon*, and an attempt will then be made (and, given the nature of today's terrorist threat, it can never be more than an 'attempt') to quantify the actual level of threat they pose. The threat is actually not as straightforward as it might appear. There are four particular types of WMD attack that a terrorist could consider employing: chemical, biological, radiological and nuclear.[46]

Chemical weapons (CW)

Chemical weapons have the theoretical capacity to kill thousands while being fairly easy to obtain or produce. CW can actually appear in the form of readily available gases (e.g. chlorine) or everyday insecticides and herbicides. The ingredients, or precursors, for 'home-made' CW can be ordered easily enough from reputable outlets or produced domestically. More refined CW can be stolen from civilian research facilities or from military storage sites, particularly in the states of the former Soviet Union. 'Rogue' states which manufacture their own may pass them on to non-state actors either for profit or for ideological/political/religious motives.

CW can have effect through inhalation, absorption through the skin or eyes, injection by flying glass and debris, or by ingestion. There are four classes of CW: nerve, blister, blood and choking.

Nerve agents

These target a victim's nervous system, and a single drop on the skin can be enough to kill. Many pesticides are in this family of chemicals, but in very dilute form. The most famous nerve agents are those whose possible use caused so much anxiety during the Cold War: sarin, tabun and soman.[47] It is technically possible for anyone to make an agent such as sarin through mixing commercially available products. The process, however, is complicated.[48] The Japanese millenarian sect Aum Shinrikyo did manufacture some sarin and spread it as a vapour from a truck in an attack in Matsumoto in 1994 (seven dead).[49] The next year, and more famously, several members of the group placed parcels containing sarin on the floor of subway carriages in Tokyo, and as they got up to leave, used umbrellas to pierce the parcels and release the vapour. Twelve people died and some 5,000 were injured.[50] The subway was chosen as the site for the attacks since it provided an ideal environment where the agent could have maximum effect. There would be crowds of people, and the agent would be trapped in the tunnel system and continue to cause casualties and not dissipate in the open air (as at Matsumoto).[51]

Blister agents

These chemicals attack the skin causing blisters and burns. If they get into the lungs, they cause secretions that result in 'dry-land drowning'. Among these are Mustard Gas and Lewisite, which were both used in the First World War. Iraq had large stocks of such weapons at one time but only ever used them in its war with Iran (1980–8) and against recalcitrant towns and villages which were not toeing Saddam's line (predominantly *nerve* agent was used at the most famous site, Halabja[52]). Blister agents are quite easy to make, but storage and dissemination are problematic.[53]

Blood agents

These target the ability of the blood to pick up oxygen and can lead to suffocation. Cyanide gases are perhaps the most well known of this type. Cyanide is commercially available and can also be made, given sufficient quantities and much patience, from such everyday objects as wool, cigarettes and plants.[54] Making a weapon in such a way, though, is far from efficient. Cyanide gas has been used before: the terrorists who bombed the World Trade Center in 1993 used it, but the gas was all burnt up in the initial explosion and had no effect.[55]

Choking agents

These attack the lungs, again causing dry-land drowning. Among the agents used here are chlorine and phosgene. The most notable use by terrorists of chlorine gas was by the Tamil Tigers in Sri Lanka in 1990. This strike was opportunistic, in that the Tigers discovered chlorine in some tanks and used it against a nearby government fort. The gas injured some sixty people, but was actually more effective in the panic that its use caused. It was never used again by the Tigers, however, because it did not meet with the approval of those trying to raise funds abroad for their cause. Some Islamist terrorists, moreover, were arrested in Jordan in 2004 and charged with planning an attack using a bomb consisting of 20 tonnes of explosives and choking agents. The device was designed to create a toxic mushroom cloud over Amman.[56] In terms of trying to build home-made versions of choking agents, it is fairly pointless, since they are so freely available (e.g. chlorine).

Biological weapons (BW)

Biological weapons can be deadlier and longer-lasting than CW. BW are composed of living organisms or their by-products. There are two classes of biological agents.

Pathogens

These are disease-causing organisms. They appear in the form either of bacteria (e.g. anthrax) or viruses. Notable viruses used will cause plague, smallpox, Lassa Fever, Ebola and Marburg disease. The most common virus used would normally be smallpox, given its lethality, its hardiness and the ease with which it can be disseminated.[57] Smallpox is very difficult to produce, however, and only major state players will have the capacity to do so.[58]

Toxins

These are poisons which are produced by living material.[59] Some of these toxins are very effective even in small quantities. Examples include botulinum toxin, which is the single most poisonous substance known. It paralyses muscles, leading to asphyxiation.[60] Ricin is another BW and can be made quite easily from castor oil beans. It can only be truly effective as a deadly agent, however, when injected into a victim. In 1978 the Bulgarian dissident Georgii Markov was killed in London by a ricin-tipped umbrella wielded by a member of his country's secret service.[61] Ricin thus hardly offers much to the terrorist. One may as well stab victims as inject them with ricin.

BW have been used by what might be considered 'terrorists'. In 1984, for example, a religious cult in Oregon wanted to engineer a low voter turn-out in local elections and so introduced salmonella into food at a local restaurant. This made some 751 people sick.[62]

The threat from CW and BW

Both chemical and biological agents are, of course, theoretically very dangerous as the deliverers of mass-casualty situations. But we need to be aware that actually producing effective weapons from agents that may kill a few animals in a laboratory is not easily done.[63] We are familiar with the use of CW in the First World War, and they certainly had an initial impact. Once the surprise factor had worn off, however, they ceased to be truly effective. Moreover, logistically it took a lot of agent to produce just a few casualties, and only with the resources of a state could the requisite volumes of CW be produced.[64] The principal drawback of these agents, then as now, is that to have utility as a weapon, they need to be in the form of a gas or vapour. Thus they can be quite easily dispersed in the atmosphere and lose their potency.

With BW such as anthrax, it would be theoretically possible to take 110 lbs of it and bring about the deaths of some 100,000 people in a city of 500,000.[65] This can only work, however, when the anthrax is in dried spore form where such spores can be inhaled. Thus the spores need to be of a certain weight so that they will hover in the atmosphere, neither too heavy to fall to the ground nor too light to fly away. The weather must also play its part; it must not be too humid, otherwise the spores cling together and fall to earth. Other factors are influential. For instance, if spores are dropped over a city from a plane, then they will normally be forced harmlessly upwards by the warm air constantly rising from built-up areas. Additionally, manufacturing spores that can survive for any length of time is very difficult.[66] Thus getting anthrax to 'work' is tricky. Even with the fulsome backing of state laboratories, for instance, all that Saddam's scientists ever came up with was a quite useless liquid anthrax slurry.[67] Indeed, the only time when anthrax has had any noticeable impact as a weapon was in the post-September 11 attacks (five deaths and eighteen cases). The type used there, however, was one produced to the highest standards by a US government laboratory.[68] The mystery still remains as to how anthrax from such a laboratory came to be used.[69]

The use of smallpox as a weapon has great potential for the terrorist. If spread unchecked, it could create a pandemic in a world that no longer has enough smallpox vaccinations (the naturally occurring virus was eradicated in the 1970s, so there is no point in holding stocks of vaccine).[70] It is virtually impossible to produce smallpox, though, and the only (admitted) holdings of the virus are in two laboratories: one in the US, the other in Russia.[71]

Although a city's water supply might appear as an enticing target for CW and BW attacks, a huge amount of agent of any description would be required. Moreover, water purification systems will account for many alien chemicals and organisms.[72]

The activities of Aum in Japan exhibited the clear difficulties of producing effective weapons from chemical and biological sources. It had the money ($2 bn of funding) to pay for laboratories and for Japanese scientists to manufacture the agents, but practical problems arose when it came to going out and creating some *impact* with them. The sect tried to disseminate both anthrax and botulinim toxin without result in ten attacks which nobody noticed, and achieved 'success' – and that limited – only when it turned to chemical weapons such as sarin.[73]

Having BW and CW sitting in a container in a laboratory or in a back kitchen as a potential threat is one thing, having them out in the open air and creating death and panic is quite another. While it is not too difficult to make or to obtain most chemical and biological agents, the actual problem lies in trying to *weaponize* them. Thus while they have a theoretical capacity to create shattering impact, turning theory into practice is probably well beyond the wit of the vast majority of terrorist groups. Of course, this does not mean that they will *never* be used in some form. And the very idea that they might will be exercising the mind of many a counter-terrorist expert for many years to come.[74]

Radiological weapons

The radiological bomb, or, more technically, the Radiological Dispersion Device (RDD), may prove to be the terrorists' most effective impact weapon. Basically the RDD (colloquially a 'dirty bomb') consists of an IED charge linked to a radioactive source. The radioactive material used can normally be obtained fairly easily. Hospitals, medical research facilities and universities all have such material (such as strontium 90 and caesium 137) under less than comprehensive guard.

The threat from RDDs

When an RDD explodes, the resultant 'fall-out' would, in theory, spread radioactive material over a large area, causing contamination of both people and infrastructure such as buildings, roads and water supplies. Large-scale evacuations would need to be undertaken, and the areas contaminated might be uninhabitable for years. Thus, while not causing many immediate deaths, such bombs would generate widespread panic and dislocation. In terms of what the asymmetric warrior wants, and if they are as effective as some believe, then the RDD promises much in terms of large effect for small outlay.[75] Moreover, the possibility of their use creates the sense that any future bomb in a Western city (and some major European cities are quite 'used' to bombs) could be radiological in nature. Where once passers-by might rush to the aid of bomb victims, there might now be a mass movement in the opposite direction as civilians attempt to escape the scene of any bomb. Just as any plane hijack, since September 11, is now treated totally differently, we are getting to the stage where the nature of bomb attacks has likewise to be considered anew.

No RDD have been planted as yet. However, a Chechen group did leave an explosive device attached to a caesium source on a park bench in Moscow in 1995. The bomb was not armed, though. It was seen as a warning to the Russian authorities that, if they wanted to, the group could have employed a 'dirty' bomb for real.[76]

Producing an RDD within a country like the United States or any Western state would be difficult given the publicity over the theft of any radioactive sources and the logistics problem of dealing with the source itself. A ready-made RDD, however, could be imported into these countries fairly easily through sea container traffic. It has been estimated that if a dirty bomb were discovered or actually exploded in a container in a US sea port, then all ports in the USA would be closed as a precaution. According to one war game, if a dirty bomb went off in the Chicago port facility, then the economic losses would total $58 bn: a consequence of no little impact.[77] A terrorist attack on a nuclear plant itself is also a possibility, and might cause a Chernobyl-style release of radioactivity. Such plants, however, are usually very well guarded.[78]

Nuclear weapons

Certainly, the possibility exists for terrorists to acquire actual nuclear weapons and to use them. If it is taken as read that certain groups want to create impact and to kill as many people as possible, then they will want to obtain the most efficient means of bringing that about, i.e. a nuclear bomb.

The threat from nuclear weapons

It appears to be practically impossible, however, for the terrorists themselves to build a nuclear device; production requires a sophisticated manufacturing infrastructure.[79] It is possible to steal a weapon, but this is unlikely; such weapons tend to be too well guarded.[80] It is possible to buy one (say, from a Russian source), but logistically this would be difficult. There are supposedly Russian 'suitcase nukes' available (actually called Atomic Demolition Munitions – ADMs), which can fit into a backpack. Russia built some 132 of these in the 1980s, and 100 are allegedly 'missing'. This, however, is probably an 'accountancy' loss in reality, and anyway, with a limited shelf-life, they would now be past their 'sell-by date'.[81] Pakistan is another possible source of a complete nuclear weapon (especially if an Islamic government were to take power in Islamabad), but even then it would have to be handed over to the terrorists complete with its codes. Any nuclear device is given a safety lock code which is known to very few people.

It is possible to make an Improvised Nuclear Device (IND) – or 'poor man's nuclear bomb' – which is not a nuclear bomb as such (it has a distinctly lower explosive potential), but would nonetheless be pretty effective. There would still be the need, though, for millions of dollars and probably state backing to produce an IND.[82]

Understanding the threat

In discussing the possible use by terrorists of any sort of WMD, we need to be wary of exaggerating the threat. To employ such weapons, there needs to be a combination of technological ability, opportunity, a lack of restraint (usual religious in nature), and a slice of luck (weather, for instance). Getting such a combination is quite rare. There is, moreover, no real evidence that any terrorist group of this century has got far with research – merely interest. It is clear that Al Qaeda in Afghanistan conducted experiments with WMD, but not that they produced any. It must be remembered, too, that Aum Shinrikyo carried out ten unsuccessful attacks before the Tokyo subway devices, and this was a group blessed with huge financial resources and technical ability. And even the subway operation did not kill that many people. The terrorist may be left with the sense that there is not much point in going to all the trouble of trying to obtain WMD. In the end, sufficient – and guaranteed – impact may come about through just using 'normal' IEDs (or aircraft, or whatever is easiest to hand). However, we must always bear in mind that the promise of WMD to deliver mass casualty situations will always be acting as a spur to their eventual use by the terrorist asymmetric adversary.[83]

Responding to the terrorist asymmetric adversary

Having established the parameters of the threat that the terrorist asymmetric adversary poses, it is possible now to propose some responses or counters to this threat. The first and most fundamental problem for the Western liberal democracies in dealing with terrorism is, of course, that they *are* liberal democracies. They cannot take draconian anti-terrorist measures that impinge too harshly on the everyday lives of their own populations. And whereas the terrorist, to quote Rumsfeld again, is 'unburdened by fixed borders, headquarters or conventional forces', those that oppose them are burdened by all three.[84] The democracies have to respect state borders and cannot intervene wherever they would like. They have headquarters – or bureaucracies – that tend to degrade responsiveness. They also have conventional forces which, for the most part, are not crafted for chasing – either at home or abroad – after will-o'-the wisp enemies such as the small, nimble and determined terrorist adversary.

Despite the shackles, however, there are steps the liberal democracies can take. Two particular strands should be considered: we may call these 'defence' and 'offence'. Defence covers all the protective measures that can be taken to prevent, or to lessen the impact of, any particular terrorist attack. Offence will be employed to pre-empt any actions by the terrorist so that the likelihood of their carrying out any attacks falls sharply.

Defence

Defence could start with some 'big picture' approach. The liberal democracies may try spreading their wealth to the underdeveloped world in the pious hope that if poverty were to be reduced abroad, then so might anti-Western sentiment. The expectation would be that 'when social conditions are attained that make life more worth living for than dying for, then [terrorism] will fade into history'.[85] This approach could be a very expensive one and may actually provide little benefit. For the September 11 hijackers, of course, were not poor; they were driven by more fundamental motivations. And it is these motivations that we cannot change. As Laqueur points out, 'there is no known cure . . . for fanaticism'.[86]

Another line of defence against any terrorist attack is diplomacy. All states would say that they employ diplomacy as a primary protective measure. If dialogue is entered into and if agreements are reached, then, so the theory runs, aggression does not take place. When states deal with terrorist organizations, though, the tool box of possible defensive measures may not include diplomacy. Governments have in the past negotiated with terrorists (the British with the Provisional IRA, the US with Lebanese groups, etc.[87]), but the Islamist terrorist of today is of such an order and characterized by such zeal that it becomes difficult to entertain thoughts of negotiation. Al Qaeda's drive, for instance, is not really towards an achievable political end: 'Its objective is metaphysical: a titanic struggle between "good" and "evil" forces.'[88] Not much common ground, then, for diplomacy to exploit.

This is not to say that diplomacy does not have its place. Diplomacy can be used to persuade certain *states* that sponsoring or harbouring terrorists is ill-advised. And other small states, which want to tackle their own indigenous terrorist groups but lack the capacity to do so, can be assisted. Their military and civilian personnel can be given the requisite training and equipment.[89]

Linked to diplomacy is the idea that more general engagement policies and charm offensives could be employed. These might undercut the hatred generated for the West in the Muslim world. 'Terrorism', as one observer puts it, 'is not ubiquitous and neither is it uncontainable, but the potential for its occurrence is virtually as widespread as is the manifestation of bitter political antagonisms . . . reduce the latter and you will reduce, though not eliminate, the former.'[90] The methods used in such 'reductions' can be wideranging: from 'community outreach' operations all the way up to building fewer of those 'provocative' fast-food outlets.[91]

While certain measures may chip away at the edifice that is anti-Western sentiment in Islamic communities, the sores run deep. There seems to be no predisposition for the acceptance of any 'hearts and minds' campaign.[92] This does not mean, of course, that attempts cannot be made to engage. Through engagement comes greater understanding, and through greater understanding comes not only an appreciation of the feelings of alien cultures, but also an appreciation of the nature of the opponent. As a recent official British publication put it, a level of defence against terrorist attacks can emerge through the creation of a degree of appreciation of 'the causes, motivations, intentions, capabilities, organisational structures, and value sets' of possible terrorist opponents.[93] Clearly, however, the British got it wrong in their levels of understanding of how terrorists operate in the London bombings of July 2005. The UK authorities had actually lowered their warning levels prior to these terrorist attacks. They seemed to have no idea that they would draw a terrorist outrage. And this even when the G8 summit – a prime terrorist target given that the eyes of the world would thus be on the UK – was due to start on the very day of the 7 July bombings.

More prosaic defensives measures include restricting access in target cities, placing physical barriers around buildings, and having a greater police presence. Steps taken also include some that infringe civil liberties: more random checks of people, more lines in airports, more calls for ID cards, and more border controls. But care needs to be taken in getting the balance right. The threat posed by terrorists should never be such that they can have profound negative impacts on free societies. Fear of terrorism should never undermine what democracies are all about. Indeed, clamping down hard may make the problem worse. British heavy-handed actions in Northern Ireland, for instance, in the early 1970s actually created an IRA threat where none had existed at the time.[94] On the other hand, democracies should never be soft touches. A salutary warning comes from Japan. Here, in the 1990s, the police waited too long before moving against Aum Shinrikyo because of laws prohibiting interference with religious organizations. Despite knowledge of what the organization was doing, only after the subway attack was action finally taken against the sect.[95]

The most dreaded attack is one using WMD. The fear can be reduced, of course, if sufficient preparatory measures are taken. The first port of call here is to ensure that treaties such as the Nuclear Non-Proliferation Treaty are adhered to.[96] Then there is the need to maintain the requisite level of security measures at potential sources of WMD – nuclear plants, factories, laboratories and the like. The next step has to be the creation of adequate emergency service provision such that casualties of WMD can be cared for properly. Hospitals, for instance, need to have well-trained staff with the right equipment. Medical personnel need to be aware of the symptoms of WMD injuries, so that rare wounds and illnesses can be recognized and tackled early (which patently they were not in the post-September 11 anthrax attacks[97]). Vaccinations also need to be readied and on hand. The public at large should be educated to ensure alertness, while avoiding the idea that the use of WMD is just around the corner, which might induce a degree of panic.

All these defensive measures are fairly simple and straightforward. They do, however, cost money. The US in 2004 allocated to the Department of Homeland Defense the sum of $6bn to defend *just* against biological terrorism.[98] With such figures involved and with budgets tight, there is a natural reluctance in places like the UK to invest in capabilities – particularly when they might never be needed. Hospitals in Britain, for instance, have been paring down excess capacity in recent years in order to be more 'efficient', and thus have left little slack in the system to cope with major incidents such as WMD attacks.[99]

Defensive measures work best, of course, when you know what the terrorist will do. Resources can then be targeted to deal with a known threat. But 'knowing' requires good intelligence. Where the 'old' terrorist was concerned, gaining intelligence was easier than with today's version. The history of terrorism tends to be a story of the threat coming from those dedicated to political change in individual countries (Red Army Faction, Red Brigade, ETA, IRA, etc.). These terrorists would be understood by the security services of their own countries, who would then be able to deal with them. But now the situation has changed. It has changed because the challenge from the terrorist has become much more widespread. There exists today an Islamist threat that spans the globe, employing terrorists who are more geographically widespread and far more mobile then they ever were, and who use funding sources far more diverse than at any time hitherto. And because this menace is now so wide-ranging, the response to it must also be wide-ranging; it is a transnational problem requiring transnational solutions. Co-operation across state borders is thus vital. This is especially true of defensive measures that look to prevent the terrorist from gaining the wherewithal to have the desired impact. If the spread of weapons across borders, especially WMD, is limited, then the terrorist will present a much reduced threat.[100] And while acknowledging the need for international collaboration, it must not be forgotten that domestic (inter-agency) partnerships are also vital. This has been lacking in recent years as turf wars undermine liaison between, in the case of the US, the likes of the CIA, FBI, NSA and DIA[101] – to name only some of the agencies involved in US counter-terrorism.[102]

The problem here, though, is that co-operation across a wide spectrum of agencies and countries relies on an agreement that a mutual enemy actually exists, on what the threat actually is, and on who the terrorists actually are. 'Terrorism' is a subjective term, not an objective one. There can never be an across-the-board definition of terrorism or of terrorists, because views always vary as to where terrorism ends and, as the saying goes, freedom fighting begins. If different states cannot agree on who the terrorists are, then trans-national agreements will not work.[103] This inability to define the terrorist caused many a diplomatic spat in the days of the 'old' terrorists (when, for instance, IRA 'terrorists' could take refuge in the US). Now, though, given the nature of the terrorist threat and its ubiquity, there is a greater degree of collaboration between Western security services. As the head of Britain's secret intelligence service, MI6, put it, 'International co-operation to combat the terrorist threat has never been closer or more productive.'[104] However, there are still countries on the margins of the Western powers who are not singing from the same hymn-sheet. Some, like Saudi Arabia, have their own reasons not to co-operate. Aware that groups like Al Qaeda have a good deal of support within the country, the Saudi authorities have something of a *laissez-faire* attitude to apprehending known terrorists. Better to offend foreign powers than to create domestic unrest.[105]

The generally close-knit nature of the 'new' terrorist groupings means that they are almost impervious to the human intelligence (HUMINT) resources that anti-terrorist forces used to rely on. For Western security organizations to actually place intelligence operatives inside such closed groups as Al Qaeda was and is extremely difficult.[106] Today's terrorist is also now wise to the capabilities offered by signals intelligence (SIGINT). To avoid interception of communications traffic, the terrorist will, on the one hand, make use of sophisticated devices that encrypt communications and, on the other, communicate via such low-tech and non-interceptible means as 'runners' carrying messages in their heads or on bits of paper. By actually being 'backward', the terrorist can subvert technology. As one US intelligence officer put it concerning operations to seize Al Qaeda suspects in Afghanistan: 'There was an over-expectation by us that technology could do more than it did. Al Qaeda are very smart . . . Our intelligence is hi-tech – they went back to primitive methods that we Americans cannot adapt to.'[107] The US and its allies became so used, throughout the Cold War, to employing SIGINT means to find out what their enemies – including terrorists – were doing that virtually all intelligence-gathering investment went down that particular avenue at the expense of other means and of 'redundancy' (i.e. back-up if primary means fail). There is certainly now no capacity in the SIGINT-collecting world to check on notes in pockets. Here is an example of the way in which the asymmetric adversary can downshift to overcome and perhaps totally negate a Western technological advantage. It is the action–reaction model.

Good intelligence will certainly provide a safeguard, specifically where WMD attacks are concerned. While it will always be difficult to find out what terrorist groups are planning, it should be relatively easy to find out if they will be using WMD. For groups trying to acquire WMD create a profile. In attempts to purchase WMD, they will ask too many questions; in attempts to steal materials, they will be too obvious; and if they want to manufacture their own, they will create a visible infrastructure – laboratories and the recruitment of scientists. It is such signatures that intelligence organizations will pick up on, and defensive action can then be taken.[108]

It is, of course, not only in the realm of defence that intelligence on the terrorist foe is useful. It is also essential in order to take offensive action. For given the nature of the terrorist threat in the current era, there is also a need to go beyond defensive measures. Where Islamists are concerned – with their promises of mass devastation – the liberal democracies cannot sit still and wait to be attacked;

offensive action is also called for. Terrorists need to be physically targeted in their 'lairs', in order to deny them ease of preparation, to disrupt their planning procedures, to degrade their capabilities, and to destroy their infrastructure.

Offence

The first offensive measure, and perhaps the least controversial, is that aimed at cutting off the funds of the terrorist. Patently the targeting of terrorist coffers can produce results.[109] 'Financing', as Bill Rammell expresses it, 'is the lifeblood on which terrorists survive. Without money they can't train. They can't plan. They can't travel. And they can't attack.'[110] True, but we need to be aware that the cost of mounting terrorist outrages can be fairly minimal. The September 11 operation did not cost that much to put into effect, yet caused an inordinate amount of damage. The Provisional IRA's operation to put a bomb in the City of London in 1994 cost about $3,000 (and led to a repair bill of some $1 bn).[111] Most recent large bombs have been made from ingredients no more complex than fertilizer and diesel, and smaller ones from the likes of nail varnish and olive oil![112] The costs involved in mounting terrorist attacks are certainly not prohibitive.

While Western security agencies can seek to limit the financing of terror, notably to reduce the ability to obtain large-cost items such as WMD, in many ways they would be locking the stable after the horse has bolted. The expensive infrastructure of the Al Qaeda training camps that existed in Afghanistan in the 1990s has done its job, in that it has created a cadre of *trained* terrorists who have now spread to the four winds since *Operation Enduring Freedom* and who have now taken their skills with them to pass on to others.[113]

One of Al Qaeda's skills is the ability to move finances around. While it may be possible to freeze certain bank accounts and seize assets, the sponsors and bank-rollers of the terrorist have adopted new methods of financing and have become more adroit with the movement of funds. Here again is the relative advantage of the asymmetric player: the ability to be flexible and to change and adapt quickly when put under pressure. One very flexible means of cash transfer practised in the Muslim world is that known as the *hawala* (or 'trust') system.[114] This has the capacity to involve so many different players that intercepting the passage of funds for nefarious purposes would be well-nigh impossible.[115] This is not to say, however, that everything should not be done to limit the passage of terrorist funds. It is important that this is done: 'the single most important initiative taken by the majority of European states has been the introduction of measures that may be used to suppress the financing of terrorism'.[116] We must be wary, though, of thinking that we have a panacea in such initiatives; where there is enough fervour, there will always be enough funding.

Offensive action can also take the form – in the domestic realm – of arresting suspected terrorists before they have taken any action. Such a step is fraught with civil liberties issues and risks inflaming Islamist sentiment rather countering it. Again, as an example, the British in 1971 in Northern Ireland locked up without trial all *suspected* IRA terrorists under the Internment system, but quickly realized that they had made a huge mistake as they tried to deal with the backlash they encountered both in Ireland and across the world.[117] The anti-terrorist campaign in Northern Ireland was probably set back 20 years by this one act. The arrest, or elimination, of even one person who is innocent *may* create many more problems than the jailing or elimination of many known terrorists actually solves.

Direct offensive action can be taken abroad in the form of kinetic attack, i.e. the use of military muscle. Such action was evident after the terrorist attack on the Berlin discothèque in 1986 when US aircraft bombed targets in Libya. It also occurred after the East Africa embassy bombings in 1998 when the US launched missile attacks on Al Qaeda camps in Afghanistan and on a pharmaceuticals plant in Sudan. Such activities, however, carry some 'baggage' in terms of international law. These acts by the US were technically illegal under customary (i.e. unwritten, but accepted) international law.[118] The right of 'self-defence' under such law, which the US used as a reason to carry out such raids, did not cover *ex post facto* actions, i.e. 'retribution'. However, the fact that the US in its actions was seen to comply with two of the most fundamental of the 'just war' principles – 'necessity' and 'proportionality'[119] – meant that most states accepted that such actions were, in fact, 'legal'. The actions carried out here by the US, and their general acceptance, have meant that customary international law has *now altered* to include the right of 'retribution' for terrorist attacks so long as necessity and proportionality are applied. Thus there were no real legal complications surrounding the US-led, post-September 11 attack on Afghanistan to destroy Al Qaeda camps.[120]

However, restrained retribution is one matter, 'pre-emption' is another. No state should initiate attacks before it is itself attacked; Article 51 of the United Nations Charter is clear on this.[121] However, pre-emptive action can be applied if a state knows that it is about to be attacked. But to undertake such 'legal' pre-emptive action, both customary and extant international law agree that this action must be in accordance with the concepts of necessity, proportionality *and* 'last resort'.[122] Perhaps, for instance, the Israelis could make a case for their 1967 pre-emptive actions before the Six-Day War, but their attack on Osiraq in 1981 becomes harder to justify.[123]

The importance of the idea of the use of pre-emptive measures against *terrorists* today lies with the fear of mass-casualty – including WMD – attacks. Can any state wait to be attacked if the consequences can be so profound? Measures may need to be taken to thwart such attacks and disrupt the plans of the terrorists.[124] The undertaking of such activities is clearly set out in the 'Bush Doctrine' of 2002.[125] This, in essence, states that the US has the right to take pre-emptive military action against terrorists if there is evidence that American lives will be endangered if it takes no action.[126] 'We must', as President Bush put it, 'take the battle to the enemy, disrupt his plans, and confront the worst threats before they emerge.'[127] Thus the US and some of its allies are now acting according to the premiss of 'anticipatory self-defence'.[128] This concept appears to be doubtful under international law.[129] There are two issues here. One is that if the US does act militarily in accordance with the logic of anticipatory self-defence, then it may have a hard time proving to both friends and enemies that such action was actually necessary.[130] The equivalent of a smoking gun may be hard to find. The second point is that once states start operating outside international norms, then they will inevitably lose some of the international *co-operation* that is a vital part, as has been noted, of any counter-terrorist measures.[131] If certain key states or international bodies cannot agree with the aggressive and perhaps 'illegal' (by whatever standard) actions of a 'reactionary' US and some of its close friends, then they may stand in opposition to them.[132] The terrorist's life could then be made a lot easier. The British, with their policies in Northern Ireland in the 1970s, found that both of the above consequences came to pass.

Having pointed out the problems with pre-emption as a form of offensive action, it is necessary, though, to add that international law, be it customary or in the statute book, was created according to a very different logic than that pertaining today. Such laws were not formulated at a time when terrorists had the possibility, through possession of WMD, to create untold destruction and havoc. With the existence of *possible* intent and *possible* capability, then, perhaps states do have the right to assume worst-case scenarios given that those scenarios could be so devastating. Can you really wait to be attacked with a nuclear bomb and *then* take action?

There is one further problem with pre-emption: it has the capacity to be counter-productive unless it is carried out with some subtlety. One of the recurring concerns about the use of Western militaries against asymmetric adversaries is that they tend to be rather blunt instruments. Current military structures and doctrines were formulated to deal with the Cold War battlefield where the enemy, above all, would be visible – either to the naked eye or to some form of sensor. Terrorists today are not quite so obliging. Given their lack of profile, they have the capacity to disappear almost completely. As Colin Gray puts it, 'Even a country as powerful as the United States requires that its enemies have map co-ordinates as a necessary condition for chastisement.'[133] And when that necessary condition is absent, and when blunt instruments are employed to try and strike them, then the inevitable result is 'collateral' damage and all that entails.

To engineer the subtlety required to ensure that pre-emption has its required results, three particular factors are essential: having the correct intelligence, so that the right target sets are selected; having the requisite military skills to hit those targets; and having the 'intelligence', in a more cerebral sense, to understand the effects that would be created and to have a plan to deal with their consequences. For hitting the wrong targets or not hitting them accurately enough when acting pre-emptively can make the situation, and thus the terrorist threat, worse. If innocent people are killed, if questions are asked, if public support wanes, and if an increased level of hatred is engendered, then it was all for nought.[134] When acting pre-emptively against the terrorist foe, it is vital to prevent actions at the tactical and operational levels from becoming strategic issues.[135] This theme will be returned to later in the book.

Stopping the terrorist

The ultimate response to the terrorist asymmetric adversary has to come in the way in which the liberal democracies undermine the goals of the terrorists. This is principally a question of the targets of terrorism – the populations of Western countries – displaying a suitable level of resolve and of vigilance. In terms of resolve, the terrorists must be shown that their attacks have little *impact*. The goal, after an outrage, should always be to carry on life as normal as if nothing had happened. The people of London showed this to good effect in July 2005. After a bomb that killed fifty-two people, Londoners just got on with their lives. The next day the Stock Market rose 200 points, the media moved on to other things, and the whole affair was treated with 'relative indifference' by Londoners.[136] If such attitudes are taken, then the terrorists will be denied the impact they most crave; without *impact*, terrorism is nothing.

Vigilance is also essential. The vigilance of governments, of security services and, most of all, of ordinary people will provide the greatest protection against terrorism. When people are alert, terrorists can never act with impunity. Vigilance also negates impact. The terrorist will always be looking for factors which contribute to impact, and one of these factors is surprise. Impact comes from the fact that terrorist outrages appear against a background of peace; we do not expect them, they are a shock. Thus terrorists in liberal democracies rarely follow one attack with another; there is no point, since shock value has already been lost.[137] There will then be long periods when the terrorist does not strike. The terrorists, as asymmetric adversaries, have what we lack: the quality of patience. For it is in these long periods of calm that target states let their guard drop and lose their vigilance.

Finally, there needs to be an appreciation in Western states that, in responding to the threat of terrorism, there is no ultimate answer. Any attempts to fight a 'war on terror' may be deemed unwise. It is not a 'war' against terrorism; it is a struggle or campaign. The vernacular of 'war' requires that a point of victory be reached. But the terrorist can never be totally defeated, because in attempting to totally eradicate the menace, the means that would have to be used would inevitably create even more terrorists. Draconian laws and heavy-handed military action are, as has been proved throughout history, manna from heaven to terrorist organizations. They want states to overreact. As one British government minister put it, 'Asymmetric warfare can wreak its greatest damage by producing an ill-judged response by the state.'[138] Terrorism is best treated as a problem, but not as a major threat. The risks from terrorism, as a foremost analyst puts it, 'cannot be eliminated, only contained and managed'.[139]

Conclusion

The terrorist is the asymmetric adversary with the highest profile. Few people in the West have not been touched in some way by terrorist action in the last few years. In the past, most Western states have had some experience of terrorism and learnt how to deal with it, or at least how to live with it. But that was 'old' terrorism, mainly political in nature with mainly political solutions. The possibility always existed that a campaign would end if 'peace processes' began or if just a few of the terrorists were arrested or killed. But the main threat now is from Islamist terrorists, and is of a completely new order. Their type of terrorism cannot just be ended by political compromises or a limited number of incarcerations. For where once there were just isolated small groups, there is now a network of groups with a substantial number of affiliates and hangers-on across a number of states. And they are incredibly committed to their cause. They are zealots driven by a sense that their culture is under threat, and that they suffer injustices at the hands of the West, and especially at those of its 'leader', the US. These Islamists also have a range of assets available to them that previous terrorist organizations lacked. They have access to a wide array of funding, weaponry and communications technology, which, when combined with their unbounded fervour, makes them a daunting adversary, not just now but also for many, many years into the future.[140]

We need to be careful, however. The intent of today's terrorists to cause great destruction is not *always* matched by their capabilities. There is much dark discussion of the use of WMD. These, though, are very difficult, as Aum discovered, to field as effective weapons. The question the terrorist then has to ask is why spend all that money and invest all that time in procuring WMD when there are far simpler ways of creating the requisite impact? The London bombers of July 2005 with their nail-varnish devices would attest to that.

Responses to the terrorist asymmetric adversary have to be a mix of defensive and offensive measures. Defensive measures will be mostly mundane but vital. They will rely predominantly on the ability of security services, police forces and military organizations – with help from ordinary citizens – to maintain an adequate level of vigilance. Offensive measures will also be part of the equation given the fact that the threat is so severe. Co-operation will be vital too. Domestically, in Western states there must be a wide-ranging alliance of security agencies and military organizations to counter any threats. There must also be co-operation across borders. The days of terrorist groups and their activities being confined to one country are gone. The problem is now international, and it needs international responses. And because these responses rely so much on international co-operation, the big players then must have very similar hymn-sheets in front of them. If any one state attempts to go off message and tries to 'solve' the problem on its own, then it risks doing more harm than good. For in tackling the terrorist asymmetric adversary, we must be careful. Countering terrorism has to involve a package of measures, but a package that has as its ultimate goal the *limiting* of terrorist action, not its total elimination. In striving for absolutist endings, we risk actually exacerbating the problem. This can happen with pre-emptive action abroad, and it can also happen domestically through the imposition of draconian internal security measures. Such action will risk alienating allies and our own populations, and perhaps be divisive enough to drive domestic minorities – in places like the US and the UK – into the welcoming arms of the terrorists. The terrorist asymmetric adversary presents a problem that needs to be managed and lived with, not one which has to be smashed into oblivion.

3 ASYMMETRY AND INFORMATION WARFARE

Introduction

We live, apparently, in an 'information world'. Where once the human race relied on word of mouth for information passage, we now rely – via smoke signals, 'snail' mail, heliographs, telegraphs, telephones and radio – on such modish technologies as microwave, fibre-optic and satellite links. The success and ubiquity of information technology (IT) has changed societies across the world in a variety of remarkable ways. With the current capacity for the swift and unhindered passage of information there exist now, among other benefits, home computers, mobile/cellular phones, 24-hour news channels and automated banking. The pace of life is faster, as the speed of decision making, based on information flow, has increased.

That fundamental pillar of human endeavour, warfare, has likewise seen an increase in the speed of information passage. Throughout recent history, the ability of military organizations to bring together and control greater mass and to act more swiftly in a more co-ordinated and targeted fashion has improved. The telegraph allowed the American Civil War and the Franco-Prussian War to assume the proportions that they did, and to be conducted with the dynamism that they were. Without radio communication, German *Blitzkrieg* tactics would have been impossible. Without information from radar, Great Britain might not have won the Battle of Britain. Moreover, without the Internet and satellites and a host of other information force multipliers, the recent Gulf Wars might have descended into drawn-out and mutually punishing slug-fests.

The West now, of course, has military organizations that are very efficient and very effective, in large part due to the amount of information that can be gathered and passed in limited time frames. Information is made available more readily than hitherto, allowing decisions, suited to the environment, to be made in a timely fashion that facilitates the destruction of the enemy whilst aiding the defence of friendly forces. All this is encapsulated in the US military's striving to enact what is known as the Revolution in Military Affairs (RMA). The RMA is 'the application of new technologies into a significant number of military systems combined with innovative operational concepts and organisational adaptation in a way that fundamentally alters the character and conduct of conflict'.[1] The proponents of the RMA say that it will provide, and to a large degree is already providing, a new form of warfare that makes unparalleled use of IT.[2] A vital component of the RMA is the ability to generate network centric warfare (NCW) or, in British parlance, a network enabled capability (NEC). NCW/NEC 'enables instantaneous data distribution, resulting in a common operational picture shared by separate units, allowing for better informed decisions at any level of command'.[3]

Among the more vital contributors to the RMA are the Internet (itself invented by the US military) and satellite-based technologies. Satellites provide a cornucopia of increasingly accurate images of the Earth and ensure better command and control through the smoother and more secure passage of communications. Beyond communications, perhaps chief among the assets provided by satellite technology is the Global Positioning System (GPS). The GPS consists of twenty-four satellites orbiting at a height of 11,000 miles. These are arranged so that any point on the Earth (or above it) has a line-of-sight link with at least four satellites, which are then able to provide data to fix that point's exact position. The GPS allows for the accurate positioning of everything from ballistic missiles to individual soldiers.[4]

The RMA also makes use of Unmanned Aerial Vehicles (UAVs[5]), which can be guided by the GPS. UAVs will observe from above and, through video links, transmit back real-time images of events below without risking pilots' lives. There is thus, on today's battlefield, the capability to find the position of an opponent more easily, at reduced cost, and with little risk. Once located, links – often using Internet technology – between sensors and increasingly accurate shooters (e.g. PGMs) supposedly ensure the swift and efficient destruction of the opponent and his assets. The RMA, with IT at its centre, offers control of the battle space; it offers the promise of quick victories against enemies who lack the same capabilities.

However, while Western societies and their military organizations have gained immeasurably from their push to make greater use of information, they have presented a window of opportunity to less well-endowed opponents. Weaknesses have been created that the asymmetric adversary can utilize. For the increased availability, tempo and efficiency of the flow of information in both civilian and military realms has created *reliance*. We have now reached a point in the world's history where the most developed states cannot do without the swift and accurate passage of information. There are few, if any, essential services and systems that are not linked in some way to the information 'superhighway' of the Internet. What, though, if the Internet had a glitch? Where would we be if such Internet-reliant systems as the water and electricity supplies, the phone network and the banking system were disabled? Our reliance on the free flow of information is becoming more and more crucial, as more and more services take advantage of what the Internet has to offer. Likewise, in the military realm, where would the world's best be without the force multipliers such as the Internet, the GPS, satellites or even radio links? The more powerful the economy or the military organization of a state, the more likely they are to rely on IT. And, of course, the greater the level of reliance, the greater the level of that concomitant of reliance: *vulnerability*.

The sense of vulnerability is exacerbated by the fact that our information systems have to be open. The cornerstone of the information system, i.e. the Internet, in order to be effective and efficient, has to be accessible. It lets us in to use it, but it also lets in those bent on malfeasance. And once in, the interconnectedness of the system, in both civilian and military spheres, allows for the cascade effects of such malfeasance. Cause a problem in one area, and the possibility is created of having effects in many others. The accessibility of the Internet for civilian use is well known, but the US military also relies on the same system for much of its information flow. It needs to be remembered that advances in the capacities of modern military organizations to generate, process and disseminate information – the bases of their strength – are built largely on the civilian information infrastructure. It has been estimated, for instance, that about 95 per cent of all US military communications pass through civilian, and therefore 'open', commercial means.[6]

The turning of strengths into vulnerabilities is obviously what the asymmetric warrior is looking for. Here we have an information system on which great reliance is placed, and yet much of it is open. It allows for attack by those who would wish to cause delay, introduce deception, and create disinformation. The information system has become a battleground. The weak want to have impact and effect from interfering with a system on which such reliance is placed, and the strong wish to protect their information flow. The ranks of the 'weak' here can draw their number from a variety of actors: individual computer 'geeks', those wishing simply to draw attention to an issue, organized crime gangs, terrorist groups, firms and corporations, and even state actors. All can indulge in what is known as 'information warfare' (IW) for their own particular ends, and all can create fundamental effects. As Bishop and Goldman put it of the situation now, 'What is really new is the widening ability, due to both the changing nature of the capabilities of state and non-state actors and the increasing vulnerabilities of advanced society, to disrupt the information and networks that support crucial day-to-day workings of civilian, commercial and military systems alike.'[7] Thus, on the information battleground, as Martin Libicki stresses, 'it seems that the small have caught up with the strong and that size does not matter, at least not as it once did.'[8] The small and weak, through attacking information passage, can have devastating effects on the large and powerful in a variety of different ways and to a degree not possible before.

The asymmetric adversary can practise IW. But what exactly is 'information warfare', and how does it manifest itself? A true definition of IW is a little hard to come by; it seems to be a catch-all concept. As John Rothrock remarks, 'it remains very difficult to determine if there is anything that IW is not'.[9] A good definition of IW, though, would obviously cover the fact that IW can take place in the civilian and military realms. Being about 'warfare', it will also include something about offensive capabilities. But IW also has that other aspect of creating a situation whereby practitioners, while attacking an opponent's information, will want to protect their own information so that they are constantly advantaged. Thus there is a defensive aspect to IW. Terrorist groups, for instance, may launch their own IW attacks, but will always want to prevent the authorities from damaging and infiltrating their own information systems. Military organizations will do likewise. A good definition of IW, therefore, should take note of this dynamic. IW can thus be seen as 'Actions taken in support of objectives that influence decision-makers by affecting the information and/or information systems of others while protecting your own information and/or information systems'.[10]

While this definition catches something of the flavour of IW, it does not take into account and make clear the breadth of actors involved, or the breadth of means that IW can incorporate. A definition, for instance, needs to make it quite clear that IW is not all about cyber activity, i.e. 'virtual' attacks – a common misconception. For, indeed, 'IW is an umbrella concept embracing many disciplines.'[11] By way of example, blowing up a telegraph pole or dropping propaganda leaflets from an aircraft are aspects of IW. Thus perhaps a more comprehensive but slightly awkward definition might be: 'IW is a coherent and synchronised blending of physical and virtual actions to have countries, organisations and individuals perform, or not perform, actions so that your goals and objectives are attained and maintained, while simultaneously preventing competitors from doing the same to you.'[12]

Given the scope of IW and its prominent role in asymmetric warfare, it is probably best for clarity's sake to look at the issue under four specific headings: attacks on infrastructure, deception, electronic warfare, and psychological operations.[13]

IW attacks on infrastructure

These involve the targeting of computer networks, electronic systems and other infrastructure that supports information passage. The most familiar term used here is 'cyber war'. Cyber war is a subset of IW. Definitions of cyber war are problematical, and some authors use the term fairly loosely. One source has it that 'cyber war is the use of all available electronic and computer tools to shut down the enemy's electronics and communications'.[14] Most observers of cyber war, however, are broader in their interpretation of the term. The first to actually coin the phrase 'cyber war' (in 1993) were John Arquilla and David Ronfeldt, who seem to have come, through a variety of definitions, to the idea that simple is good. They now see cyber war as being 'a concept that refers to information-oriented military warfare'.[15] Attacks thus do not necessarily involve only virtual attacks; they can involve the physical disruption or destruction of systems by kinetic means. Thus cyber war can range from the planting of viruses within computers (where both means and target are cyber) to 'physical attacks' where, say, aircraft bomb buildings that house the computers that control, for instance, a telephone system or a radar that feeds a computer (target is cyber, not the means).[16] We need also to be mindful – although definitions like Arquilla and Ronfeldt's exclude the contingency – of the fact that cyber war can have non-military targets and be sourced to non-military actors (such as terrorists).

Attacks on infrastructure will be examined here under two headings: 'Types of Attack' and 'Sources of Attack'. These will be followed by a review of the possible responses that can be made to the threats posed by such attacks.

Types of attack on infrastructure

The types, in turn, may be considered under the headings of virtual and physical attacks.

Virtual attacks

Here is probably the most familiar aspect of IW. Virtual attacks constitute IW waged over the Internet. The main participants in this form of warfare are the 'hackers'. They want to manipulate and disrupt electronic information systems to influence an adversary's perceptions and behaviour through the corruption of their computer networks and databases. This will be done through the use of the likes of viruses, worms, Trojan horses, logic bombs, zombies, etc.[17]

Obviously, the more reliant on the Internet any particular target is, the greater the possible damage that hackers can inflict. Most of the developed world's states have IT-based economies and Critical National Infrastructures (CNIs). CNIs would include the public utilities, transportation, telephone, air traffic and banking systems. These tend to operate with Internet support, and thus, when targeted, can be vulnerable. As a US congressional panel put it, reliance on the Internet was a source of substantial economic, industrial and societal advantage, but 'it creates vulnerabilities and critical interdependencies that are potentially disastrous to the US'.[18] It has been estimated, for instance, that if several hackers worked together with a budget of a few million dollars, then they could actually engineer a Doomsday scenario that would 'bring the United States to its knees'.[19] Indeed, nervous about the possibilities of attack, in 2002 the Federal Reserve Bank changed from using what was seen as vulnerable Microsoft software.[20]

Virtual attacks on CNIs are actually fairly common. Since September 11, for example, there have been many instances of hackers from the Middle East trying to get into American power-plant systems (although with little success). On the commercial level, attacks on the Internet-based companies Yahoo, Amazon and E-Bay, through the planting of viruses in 1999–2000, are estimated to have caused $7 bn worth of damage.[21] Many of these cyber attacks, however, are actually kept secret by the firms involved.[22] The embarrassment factor can be substantial, but catastrophic loss of faith can also accrue if these companies are seen to be vulnerable.[23] Indeed, much of the world's 'faith-based' e-commerce system could come under threat if any overall lack of trust became apparent.

In the military realm, the main problem, of course, for the USA and for the militaries of other Western states is that the striving for such force multipliers as the NWC/NEC to create much improved command and control capabilities means a massive reliance on the more open civilian IT infrastructure. And while the military will use strong firewalls to prevent access and use encryption devices that make it impossible to decipher communications, systems and traffic can still be interfered with. Civilian satellites, for instance, on which the military rely so much, can be disrupted or even sent spinning out of control by hacker activity.[24] Moreover, as the US military also buys most of its microchips from commercial sources (mostly from abroad), there is the possibility that these chips may have been tampered with. Thus viruses, Trojan horses, etc., can be introduced into military systems to be activated later when and if they are needed.[25]

Physical destruction

Physical damage is usually brought about by military or terrorist action. This may involve using kinetic-effect weapons or explosives that degrade computer systems themselves or their source of information, e.g. a radar array. Directed-energy weapons can also be used which 'fry' the circuitry in computers, thereby disabling them. In this regard, there are basically two types of weapon: those that produce an electro-magnetic pulse (EMP) and those that produce high-energy radio frequency (HERF). More is known about EMP blasts and the damage they do than about HERF (see also chapter 4). EMP blasts are normally associated with nuclear explosions, but a manageable EMP weapon can be constructed and placed, for instance, on the back of a truck and directed at buildings destroying any computers inside along with their data.[26] HERF weapons work in much the same way as those using EMP. The development of small-scale HERF directed-energy weapons is cloaked in secrecy, but they seem to be available. Portable versions have appeared on the black market in the Baltic states, and one US government scientist said that he could make one using everyday materials costing no more than $500.[27] There are rumours that in the 1990s some financial institutions in London paid out huge sums to blackmailers who threatened to use HERF transmitters that would disable computers in their offices.[28]

Sources of attack on infrastructure

Attacks on infrastructure will come from various sources. It is perhaps most convenient to look at these in terms of attacks from individuals, groups and states.

Individuals

The level of development of today's IT allows very small players to produce very large effects. As James Dunnigan puts it, 'There has never been a time when war was open to anonymous individuals sitting at distant locations armed with computers and other electronic devices.'[29] Stories are legion of individuals, often very young, accessing and causing disruption to the systems of the powerful. A 16-year-old boy in the UK, for instance, accessed some 100 US defence systems in 1994.[30] Another Briton carried out the 'biggest military computer hack of all time' and made 'the US military district of Washington . . . inoperable' in 2001–2.[31] For any computer 'geek' confident of his or her own abilities much kudos can be gained among his or her friends in the hacker world by breaking into the supposedly most secure sites. It is this search for kudos among peers – rather than a desire to make money or disrupt systems – that means there is often little ill intent involved. The tendency is for individual hackers to want merely to show off their prowess, and they will target government sites since these supposedly have the best defences, and therefore the challenge is the greater.[32]

Some individual hackers, though, *are* intent on serious mischief. But they will either be professional cyber criminals or disgruntled employees or former employees.[33] Such individuals will hack into and damage, or threaten to damage, information systems. And they may employ blackmail.[34] The number of people carrying out such attacks is thought to be very small, although it is difficult to tell. They do not want publicity, and neither do the victims of their actions; again, firms do not want the world to believe that their IT systems are not secure: customers may be put off, and/or new attacks encouraged.[35]

There will doubtless be more cyber-savvy individuals coming through in the years ahead who will want to test their skills in the manner of a hooligan or a thief.[36] There are more and more computer-literate people emerging, especially from Eastern Europe and East Asia, who have the capacity to do considerable damage. It is estimated, for instance, that the number of 'cyber warriors' doubles every two years.[37]

Groups

Sub-state groups such as criminal gangs and terrorist organizations can launch more co-ordinated and more problematic attacks. In theory, they can only do as much damage as any individual, but their motivations to cause disruption can be much greater. And beyond virtual attacks, there are those gangs, with access (or threatened access) to HERF and EMP weapons, who are intent on blackmailing vulnerable firms with threats of physical destruction.

Terrorist organizations will attempt to carry out virtual and physical attacks. In 2000, for instance, Hizbollah, the Shia Islamic support movement/terrorist organization, launched cyber attacks against official Israeli government and commercial websites. With the high-tech Israeli economy based to a large degree on Internet companies, this campaign was quite effective. It caused an 8 per cent dip in the Israeli Stock Exchange. Israel, of course, could not react in kind, since Hizbollah had few computer-based resources. As one Israeli source put it, 'Their side has almost nothing to lose from this war, while ours has a lot to lose.'[38] Beyond Hizbollah, such tactics are becoming a favoured tool of Islamist groups in their struggle against Western opponents. As Faris Muhammed Al-Masri, founder of an Islamist website put it, 'As information technology comes to rule every part of life, it is no longer necessary to have rockets to destroy an electrical facility. Instead, penetrating the enemy's network and planting your code will get a better result.'[39]

Al Qaeda, as has been mentioned, has shown signs of wanting to be involved in cyber attacks.[40] This is known from computers captured in Afghanistan. There is, however, the question of the effect such attacks would have. Often virtual attacks on their own will not supply sufficient *impact*; there is usually a lack of the 'visibility' aspect of the impact equation.[41] What is considered highly likely, though, is an attack on information systems by terrorists running in conjunction with a kinetic bombing operation. The aim here would be to target, for instance, the information network of the emergency services, to slow down responsiveness to an outrage such that the original kinetic attack has greater effect.[42]

States

With the United States and its closest allies moving ahead so rapidly in terms of dominance in the information realm, it then becomes the path of least resistance for 'underdog' states to indulge in IW. Cyber war offers unique opportunities to leverage minimal assets. This was clearly seen during the Kosovo War in 1999, when Serbian hackers and their East European sympathizers launched attacks on more than 170 organizations worldwide with the aim of shutting down key computer systems in NATO countries.[43] The Serbs knew that their actions would not win the war, but IW pathways offered a possibility, given NATO's information reliance, of bringing about strategic effects.[44] The principal of these was the slowing down of the pace of NATO's offensive, in order to buy the time that would allow other avenues of defence to work in their favour – such as diplomacy and the opportunity to break down the fragile will of the NATO coalition.[45]

The Serb techniques, though, were fairly amateurish compared to what might be expected in terms of IW from a state like China. China is 'perhaps the best example of a country that has embraced IW'.[46] The authorities in Beijing have realized that future conflict with the US is not out of the question given the contretemps over Taiwan and China's general desire to become a great power. China, however, with its People's Liberation Army (PLA), does not have a conventional military that can challenge that of the US. Acknowledging this weakness, the PLA has explicitly stated that in any future war with the US a variety of asymmetric approaches will be adopted.[47] The aim would be to face the Americans not so much on *the* battlefield but on *many* battlefields and to bring about effects on a number of different levels. In pursuance of such a strategy, 'the Chinese have invested significantly in cyber warfare training and technology'.[48] Beijing is even considering setting up a fourth branch of its armed forces devoted to IW.[49] Chief among the tactics used would be cyber war against information networks within the US itself. The domestic realm is seen by the Chinese to be the Americans' soft underbelly. The potential targets include the computer systems of financial institutions, of utilities (electricity, water, telephone), of air traffic control, and of the mass media.[50] The point is that war, as the Chinese see it, would be brought home to the American *people*. It would not appear to them as some video game taking place on a distant shore and divorced from the mainstream of American life. The specificity of the threat enunciated by the Chinese authorities probably explains why they are so open with their future strategies *vis-à-vis* future war with the US. It is a warning. The warning is there from Beijing: begin a conflict with us, and you will suffer domestically; war, next time, would be up close and personal.

In terms of taking on the US military itself, Chinese generals boast that they will be able not only to introduce information-paralysing software, blocking software and deception software, but that they will also tap into enemy command and control systems. The philosophy runs along the lines of 'we need to ensure that the US military machine can only come at us piecemeal and not in a co-ordinated fashion'. For example, the PLA could alter US military databases to ensure that 155 mm shells would be delivered to artillery units using 105 mm howitzers. The US would thus be denied the use of such guns despite their not actually being destroyed. Such a form of attack is especially inviting, as US military logisticians, as well as those of other Western states, have adopted precision techniques and the 'just-in-time' philosophy. The use of thoroughly efficient computer-enabled delivery avoids slack in the system. But cause even a slight problem with that delivery by changing a few figures here and there, and precision techniques can quickly become a huge liability as they turn to chaos.[51] Strength is turned into vulnerability.

Moreover, any cyber attack need not be very thorough to be effective. With the merest inflection of cyber chicanery, seeds of doubt would be sown within any society or a military organization that is so reliant on the swift and accurate flow of information. Major effects can be achieved. Having just once added a nought to some market trader's computer data, would any figure in the financial markets, built on nothing but faith as they are, ever be trusted again? Change the figure 155 to 105, and would any military logistician continue to trust the other figures that he or she sees on his or her computer screen? If just once the imagery being sent via US reconnaissance downlinks (such as from a satellite) was manipulated by cyber means, would any intelligence picture ever be trusted again?[52] The frightening point is that the cyber attack does not have to be massive to cause mass effect; it is the following cascade effects that can often do that. And if we are so reliant on our information from technological sources, where do we go when we can no longer trust those sources?

Having said all this, the Chinese, of course, do not abjure the use of physical means in any war with the US.[53] They merely look upon future war as one in which a holistic approach needs to be taken so that they, as the weak, can go some way to level the battlefield with the strong.

What is perhaps most interesting here is the fact that if the authorities in Beijing are thinking along these lines and they see conflict with the US as inevitable, then what kind of preparation has already been made? Given that a large proportion of the integrated circuits used in the West are made in China, could these chips actually be programmed to carry out certain actions when required? It seems to be not inconceivable.[54] On the whole, though, states as such would be wary of launching huge cyber warfare attacks, given that the global system is so interconnected now; the attackers might cause damage to themselves.[55] Any general global disruption, however, caused by Chinese Trojan horses, worms, etc., would not affect the Chinese themselves so much, since their operating system of choice is Linux, not Microsoft.[56] Russia is another state which seems to have designs on causing disruption in the US through cyber attacks. US military sites have come under sustained assault from sources in Russia since 1998, which have left behind the likes of zombie programmes. The attacks are presumed to come from official Russian sources, since they only take place in the 9–5 time-frame (Moscow time).[57] In terms of physical cyber attacks, states such as China and Russia could also in the near future have the ability to target US satellites using EMP and HERF weapons. (For more on this mode, see chapter 4.)

Despite rhetorical suggestions that in the IW realm an individual attacker is empowered to the level of state actors, this is not really true. IW attacks by state actors will be more effective because states have access to more resources and have greater intelligence capabilities to deal with any defensive measures the target utilizes. They also have access to training facilities, so that attacks can be road-tested beforehand. Clearly an individual attacker is not able to do this.

Responding to asymmetric attacks on infrastructure

Obviously, infrastructure pertinent to the transmission of information such as telephone switchgear, fibre optic cables or even radar dishes can be protected from physical attack. Satellite systems can be protected by hardening (see chapter 4). The problems here are obvious but surmountable, physical assets protected by physical means. Virtual attacks on infrastructure are, however, more difficult to counter. The first question that needs to be considered is, what is the problem? Is there a distinct need for the powerful, information-rich states and their militaries to fear virtual cyber attacks on their infrastructure? As Libicki says, 'Were cyber terrorism or blackmail so easy, one or another malevolent party would have done it long ago to the United States or other advanced economies.'[58] The issue here, of course, is, how do we know that they have not already done so? There can be few detectable signatures of an attack. We also have evidence that certain corporations have secretly paid out huge sums to cyber blackmailers. Moreover, state actors such as China have no real incentive to show their hand just yet. The asymmetric warrior looks for surprise, for shock and for impact. The true asymmetric warrior bent on real damage does not poke away in pin-prick assaults, because in that way his opponent gets to know his methods of attack and can develop antidotes. The state asymmetric adversary will remain *patient*, waiting for a devastating assault with huge impact. As one Chinese general put it in regard to cyber war against the US, 'for a relatively long time it will be absolutely necessary that we quietly nurse our sense of vengeance . . . We must conceal our abilities and bide our time.'[59]

Given this situation, those charged with defending systems in the cyber realm have a difficult problem. They do not really know what form *major* IW attacks will take, so how can they prepare adequate defences? Protection of information systems is the subject of much research, and new means are constantly being developed that are designed to keep adversaries out. But one of the problems here is the sheer pace of change. Countermeasures are of their time and place. As new measures are introduced, so the hackers move on. As a recent head of the FBI, Louis Freeh, put it, '[Even] though we have markedly improved our capabilities to fight cyber-intrusions, the problem is growing even faster.'[60]

Countermeasures to hackers can take the form of firewalls, intrusion detection, strong authentication and antivirus programmes. These measures, of course, lessen the degree of access. But the very open nature and interconnectedness of the information system is its great strength. Information systems work best when access is unfettered; it has to be the 'superhighway'. Security against hacking cannot become a road block on that highway; information would not be passed quickly enough.[61] How do you restrict access, though, yet keep the strength of the system? How do you keep people out when, as one researcher put it, 'there is no longer an outside? When we are just inhabitants of cyberspace along with our adversaries?'[62]

Western militaries themselves might create a reasonable degree of protection, but they still have to use civilian IT systems. How much they should be reliant on these is a moot point. Military organizations also need to think very carefully about co-operation with civilian agencies, in order to develop countermeasures. The militaries can never keep up with the necessary countermeasures, given that they cannot keep up with the pace of development of IT in the civilian sector. Another problem is that one traditional 'general' means of military defence – deterrence – is one denied. Since IW attacks can be anonymous, then retaliation is out of the question, and the whole idea of deterrence disappears with it. If someone launches a nuclear weapon at you, then you can strike back. Not so in IW. Moreover, even if you knew the source of a major and catastrophic IW attack, could you actually retaliate, and in what way? A very serious attack may actually be seen as an act of 'war', but can you then contemplate some sort of *kinetic* retribution where people actually get killed?[63]

Another defensive tool can be the employment of individual hackers. Such individuals may actually be the best friend of the powerful. Since attacks by such people are rarely malicious, it seems appropriate that, once caught, these hackers be 'turned' to later find themselves in the employ of the authorities as 'white-hat hackers'. In essence, they are the poachers turned gamekeepers. These hackers can indicate where the vulnerabilities are, so that defences can be built against more serious and more devastating attacks. Here human intelligence is required far more than technological systems, because a human mind geared to hacking activities can *think* like an asymmetric cyber attacker, and *then* the right defensive techniques can be developed.[64]

As a final point, and returning to the constant theme of defending against asymmetric attacks, we may have to consider the fact that our sources of information, despite all our attempts, may be denied to us. We must then be able to carry on without them. Redundancy must be a part of the capacity to respond. If the Internet does not work, how do we pass our information? If there is no GPS, how do we navigate? If there are no satellites, are there then enough landline phones to allow voice communication? There must be a Plan B.

Deception

Deception is very much a part of IW, and very much an asymmetric technique.[65] It can be defined as 'a conscious and rational effort deliberately to mislead an opponent'.[66] Deception in warfare is, of course, a commonplace. As Sun Tzu, later to be read by many a strategist as the arch guru of deception, tells us, 'All warfare is based on deception.'[67] This may or may not be true. There surely have been military commanders down the centuries who have been arrogant enough, or even chivalrous enough, to believe that deception was not a necessary tool in the striving for victory. There would, however, be few underdogs in military engagements who would not look to deception as a force multiplier: 'The weaker the forces that are at the disposal of the supreme commander,' Clausewitz notes, 'the more appealing the use of cunning becomes.'[68] So it is with the modern asymmetric adversary. The vast disparities apparent these days in relative capabilities mean that the weak will be looking to use deception in whatever way they can. The weak will also be aided in this endeavour by the very fact that their opponents *are* so powerful. For the most powerful are always the most susceptible to deception, since, whether they realize it or not, power breeds arrogance, and arrogance blinds the powerful to things they do not wish to see.[69] Deception, moreover, is attractive to the weak, since it can be very cheap to practise, requiring little in the way of investment.[70] It is clearly a potent tool available to today's asymmetric warrior (see chapter 4).[71]

Deception techniques can be employed in the civilian realm, especially where financial markets and the altering of computer databases are concerned. The emphasis here, though, will be on deception in the military realm, since powerful military organizations are far more susceptible now to deception *than they have ever been*. Deception has, of course, been practised against militaries many times throughout history. The Greeks' use of the Trojan horse is one famous example, and Sun Tzu relates several instances in ancient China where strong protagonists were defeated after being out-manoeuvred by deception, rather than being out-fought by military superiority.[72] More recently, great generals such as Marlborough and Napoleon became great in large part due to their skill in the use of deception.[73] In the First World War, the introduction of radio links and photography meant an increase in the number of channels by which information could be obtained, and thus an increase in the way in which information could be manipulated and deception practised. The British, adept at deception in the First World War (using such 'sneaky' schemes as the Q-Ships[74]), were 'especially masterful' in the Second.[75] The most famous example here was *Operation Fortitude*: the idea of making the Germans think that the D-Day invasions would take place, not in Normandy, but in the Pas de Calais.[76] Some of the lesser British deception techniques were no less adroit. Serving in the army in North Africa, for instance, was one

Major Jasper Maskelyne. Being a professional peacetime illusionist, he was able to display some impressive deception skills. Among other ruses, he 'moved' the Egyptian city of Alexandria, so that German night bombers would drop their bombs on empty desert.[77] Israel also showed pronounced leanings towards the use of deception in its early wars with Arab neighbours. Once established as a regional power, however, Israel was itself the victim of Egyptian subtlety and was deceived into unpreparedness in the initial stages of the 1973 Yom Kippur War.[78]

The main lesson from these examples, and from history in general, is that there appears to be 'an inverse relationship between strength and the incentive to use deception'.[79] The weaker opponents are, the more likely they are to consider deception as a tool of war. They, in order to level the battlefield to some degree, need to use their imagination and to cajole their enemy into making mistakes.[80] In the Second World War, for instance, the much more powerful US military did not set as much store by deception as did its weaker, but more imaginative, British ally. The US had to be convinced, for instance, to go along with *Fortitude*.[81]

Today, the weak have yet greater opportunity to practise deception (see chapter 4).[82] The more means that a military organization has of obtaining information, the greater the incentive for the asymmetric warrior to 'skew' that information. The possibilities now exist, along with the usual technique of fooling the human mind, to manipulate technology such as videos, satellite imagery, and other data and computer outputs to engender misinformation and hoaxes. Another plus for those employing deception today is the fact that information is being utilized to produce quicker decision making and reduced sensor-to-shooter times. This means that there is less time available to *check* the veracity of information. Indeed, where technology is concerned, deception can engender a cascade effect. As we have seen, if false information can be supplied in one quarter (say, by hacking into logistics computers or those controlling satellite imagery), then, with seeds of doubt sown, can any source of information be trusted? And if it cannot, then what use is it?

Responding to the asymmetric use of deception

Responses to deception have to centre on the need to provide confirmation of information received. Modern sensors are good, but they are not infallible, and they need their own technological back-ups in the form of other sensors. But the ultimate sensor, and therefore the ultimate redundancy, is the human brain. Humans can often add context and depth to situations that bypass technological means. Adding context and depth can often lead to a resolution in distinguishing information from misinformation. For instance, if air forces are constantly being deceived into launching PGMs at dummy tanks, then sometimes the only way to verify what is real and what is not is to go up to the tanks and physically knock on their sides: metal or wood? Spies – another form of human intelligence – are also often vital in seeing through certain deception techniques. (For more on deception, see chapter 4.)

Such verification procedures and redundancy measures add, of course, what modern military organizations try to keep to a minimum: time. If sensors are not trusted, if other checks have to be made, and if humans have to be called into the loop, then operations can slow down. The whole point about bringing more IT into military organizations was that it was supposed to speed up the decision-making process by taking large degrees of doubt out of procedures and processes. Again, though, the great strength of speed can be turned into a vulnerability by asymmetric adversaries applying deception. Where information is concerned, the greater the amount, and the faster it comes, equates to an increased opportunity to employ deception techniques: action–reaction.

In trying to respond here to the asymmetric adversary, we are reminded of a problem that for centuries has affected powerful militaries. Power is the ability to make others do as you would wish them to do: 'the strong do what they will, the weak do what they must.'[83] Thus, when military organizations increase their power, they are conscious of their increased ability to impose *their* will on opponents. The concentration for the powerful is thus on getting what they do right, and there will be less concentration on *what the other side will do*. As Basil Liddell-Hart wrote many years ago, such thinking 'fosters a culture of soundness rather than surprise. It breeds commanders who are so intent not to do anything wrong, according to the "book", that they forget the necessity of making the enemy do something wrong.'[84] And in today's world, where the strong are relatively so much stronger, this thinking is enhanced. Our militaries give little thought to the enemy and making them 'do something wrong'; and because they do not, they do not 'mirror-image' and imagine their enemy trying to make *them* do something wrong. Today, strong military organizations must be extremely aware of the fact that their very strength encourages weaker adversaries to use deception techniques.[85]

Electronic warfare

Electronic warfare (EW) is concerned with inhibiting the flow of information by interfering with electronic signals.[86] The most basic and common form of EW is jamming. Jamming occurs when one signal is transmitted to interfere with another signal, the target.[87] EW first came to prominence in the Second World War, as British and German boffins vied with each other to degrade the other's radar systems.[88] Much research has recently gone into jamming and anti-jamming technology concerned with information from radar – both general search radar and radar linked to target acquisition. These days, however, the chief, and the most enticing, quarry for the asymmetric adversary are the GPS and UAVs. In its military uses, the GPS not only helps in many mundane ways as a tool for navigation, but at the 'sharp end' it has also become the means of choice when it comes to delivering Precision Guided Munitions (PGMs) to their targets. UAVs, too, in an era in which risking pilots' lives and putting them through long, gruelling missions is frowned upon, are proliferating. And being pilotless, they are, of course, guided by remote signals. Thus, two of the systems at the heart of modern Western military power rely on the passage of signals. And these signals are vulnerable to jamming. The crucial point here is that this jamming can be done with very simple and cheap technologies which have the capacity to neuter very expensive and very important systems. The issue of jamming of both GPS and UAVs and the responses to such jamming will be discussed more fully in chapter 4.[89]

Responding to asymmetric use of jamming

See chapter 4.

Psychological operations

Psychological operations (Psyops) use information against the human mind.[90] They target the 'opinions, emotions, attitudes, and behaviour' of 'enemy, friendly and neutral audiences', and involve altering perceptions rather than engineering outright deception.[91] Such manipulation of perceptions can be a huge force multiplier. It may involve seeking to paint one's own actions in a favourable light, those of the opponent in a poor light, or, of course, involve a combination of both.

Psyops are 'as old as the history of mankind'.[92] They were important to the likes of Gideon against the Midianites, to Genghis Khan, to the Boers against the British, and to both sides in the World Wars and the Cold War.[93] Today we see evidence of psyops being employed by US forces in ways as diverse as setting up television stations in Iraq and dropping leaflets over Afghanistan. And although in recent campaigns the strong powers, notably the US, have made much use of psyops, it is their use by weaker powers that concerns us here.

Psyops today are a very useful tool in the locker of the asymmetric warrior. As Kenneth McKenzie notes, 'Asymmetric opponents can achieve powerful effect through manipulation of the psychological element.'[94] One does not need to be powerful to get a message across, but merely to have access to the means of disseminating information. Such means in the modern era are, of course, readily available, especially in the form of the Internet and the Web. What is also an advantage today to the asymmetric adversary is the fact that when it comes to taking on the developed world's most powerful nations and most powerful military organizations, there is already in place a distinct target for psyops. There is the element of the lack of will: the lack of will to prosecute military campaigns to the fullest extent and the need to conduct 'wars of choice' with a large measure of restraint. This lack of will, as has been noted, can be seen as an Achilles' heel of the world's most powerful states. With any use of psyops, asymmetric adversaries merely have to push at a door that is already ajar. And since the lack of will is most evident at the strategic level, then that is where the asymmetric players will be looking to target their psyops, rather than on the operational or tactical levels. Their aim is always to go to the top and attempt to achieve maximum effect.[95]

In terms of modern examples of the use of psyops by weak protagonists, one might initially look at the Tet Offensive in 1968 in South Vietnam. Tet was a general assault launched by the Vietcong – with North Vietnamese backing – against US and South Vietnamese forces. The North Vietnamese leaders knew that the offensive would not result in outright victory. But they also knew that, when television pictures appeared of Vietcong guerrillas in the heart of such supposedly 'safe' cities as Saigon and Hue, then they could make the American people believe that their own troops were not winning the war. They would thus sow the seeds of doubt in the United States as to why the war should continue to be prosecuted. As Henry Kissinger once sagely remarked in respect of the Vietnam War: 'the conventional army loses by not winning; guerrillas, on the other hand, win by not losing.'[96] All that was required on the part of the North Vietnamese was an operation – a psyop – to point this out starkly; i.e. that they were not losing. This is what Tet did.[97] Many an insurgent today works on the same premiss as did the North Vietnamese.

The slickest psyops by an asymmetric adversary seen recently were conducted by Serbia in 1999: 'Serbian Information Operations carried out during NATO's *Operation Allied Force* were unprecedented in their quality and sophistication.'[98] These operations were characterized by such practices as having an advertising agency send out videos in MPEG files emailed to news agencies and opinion-formers. These videos portrayed NATO troops as Nazis, showed suffering Serb children, and members of the KLA as being associated with drug smuggling. The Serbs were also quick to produce postcards to cash in on the shock of the loss of a US F-117 'stealth' aircraft on an attack mission.[99] NATO actions – and especially their bombing mistakes – were made great use of by Belgrade, too. The effectiveness of the Serbs' psychological IW campaign was in large part due to the fact that the use of psyops by the Serbs was not considered beforehand by NATO planners, and therefore could not be properly countered.[100] Hubris, again, blinded. As Jones et al. point out, 'It happened because of an arrogant oversight that the Serbs would be effective at manipulating international opinion.'[101]

Asymmetric adversaries in their psyops today will also use outlets that were not previously available to weak actors. Take, for instance, the insurgents in Iraq and their use of psyops to appeal to a 'friendly' audience. A few years ago, insurgents in Iraq could have made all the videos they liked, but they would never have been shown by the Western news channels that dominated the airwaves. Nowadays, there are not only new broadcasting outlets, but also more televisions around the world to pick up their output. Viewers in the world's less powerful states can now receive news on their televisions refracted through a very different prism than that formerly provided by the likes of CNN and the BBC or by indigenous stations controlled by host governments. In the Arab world, for instance, there are new 'messengers' in the form of the 24-hour news channels Al Jazeera and Al Arabiya. The former is financed by the Qatar government and began broadcasting in 1996, and the latter, backed by Saudi Arabia, a few years later. Thus there is available a very different editorial slant on news, for instance, from Iraq.[102]

The existence of Al Jazeera and Al Arabiya allows people across the Arab world to see what the insurgents are achieving, what success they are having, and how the powerful forces of the West are being, perhaps, 'humbled'. Every time a bombing attack on Coalition forces is carried out, there is someone there to film it (though the film is rarely shown in the West). Such attacks are mere tactical blips in the operations of Western armies. The real victory, the strategic advance, comes with the televising of the acts and the 'encouragement' this gives to a variety of audiences across the Arab and Muslim worlds.[103]

These stations also, not unnaturally, focus on dead Iraqi civilians resulting from Coalition actions. This leaves the US 'unhappy with broadcasts that focus on civilian casualties without providing the broader context of the war' in Iraq.[104] It leads to a situation where, as one senior US officer put it, 'All people are seeing is the minaret hit by American fire and falling. They're not seeing the pictures of the fighters shooting at us from those mosques and minarets.'[105] The Coalition, with such psyops directed against it, is losing support among many Muslims. But Western forces will have to get used to operating in such an environment. The weak can now level the psyops battlefield, because they now have the capacity to get their message across in ways previously denied.[106]

Beyond actual news channels, weak players such as terrorists or insurgents in Iraq can now make use of other outlets such as websites. These can carry images including hostages pleading for their lives (and often their beheadings). These will have great shock value, and thus impact. The humbling of representatives of the West and its acolytes is designed to encourage the 'friendly' and make their enemy – Coalition members and the West in general – question missions such as that in Iraq. Using the same strategy as that adopted by the terrorists, such images are partly designed to encourage Coalition forces to overreact in retaliation, thus losing yet more support from local Iraqis and, indeed, support in the domestic realm. The Iraqi insurgents know that they will not win purely by tactical actions on the ground, but they can win, as the North Vietnamese knew, via the psychological impact of images transmitted to living rooms in the US and elsewhere.

Responding to asymmetric psychological operations

Countering the asymmetric adversary's psyops is obviously made much more difficult today, given the number of outlets and the level of technology available to them. Whatever means the powerful have to get their message across, the weak, to a large degree, have as well.

Both sides are playing on the nearest thing to a level playing field, with the weak seemingly making the greatest use of it.

One of the ironies in the way in which small players can get their message out now is actually that the liberal democracies are proving triumphant. As they 'spread' democracy, they also spread free speech. Free speech allows information – some of it of dubious veracity – to be disseminated to a wider audience and more readily than at any time previously. As the West tries, for instance, to spread democracy to places like Iraq, it is running into problems of its own making. Free speech includes the freedom to 'bash' the West, and the US in particular. As Edward Djerejian, a former US ambassador and Middle East expert put it, 'The challenge here is, how does the United States on the one hand promote freedom of the press as part of a whole process of reform in the Arab world, and on the other, accommodate the interests of the US and its troops?'[107] And there is little the US can do: 'allied commanders say that they have few defences in the information air wars against Al Jazeera's reporting.'[108]

The US has tried, of course, to counter the reporting of Arab channels. Libicki says that, while the DoD might complain that opponents of the US manipulate the media, 'the truth is that television is ubiquitous and that the United States gives as good as it gets' in terms of civil affairs and psyops teams. The US has also responded by setting up a television station in Iraq – Al Hurra. However, because all and sundry in Iraq know that it *has* been set up by the US then it is dismissed as the mouthpiece of a foreign power and has been 'singularly ineffective'.[109]

It is, moreover, not just Arab television channels that are the culprits here. European stations also report far more negative news about Iraq than do US channels. US audiences, for instance, tend not to see the bodies of civilians killed by US bombing and artillery.[110] The US, indeed, tries to avoid any emphasis on the number of Iraqis killed. As the one-time overall US commander for Iraq, General Tommy Franks, put it, 'We don't do body counts.'[111] But there has to be an appreciation of the problems that 'bodies' cause. As Anthony Cordesman puts it, 'No amount of information management can substitute for better methods of minimizing civilian casualties and collateral damage.'[112] And with the US taking one tack in terms of ignoring civilian casualties and many in Europe taking another, this can and will affect the strength and effectiveness of coalitions.

Because there seems to be a general lack of appreciation of other messages that are being put out by various parties, it seems that the US is finding it hard to counter with its own psyops programmes wherever it happens to be involved militarily. For the most powerful today have a weakness when it comes to psyops being used against them. It is that there is, out there in the contemporary world, a willing audience prone to believe the worst about the world's most powerful states. Again, when the powerful stride the world like, as Eliot Cohen put it, some military and cultural 'colossus', then they naturally generate antipathy.[113] Antipathy comes with the territory of being powerful; there is no avoiding it. Thus the US, however benignly it acts, will always be perceived to be the bully. Thus, when the colossus tries to counter psyops with psyops of its own, then these can easily fall flat. And while the US has put great effort into building a large psyops structure, getting its message across will always founder on the fact that it can be sourced back, sometimes via other players such as Coalition members, to the US.

Against such a background, those involved in psyops need to think a great deal about what they are doing. This process will involve thinking more like the opponent. We have already discussed the fact that the powerful tend not to worry about what the weak are thinking. Such a mind-set may have worked well in *normal* warfare against *normal* opponents, but this is asymmetric warfare. When the powerful are hamstrung by the restrictions of fighting 'wars of choice' against small-scale opponents, then they should put less effort into the kinetic and more into the psychological. This is especially true if there is a great difference in relative power. In essence, the powerful can be *too* powerful for their own good. Again, they allow the *usual* ways of defeating an enemy to dominate, and think less about the *best* way to defeat an enemy. The best way of defeating asymmetric opponents may include a good deal of psyops. Good psyops will be produced, though, not only by developing a good understanding of the target audience, but also by developing a good understanding of how they appear to that target audience. Here one might paraphrase Sun Tzu and point out that if you know yourself, know your enemy, and *know how you appear to others*, then in a hundred psyops battles you will not be defeated. Faced with asymmetric opponents such as the insurgents in Iraq, then, Western forces and their governments need to step outside themselves and take a long, hard look at how others might interpret their actions. Not to do so is arrogance. One of the problems with the US and the British, in particular, is that their faith in their own rectitude often blinds them to alternative perceptions of their actions (see also chapter 7).[114] Developing, though, the capability both to understand the enemy and to understand how you and your actions appear to that enemy is by no means an easy project.

Conclusion

Asymmetric adversaries have great scope to conduct information warfare against their Western foes. We in the West set ourselves up as targets because of our total reliance on information. We have put an inordinate level of faith in the ability of information passage to make a difference in our everyday lives, and our military organizations have put the same degree of faith in it to act as a critical force multiplier. The weak can create advantage for themselves by interfering with the passage of that information. And information does not just have to be stopped or prevented from reaching its destination; it can merely be changed adroitly or manipulated slightly such that its real meaning is lost. This perhaps creates more impact than stopping information altogether. One might refer here to the analogy of the captured spy. History relates that rather than being consigned to the nearest gallows, spies are more useful if they are fed with false information to send back to their erstwhile masters: if the information keeps coming, it will continue to be believed. And in our modern world there is a huge temptation to believe in the information we receive. Information is an essential ingredient in the pace of everyday life and in the effectiveness of military endeavours. Reliance breeds faith; it has to. We feel that we have neither the time to check and verify, nor, crucially, the inclination.

But if we realize that our information fails us just once, can we then maintain our faith? In the manner of a Damascene conversion, blind faith can be quickly turned to total disbelief if we see that we have been fooled. Is that figure 155 or 105? Is that a tank in the wood or one of those dummies? Can we believe the television news we are watching? Faith can be restored only if some sort of redundancy is built into information systems. There have to be back-ups and other systems to go to. With back-ups we reduce our reliance, and thus undermine the point of attacks by asymmetric adversaries in the first place. Back-ups can act as deterrents. But such redundancy is often expensive or clumsy or weighty, and thus a general hindrance; irritating speed bumps on the information superhighway. Like many a deterrent, they are costly and may never be needed.

But one day they may be needed. The real threat is not so much from the individual hacker or the terrorist organization, it is from the weak state asymmetric adversary. The likes of China have a wonderful opportunity presented to them in the shape of potential enemies who lean on information so much. Hit such a centre of gravity with care, and reliance on information can become a force disabler and not a force multiplier. In the action–reaction model, China will not look to try and match such information dominance, but will seek ways to undermine that information. And if the worst happens, and conflict of sorts does break out between, say, China and the US, then the effects will not be limited to the conventional battlefield; they will be felt domestically in ways hitherto unknown.

Our 'information world' also, significantly, creates opportunities for asymmetric opponents to create their own information. Where once the presses and airwaves were dominated by those with power, the Internet and related technologies have opened up the field. Messages that once had to be carried by word of mouth can now be disseminated much more efficiently to a much wider audience. The results can be telling, and deleteriously so, for Western power in many fields and on many levels.

We live in an 'information world'. Information passage is an integral part of the lives we live today. We undertake more activities, have access to more amenities, and move and have our being at a pace that our forefathers could only dream of. Our militaries likewise owe much in terms of their efficiency and power to information. Hopefully, our 'information world' will not come back to bite us.

4 ASYMMETRY AND AIR POWER

Introduction

To the powerful, air power has a unique allure. It is the instrument of choice in the contemporary era when Western politicians and military commanders want to gather intelligence, signal intent, bring retribution, project power, and win wars. At one end of the conflict spectrum, air power can add coercive pressure to diplomatic manoeuvrings and punish rogue states with a quick 'slap on the wrists'.[1] Further down the spectrum, air power's ultimate offer is to win wars quickly and fairly painlessly without the need to commit ground troops.[2] Moreover, given the accuracy of the weapons available today, it can aspire to accomplish missions with collateral damage and innocent casualties kept to a minimum. Air power's ability to launch its weapons from a safe distance – its stand-off capability – also keeps even pilots safe.[3] Unmanned Aerial Vehicles (UAVs) now leave out the pilot altogether and are a vital addition to the stable of air power capabilities.

Air power is thus able to provide a wide range of opportunities to Western politicians and military planners, and has produced some noteworthy successes over the last few years. In 1982 President Ronald Reagan was able to send an almost cost-free message to Colonel Muamar Khadaffi in Libya that the arm of American justice was long. US aircraft, as part of Operation *El Dorado Canyon*, struck in revenge for the actions of Libyan-backed terrorists in Europe.[4] Later, both Gulf Wars were made much easier by the Coalitions' air supremacy and by the use of cruise missiles. The conflict with Yugoslavia over Kosovo in 1999 was perceived in many quarters to have been won by air power alone.[5] More recently, the potential of the UAV has been dramatically displayed. From taking pictures of Osama bin Laden in Afghanistan to taking out Al Qaeda terrorists with a Hellfire missile in Yemen in 2002, UAVs have shown their worth.[6] In more mundane terms, air power in the form of space assets can furnish the likes of satellite imagery and the GPS system. All told, the air power of today offers a range of potentialities, from the precision required to gather intelligence and engineer surgical strikes, all the way up to providing the degree of bluntness that can blast enemies to defeat.

To understand how the asymmetric adversary can counter the effects of air power and reduce its allure, we need to start with an understanding of what today actually comes under the rubric of 'air power'. Here we can talk about aircraft, Precision Guided Munitions (PGMs), UAVs and satellites. And while these represent immense force multipliers, they do, nevertheless, carry vulnerabilities. It is towards these that asymmetric opponents must direct their energies. *As will become apparent, in the realm of air power, the asymmetric threat appears in the form of fire from the ground and action taken on the ground.* Here efforts to negate Western air power will not involve the use of aerial vehicles.

Aircraft

We must begin with the idea that today's military aircraft are expensive, and becoming ever more so. There has been a specific movement in terms of the design of military aircraft over the last few decades. These aircraft should be fast, in order to avoid opponents' counters. They should have a long range, in order to fly from distant bases and have more time to carry out their missions. They should carry lots of ordnance, to deliver a punch once they have arrived. This ordnance should be capable of being launched with accuracy a long way from the target area, so that the aircraft and its crew face less danger. Additionally, aircraft should also be 'stealthy', so that their detection is made more difficult.

The result of such design philosophies is that the ultimate military strike aircraft of today are large, fast, long-range, stealthy platforms employing PGMs. Thus the US Air Force has now, at the top of its air power pyramid, quite a small number of very expensive aircraft, such as the B-2 ($1.3 bn each) and F-117 ($150 m), but with the compensating supposition that it is very difficult to shoot them down and that they will be very efficient in the use of the payloads they carry. Each B-2 will supposedly do what it took thousand-bomber raids to accomplish during the Second World War. Other aircraft – the air interdiction variety – were originally designed to deal with the symmetrical threat offered by high-level Soviet bombers. These interdiction aircraft, in order to engage effectively in air-to-air combat, had also to be very fast, but they did not need to be as stealthy (they were and are principally defensive in nature); nor did they need to carry as much ordnance. The latest examples of such aircraft are the soon-to-be-fielded US F-22 and the European Typhoon. Thus with one type of aircraft being designed to bomb, and another being designed to intercept, this left little room, in the thinking of Cold War Western air forces, to accommodate an aircraft that could support troops on the ground, i.e. a close air support (CAS) model. Ground forces could call upon the likes of attack helicopters (Apache, Lynx) and slow fixed-wing aircraft (A-10, Harrier), but for air forces CAS was very much a secondary activity.

Whenever aircraft have been employed by Western forces in the post-Cold War era, however, their principal mission has not been air interdiction. There has been very little air-to-air combat. For those who have had to face the air power of the US and its allies have quickly realized their inability to have any significant effect in aerial battles. Both Iraq and Serbia tried to hide most of their aircraft rather than test them in combat.[7] Indeed, Western attack aircraft have actually been used in recent years almost exclusively as the deliverers of ordnance to points on the ground. In Iraq, Bosnia, Yugoslavia, Kosovo and Afghanistan, *ground attack* has been the principal mission.

Here, perhaps, is the major problem with the use of Western aircraft today. In actually trying to hit what are often very small targets on the ground, there must inevitably be a movement towards the ground; towards the targets. In such a movement, of course, aircraft expose themselves to fire from the ground, fire that most Western aircraft were never really designed to contend with. This fire comes, however, not so much in the form of the old static surface-to-air (SAM) systems such as the Soviet SA-2, or even in the form of the big mobile systems such as the SA-6 or even the more modern S-300/400.[8] Rather, the sharpest air power asymmetry appears in the acute threat from guns of various calibres (anti-aircraft artillery (AAA)) and from man-portable air defence systems (MANPADS).[9] Both weapon types, because of their size, portability and lack of any signature such as radar guidance, offer no real target to aircraft, and thus cannot be engaged effectively from the air. Any aircraft, therefore, no matter what its sophistication and its cost, if it comes close to the ground to engage targets, runs the risk of being brought down by something no more complicated and no more expensive than a heavy machine gun. More serious, though, is the MANPADS threat. There are now more of such systems than ever before available to small states, to terrorist organizations, and to rebel groups. Again, with the end of the Cold War, there are several manufacturers around the world making MANPADS and finding few takers among the defence ministries of the larger powers. They are then sold to a variety of weak-state and non-state actors who can thereby provide for themselves a fair degree of air defence. A decent anti-aircraft missile (SA-7 Strela) can cost as little as $5,000, and there are reputed to be some 100,000 for sale on the black market.[10] The most potent and most difficult to obtain is the Russian-made SA-16 Igla, which has the capacity to defeat the protection systems of most aircraft.[11] In general, MANPADS can be effective up to 15,000 feet (3,000 m).

Recent conflicts have shown that ground fire has proved to be a problematic issue for Western aircraft. In the First Gulf War, low-level sorties to attack Iraqi airfields by British Tornado aircraft led to heavy losses due to AAA.[12] Subsequent Tornado and US F-16 missions flew much higher, and sorties by US A-10 dedicated ground-attack aircraft were called off altogether after two were lost in one day from AAA.[13] In 1994 a British Sea Harrier attempting to bomb Serb tanks was shot down near Gorazde, 'displaying the limits of air power in Bosnia'.[14] Flying low, with the threats extant today, is not to be encouraged. As one US Air Force (USAF) general colour-fully summed up, nowadays flying low is 'the equivalent of being brain-dead'.[15]

Other Western aircraft, such as helicopters, were likewise designed in the Cold War for operations that did not include having to face inordinate amounts of fire from AAA. In Kosovo in 1999, the US Army's attack helicopter, the Apache, could never be used offensively ('too risky') because of the fear that they could be brought down fairly easily by ground fire.[16] In *Operation Anaconda* in Afghanistan in March 2002, some Apaches, attempting to support US ground forces, engaged in a firefight against Taliban fighters, and were forced by AAA to withdraw in a matter of minutes. Most Apaches involved were disabled.[17] Troop-transport Chinooks have also been brought down by ground fire in Afghanistan.[18] In Iraq in the Second Gulf War the fear of ground fire prevented any large movements of forces by helicopter.[19]

The Russians, the first to undergo sustained MANPADS attacks in Afghanistan in the 1980s, are still suffering in Chechnya. In 2002 Chechen rebels with a shoulder-launched missile brought down an Mi-26 helicopter in Chechnya, killing 127 people.[20] Perhaps, though, Somalia in 1993 and the events depicted in the book *Black Hawk Down* provide one of the most noteworthy examples of asymmetric engagements involving aircraft. Sophisticated Black Hawk helicopters were shot down by local Somali fighters using nothing more complicated than modified RPG-7 anti-*tank* rockets! These fighters would alter the fuses of the rockets so that instead of exploding when they hit an armoured vehicle, they would explode a certain time after being fired. This allowed them to be fired into the air and thus explode at certain heights. When launched in the general direction of a Black Hawk's vulnerable rear rotor assembly, shrapnel from the explosion of the warhead could bring down the aircraft. Thus a round that costs a few tens of dollars could bring to earth a multi-million dollar machine.[21]

No strong power wants to lose its very expensive aircraft and their expensively trained pilots – and not least to fire from mere machine guns or cheap shoulder-fired missiles.[22] This is not only tactically bad, but operationally galling, and perhaps even a strategic show-stopper. Thus the temptation is to have these aircraft flying out of harm's way, above 15,000 feet. This was certainly the case in Kosovo when NATO took on Serb forces. For it appears that orders went out that this operation should be one devoid of casualties. The only way to ensure such an outcome was to have no ground troops involved and to have the aircraft that were designed to win the war for NATO flying only above 15,000 feet.[23]

Patently, the weaker opponent gains from such action wherever it is applied. Making aircraft – be they fixed-wing or helicopters – fly higher makes them less effective in support of ground actions. Their firepower will be less accurate, and certainly the incidence of collateral damage will increase. Moreover, their ability to *observe* accurately what is happening below will also be compromised. At 15,000 feet, aircraft will not only have difficulty detecting objects on the ground, but they will also have trouble identifying them. Add then a degree of camouflage, and both detecting and identifying become doubly difficult. In the First Gulf War, for instance, many mistakes were made in the great 'Scud hunt' in the Western Desert. As Grange put it, 'Initially, the Scud hunting was done from the air only. From that altitude, 10,000 to 15,000 feet, to find camouflaged and concealed weapons systems was very difficult to do.'[24] Moreover, buses and tanker trucks, as the Iraqis intended, were misidentified as Scud missile launchers.[25] In the end, despite 1,460 sorties aimed at Scud detection and all the efforts of an entire Coalition, and using the full panoply of technical means available to the greatest powers on earth, not a *single* real Scud missile was destroyed.[26]

The fact that NATO aircraft in *Operation Allied Force* (the Kosovo campaign) were flying so high was also a blessing – in this case – to the Serbs. Playing on this fact, they became adept at hiding armoured vehicles amongst refugee traffic and employed adroit camouflage and concealment measures. What also helped the Serbs was that in fifty-four days out of the seventy-eight of the campaign, there was cloud cover. It is possible to use radar to see through cloud, but radar will produce only a reflection of an 'object'; it will not really tell you what it is: tractor or tank? With planes not allowed to fly below the cloud cover, the Serb military could operate with near impunity on the ground.[27]

Operating at high altitude also affects battle damage assessments (BDAs). Such assessments consider the number of enemy assets destroyed, and then calculations can be made as to how weak or strong the enemy has become. BDAs are vitally important, since without adequate BDAs commanders cannot undertake proper planning procedures. In the First Gulf War, lack of adequate BDA, in part due to the fact that surveillance aircraft were flying so high, was 'noted as the most important intelligence failure of the conflict'.[28] The same problems were evident during *Operation Enduring Freedom* in Afghanistan in 2001. US Navy Special Forces (SEALs) had to go physically into Al Qaeda and Taliban caves to check whether US air strikes had destroyed them – air assets could not tell. The caves were still intact.[29] The reliance on high-flying aircraft to produce BDAs led one analyst to conclude that 'The US military services and the intelligence community simply do not have a credible battle damage assessment capability.'[30]

The Serbs made great efforts to hinder proper BDA by NATO aircraft in the Kosovo War in 1999. Jugs of burning oil would be placed on top of serviceable tanks to make it appear to NATO pilots that they had already been hit. Unravelled lengths of tank track would appear next to perfectly serviceable tanks to give the illusion that they had been destroyed. The Serbs were aided by NATO's inadequacies. With virtually all Cold War investment into photo reconnaissance assets being put into satellites and high-flying aircraft, the ability was lacking to pick out equipment in woods and valleys because of the 'shadowing' effect they produced.[31] These 'useless'[32] assets had to be supplemented by the taking of 'oblique' photographs by low-flying – and thus exposed – aircraft.[33] Such missions were limited. Serb attempts to prevent proper BDA were thus very successful, in that NATO's estimation of the amount of Serb armour destroyed by air assets was grossly inflated. As it turned out, ground forces were not needed in an invasion of Kosovo; but if they had been necessary, then they would have faced far greater opposition than that established by air-delivered BDA.[34]

After the war in Kosovo the real efficacy of air power was questioned.[35] True, it seemed to have won a war all on its own, but there also seemed to be several caveats. As Benjamin Lambeth put it, 'elusive enemy ground forces belied the oft-cited claim that air power has arrived at the threshold of being able to fix, track, target, and engage any object on the surface of the earth'.[36] A US Department of Defense After-Action Report also looked at the lessons of the NATO campaign and concluded that 'future adversaries are likely to study Serbian denial and deception techniques [which] could present more advanced threats to future operations'.[37]

The final point to make about the opportunities available to the asymmetric adversary *vis-à-vis* aircraft is the fact that today's state-of-the-art front-line warplanes have become icons. The stealth capabilities and the speed of platforms such as the B-2 and F-117, allied to the general ambience of power and mystery that surrounds them, has tended to engender a sense that such technology is invincible. These aircraft have become symbols of omnipotence, both deadly and invulnerable. But the asymmetric warrior is nothing if not an iconoclast. He understands the importance of targeting these platforms, because to succeed in bringing one down means more than a simple tick in the box of a profit/loss equation; the *impact* would be enormous. If the aura of invincibility is lost, then so is much of the strategic advantage of the West in terms of the much sought-after cost-free solutions. The asymmetric warrior will put every effort into bringing down just an individual aircraft, rather than a whole range of them. To do this, they might fire all the missiles in their arsenal at one plane (or, in the days of stealth technology, where they think a plane might be), knowing that by the law of averages some might hit the target. Again, the asymmetric adversary will be thinking about the best ways to bring about the biggest effect possible on his stronger adversary. He will look to cause strategic effect through tactical actions.[38]

It must be remembered that in many cases the asymmetric adversary will be looking to counter the effects of the stronger opponent possessed of air supremacy, not so much in terms of destroying many aircraft, but rather in terms of inflicting enough damage and casualties to create the all-important pause for thought. The asymmetric adversary will use every means possible to drag out any conflict. Pause can come about even if only a single strong power is engaged. However, it is now usually the case that when Western states embark on wars of choice, they do so – in order to maintain legitimacy – as members of coalitions. And these will often be formed on the assumption that the use of aircraft will allow the operation to be quick and surgical. When it appears that it is going to be neither quick nor surgical, then these coalitions come under strain and can crack. This is what almost happened in NATO's war with Yugoslavia as the delay in neutralizing Serb ground forces allowed doubts within NATO to intensify and diplomatic solutions to take effect. In the current era, asymmetric adversaries do not have to shoot down many of their opponent's aircraft; they merely, it appears, have to nullify their effects for long enough (see also chapter 5).

Response

There are several mundane measures that can be taken to undermine an asymmetric adversary's attempts to counter a stronger opponent's air supremacy. Efforts can be made, for instance, to keep systems such as the SA-16 Igla out of the hands of sub-state groups. Israel and the US have tried to prevent the export of Iglas by Russia to Syria, and thence possibly to some sub-state actors.[39]

Beyond the mundane, there needs to be a change of focus. In order to make aircraft more effective against the asymmetric adversary, there needs to be a realization that technology needs help. It is all very well to suppose that air power can win wars, as many air strategists would have us believe.[40] This may be true. But while in certain instances air power alone can defeat states (which have fixed assets that they would rather not lose), it has far greater trouble bringing an end to resistance from those asymmetric players further down the power spectrum: insurgents, guerrillas, terrorists, etc. These have little to lose structurally and provide few targets to aircraft, and they tend to have a greater will to resist than do states – aircraft can then have little coercive effect. Where such opponents are concerned, the best results will be achieved, not by air power alone, but by a combination of air and ground forces. Help from ground forces allows aircraft to use their latent power more flexibly and in more nuanced ways. Ground troops can point out targets extremely accurately using laser designators and by planting homing beacons even when the aircraft can see nothing (as in bad weather). The ability of Special Forces (SF) to provide a ground presence in Afghanistan and thus to indicate targets precisely was, indeed, 'crucial to the success of air missions' there.[41]

Ground troops, moreover, SF or not, deserve also to be protected by air power. The helicopter has proved to be susceptible to ground fire as have most fixed-wing aircraft. Ground forces are best served by dedicated ground-attack aircraft which can provide close air support (CAS) and better BDAs.[42] The problem is, of course, that there are few of these around, and, again, the new aircraft being developed at the moment (such as the US F-22 and the European Typhoon) are aircraft designed for interdiction and thus to be fast.[43] Fast aircraft are no real use to ground forces, since their speed reduces their accuracy with their air-to-ground weapons: as one cynic put it, 'You do not win people's hearts and minds by throwing ... bombs around at 450 knots.'[44] And if these aircraft fly slowly, moreover, their design means that they become far less manoeuvrable and thus easier to hit from the ground. Indeed, planes designed to be fast can carry no armour, as armour means weight. Thus they are vulnerable to even a single bullet. What is also problematic here is that this movement towards very expensive aircraft (designed as they were to cope with the best the Soviets could produce) also means that the loss of just one would be extremely painful, even if the pilot survived. Their very expense, even if they could fly slowly enough to be effective in the CAS role, means that they will rarely be risked close to the ground (the F-22 costs about $200m per aircraft[45]). The requirement here, in this case, because losses at low level are inevitable, is for aircraft that are cheap enough to be expendable. The loss of the pilots then becomes an issue. But war is about risk; it is about people being killed. Is it not losses that make war a serious enterprise, and therefore one not to be entered into lightly?

Precision guided munitions (PGMs)

PGMs, whether launched from ground, sea or air, are an adjunct of air power. They provide for that very important element of modern air power: the ability to deliver ordnance to exact points anywhere on the Earth's surface. PGMs' accuracy provides kinetic effectiveness while avoiding collateral damage. The PGM in this respect is crucial in today's 'wars of choice': 'It seems the Western democracies have passed the point where they can contemplate using air power, or any force, in ways as unrestrained as World War II bombing.'[46]

The first PGMs were radio-controlled bombs used by the US against bridges in the Korean War. They were guided by observers in the aircraft that dropped them. Later, in the Vietnam War, bombs were guided by video, by infra-red or by lasers.[47] Today many bombs are still guided by infra-red or laser. This, though, normally requires aircraft to loiter over a battlefield continually 'painting' or 'illuminating' (with laser or infra-red beams) the target until the weapon – usually dropped from another aircraft – strikes home. Such loitering, given the exposure to ground fire, is patently a dangerous enterprise. Moreover, target-designator aircraft usually require clear weather in order to see their targets.

In the current era, however, many weapons are guided by the GPS, including such systems as the Joint Direct Attack Munition (JDAM) and cruise missiles. The JDAM is merely an air-dropped 'dumb iron' bomb fitted with a GPS-guidance kit which moves control surfaces at the rear of the weapon. Far more sophisticated are the cruise missiles. These are the most familiar PGMs and cost about $1 m each. Examples would be the TLAM (Tomahawk Land Attack Missile), ACLM (Air Launched Cruise Missile) and SLAM (Submarine Launched Airflight Missile). Unlike aircraft, which have to get close to their targets to drop their JDAMs, cruise missiles can be launched from many hundreds of kilometres away while remaining unaffected by weather conditions. And no one is required to point to the target. Cruise missile accuracy comes from systems that are not weather-dependent, being derived either from the GPS, which constantly feeds guidance information to a PGM as it moves towards its target, or via an Inertial Navigation System (INS), where navigation is maintained internally from measurements of elapsed time and speed and direction.[48] Most cruise missiles actually carry both GPS and INS, since having a back-up reduces the chance of errors. It is the GPS, though, that provides for the greatest accuracy.[49]

With the PGM, there is again scope for asymmetric adversaries to produce counters to their potency. Basically, there are four approaches to consider: jamming, deception, mobility, and the testing of will.

Jamming of PGMs

Jamming is a cheap and quite effective means of preventing GPS-guided PGMs from hitting their targets. It is a simple procedure, and shows 'how astoundingly vulnerable the common GPS receiver is to jamming'.[50] Jamming is possible because the signal from the GPS that guides the PGM is very weak. This means that it can be interfered with – and thus the PGM sent off course – by a very weak jammer. Anyone keen to prevent a PGM strike could, with an investment of about $2,000 and with access to parts from any electronics shop, build a device the size of a soft-drink can and power it by means of a normal car battery. This would theoretically provide for 25 km of jamming coverage.[51] Rather more sophisticated jammers have been constructed by the Russian firm Aviakonversiya (200 km of coverage) and were made available to the Iraqis before the Second Gulf War.[52]

However, the great strength of PGMs – their accuracy – can actually be turned around and made into their greatest weakness. The PGM only has to be sent off course slightly for it to have no effect whatsoever. This rarely happened with Second World War bombing runs, when at least some bombs would usually land on the target. But when you only have one, it is vital that it hits its target. Indeed, making the PGM miss raises other issues. Publics sold on the idea of the surgicality of air power will be concerned when PGMs do not strike their proper targets and create collateral damage elsewhere. If jamming causes a cruise missile to hit a hospital rather than a secret police HQ, then questions are bound to be raised. The quandary is summed up by Sheila Melvin: 'By vastly reducing the number of misses [through the use of PGMs], precision leaves the United States open to greater criticism when a mistake happens.'[53] Criticism, again, will create pause.

States which fear the West's arsenal of PGMs will invest in jamming technology. The Chinese, and especially the Russians, will develop jammers of increasing sophistication, and they will sell these to small states and even to sub-state actors.[54] The dynamic is clear, and it is a familiar one in the realm of asymmetric warfare. As the West, and especially the United States, gets more and more sophisticated weapons (in this case the PGM), other players will not try and match them with similar technologies; rather, they will look to develop counters that are *dissimilar*. As PGMs, in this case, become more sophisticated, then so will the jammers.

Response to jamming

With the multiplication of GPS usage throughout the US and other Western militaries, it is obvious that better anti-jamming capabilities need to be acquired. This has been recognized.[55] It is vitally important to prevent the jamming of the GPS, not only in terms of the use of PGMs, but also across a broad spectrum of other GPS-linked military applications, especially navigation. The ubiquity of the reliance on the GPS means that at all times there must be total faith in its efficacy.

For the stronger powers, the first protection against jammers is their physical destruction. Jamming signals can be picked up and HARM (High-speed Anti Radiation Missile) missiles can be targeted at their source, as they were in the Second Gulf War. It is reported that many of the initial US air strikes on Baghdad in the 'shock and awe' phase of the campaign were designed specifically to destroy the jammers, so that Coalition PGMs could hit their designated targets.[56] This is the problem with powerful jammers: they give away their location, and can then themselves be targeted.[57] The jammers, however, can be detected only by a special type of aircraft (i.e. electronic warfare (EW)), and these are few in number in the US inventory. The US Air Force, for instance, is having to use the US Navy's EA-6 aircraft, since it has none left of its own after recent retirements. But these EA-6s, being very scarce assets, have many other important missions besides trying to locate just a few very unsophisticated and very cheap jammers.[58]

Another means to counter jamming is, of course, the use of redundancy. Having GPS and INS working together on the same missile allows for one system to back up the other. Most cruise missiles, while looking to GPS for the pin-point accuracy, will often have to rely on the less accurate INS for final run-ins to targets where jammers may be prevalent. Missiles can also be fitted with jamming-resistant antennae, but these only work looking forward and deal with jammers co-located with targets (this is the natural place for them to be to protect the target). But if the jammer, is operating away to the side of the missile, and is not co-located with the target, then countering it becomes more problematical.[59]

Another defensive method is to have GPS satellites produce a more complex signal that resists jamming. For this, though, we will have to wait for the next generation of GPS satellites to come on station. Additionally, a temporary, more powerful transmitter, such as that carried by a UAV rather than a satellite, can be put in place over a specific area to create a spot-beam GPS signal that is too powerful to be jammed. Pseudo-satellites are also being developed, which can be launched into space when the ones in place are being jammed.[60]

The final redundancy, and the one which features heavily in ensuring that technology associated with air power actually functions as it should, is to have SF ground troops in place either to 'paint' the targets with laser designators or to attach homing beacons to them. Both will draw in missiles while circumventing any jamming.

Deceiving PGMs

While jamming offers one particular avenue for countering PGMs, such weapons present another weakness that allows for their potency to be blunted. The very accuracy of PGMs encourages the asymmetric adversary to employ the tool of deception. Dummy aircraft, tanks, guns, missiles or whatever can be constructed fairly cheaply, and can be used to attract attack by PGMs while protecting real assets. These dummy targets can waste a significantly finite resource. Cruise missile PGMs work on a certain philosophy: they are relatively few in number, because they are expensive, but the expense can be justified by the fact that only a small number will be needed, given their accuracy; it is a question of quality over quantity. The asymmetric adversary's window here, of course, is that if enough false targets are constructed, and enough PGMs are wasted against them, then inventories can be quickly exhausted such that offensive operations may be halted.[61] This almost happened in *Operation Allied Force* in Kosovo in 1999. Here the Serbs, building on skills developed to help thwart an expected Soviet attack during the Cold War, constructed the likes of balsa wood Mig-29s, inflatable tanks, dummy artillery pieces and even false bridges.[62] NATO aircraft flying too high could not distinguish real from false, and GPS-guided bombs and missiles were fired at the wrong targets. Techniques were employed which, as well as deceiving the human eye, also defeated technology. Imitation planes or armour were made to look very real to NATO infra-red detection devices through the generation of false heat signatures. Primus stoves together with strips of metal foil were used to indicate the presence of an engine. Such ruses were especially effective in wooded terrain, where distinct heat signatures are masked quite effectively by foliage.[63]

The second promise that comes with deception is the fact that, because the PGMs almost always hit their targets, then faulty BDAs are made. If a target is destroyed, then intelligence assessors have to work on the assumption that it was real, otherwise they would never be able to give their superiors any kind of BDA. No commander wants to hear from his intelligence people, 'Well, we think we've destroyed x number of targets but we can't be sure if they were actually real.' How then could any assessment be made as to what opposition was left, and how could any future plans be made as to offensive action if the enemy's strength is unknown?

Again, with deception in mind, PGMs give greater incentive for weak adversaries to adopt camouflage and concealment measures. Camouflage, obviously, has always been a factor in warfare.[64] In the recent past, though, it has been possible to get around camouflage to some degree by letting quantity substitute for quality. During the Second World War, for instance, if the Allies suspected that enemy forces were located in, say, a wood or a village but could not be seen, then bombing the whole wood or village would be an option. The philosophy would be, 'Let's bomb it anyway, just to be on the safe side.'[65] Technically, it is known as 'reconnaissance by fire'. But nowadays, with the fear of collateral damage, targets have to be struck with pin-point accuracy by PGMs. But the PGMs, as well as being fooled by dummy targets, can also be fooled by camouflage. PGMs cannot be wasted on targets that have not been adequately identified and may or may not be significant or, indeed, innocent. Thus PGMs, given the psychology behind them and their limited numbers, need 'more and better quality targeting information than more conventional (unguided) weapons'.[66] Without such information – intelligence – to provide targets, PGMs are effectively useless.[67] If targets cannot be ascertained correctly, given a combination of good camouflage and concealment techniques, and the fact that it is hard to pick out anything when surveillance platforms are having to operate above 15,000 feet, then intelligence will be wrong. And if intelligence is wrong, then the PGM is merely a lump of metal that can make a very nice hole in the ground. The asymmetric opponent can thus quite effectively negate one of the supreme assets in the armoury of the militarily powerful – the PGM.

Response to deception

The asymmetric adversary will be employing deception techniques to undermine the effectiveness of PGMs principally because the PGM is a weapon that relies so much on target intelligence. One means of reducing the effects of camouflage and concealment is obviously for observation aircraft to fly lower to get a better target picture. But this seems to undermine the point of PGMs, which are designed to be fired from a long way away so that no friendly aircraft need be endangered. Another way around the problem may be to develop better technology that can see through deception and camouflage and concealment measures. But, as ever, such technology will always be thwarted eventually in accordance with the action–reaction model. Build a better technology, and the enemy will do something to negate it. Maybe there needs to be greater awareness on the part of the strong of the art of camouflage and concealment. It is only by appreciating the art that it can be countered effectively. The problem, however, is one of incentive. Since the strong powers do not have to think about camouflage and concealment measures themselves to any great degree, then they cannot truly understand the skills that are being used against them. Thus they have little idea how to counter them.

Again, as is so often the case in dealing with the asymmetric player, perhaps the human needs to be brought back more into the loop. SF on the ground can make better judgements about concealed targets than can satellites or high-flying aircraft – no matter how good their sensors. They will provide the good target intelligence that PGMs need, and they will ensure that they are neither wasted nor cause collateral damage. Once identified correctly, then SF can, again, 'paint' the targets or plant homing devices that ensure hits on 'real' targets from air-delivered ordnance.

Despite all the high-technology means available in Afghanistan during *Operation Enduring Freedom*, it was troops on the ground who provided the best targeting intelligence. As one of the US Air Force's top analysts put it, ground troops were 'our most versatile and highly sophisticated sensor . . . they dramatically enhance overall air power and bombing effectiveness'.[68] What Afghanistan also illustrated, however, was the fact that pilots and ground troops need more training time together. For having emerged from an era in which air power on its own was put forward as the means to win wars, the reality is now that air power needs some help. It had never really been acknowledged before that air and ground had to work in harness; now it has to be. More effort needs to be put into air–ground co-ordination.[69]

Thwarting PGMs through mobility

The ability to be small and mobile is also a crucial asset against air supremacy. PGMs guided by GPS are useful only against fixed targets. If the target moves after the GPS co-ordinates have been put in, then it remains safe: the 'lesson is that modern air power . . . cannot kill mobile systems'.[70] Hence the great virtue of mobile Scud missiles rather than those fired from fixed sites, of radars mounted on trucks, of jammers mounted on vehicles, etc., etc. Mobile systems are very hard to fix and destroy with PGMs.[71]

Response to mobility

In dealing with small and flexible players, then, the strong must, to a degree, try to be flexible in their responses. If the asymmetric adversary employs mobility, then the strong have to develop ways to deal with it. SF have a role here, too. They can be seen as an adjunct of air power that provides flexibility. SF can gain the necessary up-to-the-minute intelligence that ensures that air power assets are employed effectively. If SF are on station, then they can advise if targets have moved and where they have moved.

Flexibility, too, has to come in the shape of allowing aircraft to take on targets of opportunity. This will involve patrolling aircraft seeing targets themselves or being told where they are by ground forces. Such patrolling – 'loitering' – above battle spaces will, of course, be dangerous, but if such tactics are applied, then weapons systems in transit cannot move around with impunity as they did during the Kosovo War in 1999.

Degrees of will and the PGM

A final 'weakness' that the PGM has involves asymmetries of will. It is a given that the 'wars of choice' that the West seems to engage in these days have at their core the need to avoid casualties. Given the fact that one of the PGM's main selling points is its ability, through accuracy, to avoid collateral damage, then all the weaker party has to do is to adopt defensive procedures that take into account the psychology of its more powerful opponents. It will be tempted to adopt 'hugging tactics' to prevent the destruction of valuable assets. Civilians (volunteers or press-ganged), or even prisoners of war, can be gathered around likely targets. Western forces will then not dare attack them. Moreover, position a tank, a vehicle, a gun, etc., next to a hospital or a school, and can any PGM be fired at it? If a building housing troops has refugees on its top floor, then can it be targeted?[72] Such tactics work. The Bosnian Serbs, in gathering captured UN personnel around likely targets, used 'hugging' methods in 1994 and 1995 to weaken NATO's bombing campaign.[73] The Serbs themselves employed the method in the war in Kosovo of 1999, using both un-willing Albanians and willing Serbs to protect some high-value targets.[74]

This movement to 'hug' is in direct response to the accuracy of modern weapons allied to a liberal mind-set. The PGM's accuracy is supposed to stop collateral casualties, but asymmetric players will play on the very fact that the weapons are so accurate by ensuring that there will, in fact, be casualties. And they will use media outlets to make sure the democracies know what the consequences of their actions will be: 'Look! We have these people at your target sites.' Pause for thought – the thinking time that undermines the will to continue campaigns and one of the prime objectives of the asymmetric adversary – is again created. Liberal democracies can have very powerful armed forces, but being a liberal democracy means that with such power come constraints. As has been noted, 'US sensitivity *invites* adversary practices designed to put at risk the very civilians the United States seeks to leave unharmed.'[75]

Response

If asymmetric adversaries use one of their primary weapons – the ability and willingness to play 'dirty' or to act 'unfairly' – then there is little Western militaries, as representatives of liberal democracies, can do. They have to adhere to their self-imposed rules. Indeed, this inability to respond encourages the 'not fighting fair' remarks; for the resort to such rhetoric implies a last refuge of the truly impotent.

Unmanned aerial vehicles (UAVs)

UAVs (or drones) are small, pilotless aircraft controlled by a remote operator sited often hundreds of miles from the vehicle itself. UAVs are becoming an increasingly prevalent aspect of air power. They are ideal for surveillance and reconnaissance tasks since they have several advantages over manned aircraft. They have the ability, far more than any piloted craft, to fly more slowly and loiter above target areas and gain good imagery of objects and of movement below. Given their slow speed, UAVs, compared to manned aircraft, can fly for much longer (up to 24 hours), and they do not have to carry the weight of a pilot or all his or her accoutrements – such as an ejector seat. UAVs are cheaper than normal aircraft, and are thus more expendable. Their ultimate advantage, though, is the fact that they do not have the physical presence of a pilot: UAVs have no problem with crew fatigue and are able do the 'dirty, dull and dangerous' work that pilots are keen to avoid.[76]

The first effective battlefield use of UAVs was in 1982, by the Israelis in Lebanon's Bekaa Valley. Reconnaissance drones were able to send back TV images of the movements of Syrian forces.[77] Nowadays, virtually all Western militaries employ UAVs to some degree, and the US has especially sophisticated ones in the form of the Predator and the larger Global Hawk. Smaller, tactical versions such as the Desert Hawk are used by front-line forces to provide a view 'over the hill'. Recently, steps have been taken to move UAVs from being merely passive to acting more aggressively. Some can now be deemed to be Unmanned Combat Aerial Vehicles (UCAVs); i.e. UAVs that can deliver ordnance. In Afghanistan, Predators operated by the CIA became the first unmanned aircraft to fire weapons operationally.[78] A Predator was also used to kill some Al Qaeda terrorists in Yemen in 2002, when it launched a Hellfire missile from 10,000 feet at a vehicle on a road below. This UAV was controlled from Djibouti some 350 miles away.[79]

UAVs and UCAVs do provide a definite plus in that they allow for reconnaissance and sometime strike missions to take place without risk and at little cost. They have their drawbacks, however. Athough we have become used to seeing them work very well in the clear skies of places like Iraq and Afghanistan, they are very much hindered by any sort of bad weather. In windy conditions they have difficulty both taking off and landing. Crashes are common.[80] Their slow speed also means that they are vulnerable to ground fire.[81]

The fact that, as one US officer put it, UAVs are 'fraught with both blessings and curses' means that avenues of attack for the asymmetric adversary are available.[82] There are four particular characteristics of UAVs that make for vulnerability. The first is obviously that they are slow, and can quite easily be shot down by AAA or missiles. The second is that they are noisy. Any adversary will know that they are operating (unless they are at the 60,000 feet cruising altitude of the Global Hawk) and will take precautions to hide or mask what they are doing. In fact, knowing that they are being observed allows those being observed to turn the tables. They can purposefully give a false picture to the UAV (for instance, deliberately show some assets – personnel numbers, equipment, etc. – but hide the bulk). The third drawback is that UAVs provide only a limited view of what is around them; the video they send back is like 'looking through a soda straw'.[83] This would not really be a problem if the UAV was looking, as its designers originally intended, for rows of Soviet tanks. For the UAV, like 'virtually all current data collection technology was developed to find conventional forces'. However, with the current demand to find unconventional forces – who have little in the way of hardware and 'profile' – UAVs may not be the most suitable tool.[84]

The fourth point is that because the UAV has no pilot and is controlled from afar, the link with its remote pilot becomes vulnerable, again, to jamming.[85] As the move continues away from manned platforms to unmanned ones, a definite Achilles' heel is appearing in the form of the reliability of communications between pilot and UAV.[86]

Response

One of the fundamental problems with UAVs is that to do the job they do – mostly reconnaissance – they need to be a stable platform with a long loiter time. Both requirements lead to UAVs being slow: a slow-moving vehicle provides good imagery and preserves fuel. This means, of course, that it involves no special skill to shoot down a UAV. This aspect of vulnerability becomes more apparent as the temptation grows to add more and more capabilities to the vehicles (such as the ability to carry missiles). This dynamic, to 'improve' technologies that were originally designed to be as simple as possible, has been repeated time and again in recent military history.[87] Here with the UAV, as in other cases, it means the undermining of much of its *raison d'être* – that as a cheap, disposable model plane, its loss can be countenanced. But losses become more and more of an issue as their cost soars. UAVs need either to be made more survivable or to be kept as cheap as possible.

UAVs need to be quieter. The best observation and reconnaissance are done in secret when the people being observed are acting naturally. Anyone who can hear a drone will act knowing that they are being observed and will take precautions and often ensure that false information is reported back.

The general dynamic towards letting technology substitute for human input is again an issue with UAVs. These machines have a role, but they are not the total answer to the problem they are trying to address. SF on the ground can, in many instances, do a much better job than UAVs. They can provide the sort of observation that is done in all weathers and done clandestinely, and thus more effectively (but over a distinctly limited area). They, along with UAVs, must form part of a package of reconnaissance and strike capabilities.

Although there has been little evidence so far of the signal to any UAVs being jammed, it is only a matter of time before this starts to happen – the more UAVs that are employed, the more development there will be into thwarting them. Thought has to be given to anti-jamming systems for use with UAVs.

Satellites

Satellites are a very important dimension of air power. They provide sensors, communications links and guidance systems (GPS) on platforms that are permanently on station and so far above the Earth as to be, theoretically, invulnerable.

There is little that very weak asymmetric opponents can do to counter the capabilities offered by satellites. In some cases it is possible (by looking on the Internet) to find out when certain observation satellites will be overhead. Actors can then use that knowledge to engage in deception techniques, much as they would with UAVs. Prior to *Operation Desert Storm*, for instance, Saddam's forces kept their preparations for war to certain times of the day in order to deceive US satellite observation.[88] Hackers, as we have seen, can also interfere with satellites.

More capable asymmetric adversaries, however, have greater scope to counter satellite technology. For satellites are not as invulnerable as they were once perceived to be; they can be damaged or disabled by several means. Perhaps the most likely is through the actions of weapons that emit either an electro-magnetic pulse (EMP) or a blast of high-energy radio frequency (HERF).[89] As noted earlier, both have the capacity to destroy electronic equipment by, in essence, 'frying' the satellites' circuitry. The EMP or HERF emissions can come either in the form of directed-energy weapons (EMP or HERF) fired from one satellite towards another, or in the form of the emissions (EMP) from a nuclear explosion in space. A massive EMP generated by a high altitude nuclear explosion (HANE) will disable all unprotected electronics in the line of sight either on the ground or in space – including those on satellites.

This issue of the effects of EMP first came to light in one of the early nuclear tests in 1962. A US device was exploded 400 km above Johnson Atoll in the Pacific and produced an unexpected by-product. The blast not only disabled all seven satellites then in orbit, but also managed to blow the lights, disrupt phone services, and interfere with radio stations in Hawaii, 1,300 km away.[90] The origin of these effects was initially a mystery, but was later sourced to the EMP produced in the nuclear blast. In addition to an EMP's line-of-sight effects, the electrons and protons released by a nuclear blast will also be speeded up by the Earth's magnetic field to produce a belt of radiation which moves through space (known as the Christofilos Effect). This again will damage the electronics of satellites, but this time all around the globe. It is estimated that a 10 kilotonne nuclear device set off at high altitude would knock out 90 per cent of low earth orbit satellites within a month and have a lasting effect of two years.[91]

Many military satellites are, of course, 'hardened' against the effects of EMP and HERF emissions. This hardening involves the use of metal plates to protect vulnerable circuitry. Civilian satellites, however, are not hardened. They have to pay their way, and it is not economical for civilian companies to add the cost that comes from putting the extra weight of EMP-hardening into orbit. The problem for the US military, though, is that while it may have hardened many of its own satellites, there are times when some 95 per cent of its communications traffic is distributed through *civilian* satellites.[92]

Obviously, an asymmetric adversary such as a terrorist group is not going to launch a nuclear device into space. But a weak state adversary possessed of a small number of nuclear weapons and wanting to have a strategic effect on an enemy such as the US might consider using them – not against US territory or ground-based assets *per se*, but actually in space. If the US loses many of its satellites, it loses much of its technological edge over weaker adversaries. As one analyst put it, an EMP blast would be 'an attractive equalizer for a less sophisticated military opponent'.[93] Such opponents might also consider placing directed-energy weapons in space. These would take the form of satellites fitted with a weapon capable of producing a unidirectional EMP blast. Ground-based weapons – such as lasers – could also be developed. The Chinese are known to be developing ground-based lasers and, through a burgeoning space programme, the ability to deploy EMP weapons which can blind or destroy satellites.[94] The Chinese, with far fewer of their own, would be less affected by any general removal of orbiting satellites.

The US military are certainly concerned about the vulnerability of their satellites. A recent CIA report says that by 2015 several countries will have technologies such as space-object tracking facilities and directed-energy weapons.[95] A Congressional Space Commission also suggested that there was the possibility of a 'Pearl Harbor' in space, so vulnerable are US assets.[96] It is considered to be a 'a major issue' in the US as to 'whether the key sensors and communications systems associated with the US's next generation of reconnaissance-strike and battlefield situational awareness systems will have to be made resistant to the effects of electromagnetic radiation generated by the high-altitude use of nuclear weapons'.[97]

Response

The simple and straightforward response to the possibility of asymmetric attacks on satellites is to harden all of them. But even in the case of military satellites, the introduction of hardening procedures has been, according to one Congressional Panel, 'spotty'.[98] It is all about cost. And hardening is also a procedure that most commercial companies, patently, will not entertain, given, again, the cost *and* the extreme unlikelihood of aggressive action against their satellites.

Redundancy can be employed in terms of having high-flying UAVs to replace knocked-out or damaged satellites. The UAVs can undertake the roles related to image gathering, communications and GPS, etc. Using UAVs, however, could only ever represent a temporary measure; these cannot be kept operating indefinitely above the Earth and, what is more, covering the entire Earth's surface.

A further difficulty in relation to attacks on satellites is how they are supposed to be deterred. For instance, in the case of a nuclear explosion in space perpetrated by, say, North Korea, that destroyed many satellites, how would the US react? The same scenario can be played out if a Chinese weapon destroyed several US satellites. If no one was killed, how could the US retaliate, if at all? And because the idea of retaliation is such a moot one, is there the capability to deter attacks on satellites in the first place?

Conclusion

Air power can win wars. If used in the right way and against the right enemy, the 'shock and awe' provided by accurately delivered ordnance targeted in the right places will subdue the 'right' enemies. It appears, however, that the right enemy in this case is a symmetrical one, one with an established infrastructure, a population to consider, and assets to lose. If the enemy has no infrastructure, no population to consider, and few assets to lose – i.e. if it is an asymmetric enemy – then the efficacy of air power is less clear-cut.

However, former USAF Chief of Staff, Gen. Ronald Fogleman, has said that air power was the 'force for choice' when dealing with the asymmetric adversary.[99] Many air force officers, such as Fogleman, like to think that they use their air power capabilities in nuanced ways. They indulge in Strategic Persuasion Orientated Targeting (SPOT). Here air planners carefully work out where to deliver ordnance, so that they hit those targets which will apply most coercive pressure on an enemy. SPOT is a form of centre-of-gravity analysis: strike where the most pain will be felt, such that the enemy has no option but to yield.[100] But what if the enemy does not yield? What if they do not care about coercive pressure or, indeed, pain? What if their zeal is of such an order that they care not whether they live or die or whether those around them live or die? For such adversaries the concept of coercion has no meaning. What if, moreover, the opponent is nimble, mobile, clever and adroit enough to avoid the threat from air power – and SPOT bombing – completely? And what if SPOT bombing has some of its target sets denied because the West's employment of air power is circumscribed by the restrictions placed on it by the general lack of will to take and inflict casualties and by the restrictions of international law? For a variety of reasons, air power, when used against the asymmetric adversary, lacks credibility.[101]

Its lack of credibility is increased by the fact that many of the aircraft being used today are ill-suited to countering the asymmetric adversary. Aircraft designed for interdiction or as bombers are not the tools of choice here. The interdiction aircraft will very rarely be needed, since no weaker adversary will expose their own aircraft, if they have any, to the air capabilities of the US and its close allies. The bombers, moreover, while very capable, are not capable of attacking ground targets with *sufficient* precision. What is more, the sheer expense of these aircraft, especially if they have stealth technology, means that often they make themselves too expensive to risk in combat. Even lower-order technologies such as the dedicated ground-attack aircraft – the A-10 – and helicopters are often considered too valuable to risk being sent in to attack targets on the ground. Add in the fact that the lives of pilots have become so valued, and one is then tempted to ask how air power can be the 'the force for choice' when tackling the asymmetric adversary.

Air power can be very useful, however, if used in conjunction with ground forces. The efficacy of air power can only truly be enhanced to become the 'force for choice' that can strike small, nimble opponents when its ordnance is guided by good intelligence and by the marking of targets – especially mobile ones. Both of these can only be provided by troops on the ground: 'Airpower often cannot perform to its potential without a credible ground component in the campaign strategy.'[102] Moreover, the air campaign in *Operation Allied Force* only began to have significant effect once truly coercive pressure was applied in the form of ground troops massing on the borders of

Kosovo. This fact was recognized by senior air force personnel. As Gen. Merrill McPeak, former Chief of Staff of the USAF, said when commenting on the fact that ground troops were initially held back in Kosovo in 1999: 'In a major blunder, the use of ground forces was ruled out from the beginning. I know of no airman – not a single one – who welcomed this development'.[103]

Often the ground component will consist of SF. These can guide in weapons more accurately and can adjust targeting to deal with the mobility of asymmetric adversaries. SF work, though, calls for high degrees of skill and training, and again, it is risky work. The risk is not only for the SF troops *in situ*, but it can also extend to cover those who insert them in the first place. SF insertion will involve risks to the likes of transport aircraft, helicopters and submarines.

It should also be borne in mind that if troops are on the ground and taking risks to guide aircraft to targets, then those aircraft should be fit for purpose. There is an argument for building less 'state-of-the-art' machines and more 'cheap and cheerful' ones that, since operations close to the ground are so dangerous, can be deemed to be expendable along with the pilot. If ground troops are dying in their hundreds in operations against asymmetric adversaries, then why not the odd pilot here and there?

For the foreseeable future, Western air power appears to be facing only one particular challenge: an asymmetric one. Whether the opponent is a terrorist group, insurgents or even state actors, they will be putting inordinate effort into trying to counter the West's air power assets. They will use MANPADS, deception and jamming, and maintain mobility. And they will, in future, be more adroit in their use of all of these capabilities, because they have to be. They are reacting to what the West has, and are going in the only direction they can. The likes of the US can field better and better aircraft, PGMs, UAVs and satellite systems, but, as ever in the action–reaction dynamic, their smaller opponents will always find new ways to level the battlefield.

5 ASYMMETRY AND SEA POWER

Introduction

Traditionally, sea power is all about control of the oceans – or the Sea Lines of Communication (SLOCs) as the naval strategists would put it. Down through history the ability to influence the passage of trade, and thus the creation of wealth, has been the goal of those nations who have built large navies. Controlling trade meant the free passage of one's own goods and the ability to hinder those of rivals. In ancient times in the Mediterranean it was the maritime powers such as the Phoenicians, Persians and Romans that held sway. Nearer our own times, the Dutch, Portuguese and Spanish navies and then Britain's Royal Navy helped immeasurably in attempts to build and maintain world trading dominance, to create geographically diverse empires, and, in Britain's case, to ultimately generate a worldwide *Pax Britannica*. There would, arguably, likewise be no *Pax Americana* today without the enormous US Navy that filled the void left by a twentieth-century Britain in decline. This was a US maritime force, however, whose ultimate size was a function of its desire to thwart the Soviets rather than any great wish to control the oceans for the purposes of trade. But whatever the reasons for its establishment, there is present now in the twenty-first century a US Navy that is unchallenged in its size and sophistication.

These navies, of whatever era, were built around the not unreasonable idea that the bigger and better armed their main fighting vessels were, the more effective they would be. First, the goal was to build bigger ships. This was in order that they could carry more and more men and develop more and more speed and manoeuvrability (e.g. the move in the ancient world from the bireme to the trireme, and then to quadriremes, quinqueremes, etc.[1]). Subsequently, size was needed so that vessels could carry more and more guns (e.g. the three-decked 'First-Rater' of Nelson's era). Then, as wood gave way to steel and the steam engine, it became a question of creating in warships the best combination of armament, armour and speed. By the early twentieth century, the *Dreadnought*-class of battlecruiser became perhaps the apotheosis of this drive to balance the three characteristics. With the dawn of the aircraft carrier era, though, big guns gave way to the potential offered by the strike capabilities of floating air bases. These themselves become larger with the striving to squeeze more and more aircraft on to a platform whose size became circumscribed only by the need to dock at certain ports and to move through channels such as the Suez Canal. There was, however, one sure sign of progression over time: whatever the platform, the tendency was to get bigger and bigger.

Being big, of course, for most of maritime history, was a 'good thing'. In the nineteenth century, though, technological advances appeared that began to allow smaller naval powers to introduce truly effective asymmetric means of challenging the big-is-beautiful mind-set. The late nineteenth-century evolution of the torpedo boat and the submarine meant that small vessels were now able to inflict significant damage on much larger surface craft. The calculus of the traditional naval engagement became irrevocably altered.[2] The torpedo boat, while not as prominent as the submarine, has shown itself capable of being very effective. It first posed a real threat during the Russo–Japanese War of 1904–5.[3] The Russians were so nervous about the dangers posed by Japanese torpedo boats that their Baltic Sea Fleet, just after setting off on its epic journey to East Asia, opened fire in the North Sea on what they thought were Japanese torpedo boats. They were, in fact, British trawlers.[4] And while submarines initially appeared in the American Civil War, they first came to real prominence in the First World War. Here Britain, despite having a huge advantage in terms of battleships and a surface fleet, was almost brought to its knees in economic terms in 1917 by the ability of German submarines to disrupt supplies coming across the Atlantic from North America. This same scenario was to be repeated in the Second World War.[5]

By the time of the Cold War, the threat from the submarine was no longer asymmetric: it was *the* threat. Soviet submarines armed with ballistic nuclear missiles had the ability to deliver untold destruction on NATO countries. Their presence meant that many of NATO's warships were designed specifically for anti-submarine warfare (ASW). And since the submarines operated in the reasonable safety of the deep oceans, where they could hide and remain ready to fire their missiles, the counter-submarine vessels were likewise designed to operate there as well. They had to be of a certain size so that they could both operate in the rough seas of the open ocean and have enough space to accommodate all the technological systems – radar, sonar, missiles, electronic counter-measures and the like – that such ships needed. Indeed, the British Royal Navy's only real mission during most of the Cold War was to sink Soviet submarines in the Atlantic. US aircraft carriers – the mainstay of US naval power and its ability to control the seas – were also designed to operate out to sea away from the dangers of shore-based aircraft.[6] These carriers, of course, also had to have their large attendant ocean-going guard ships with their own specific tasks, be it ASW or as vessels designed to counter air attack. It was rare, therefore, for ships in the naval arsenals of the West to be designed to operate in the littoral, i.e. in that area a few miles out to sea from the shoreline.[7] There was no real point in having fighting ships designed to operate close inshore. What job would they do?

In today's world, however, the navies of the likes of the US and the UK are not being called on so much to operate in the open oceans. Western navies 'no longer just roam the seas looking for fights with other navies', and gone are the days when a host of Soviet submarines would be cowering in the depths ready to rain down nuclear holocaust.[8] There may be a few Russian boats left, but their threat, even given a diplomatic breakdown, would be desultory at best, given the current state of the Russian Navy.

There are now new missions for the Western naval powers. The need in the current era is not to have ships far out at sea; rather, the need is for them to be closer inshore supporting the landings being made with increasing frequency by expeditionary forces. As NATO's commander, Gen. James Jones, said in 2005, 'NATO's future lies in amphibious, expeditionary warfare.'[9] This being so, NATO's ships will have to operate in that area – the littoral – that they conspicuously avoided during the Cold War.

Before looking at the characteristics of expeditionary operations, we need to be aware of the reason why the littoral has assumed such importance and why expeditionary operations are necessary. Wherever one looks today, many of the world's problems appear on coastlines. One of the side effects of globalization has been the phenomena of people moving from rural areas to the cities, and many of the world's cities, as it happens, are on coastlines. Sometimes this movement is all about the need to seek better jobs (most notably in China), sometimes to escape starvation, and sometimes just to reach a place from which it is possible to escape abroad.[10] One has only to read Robert Kaplan's article entitled 'The Coming Anarchy' to understand how coastlines, in his case that of West Africa, attract migrants and refugees, and the effect they have on the local society.[11] One consequence of such effects was the need for British troops to be sent to Sierra Leone in 2001 to quell the unrest there.[12] In Europe, many of the southern tier of countries are concerned about incipient problems in North Africa and how these might spill over into the EU in the form of a swarm of seaborne refugees.[13] Such problems were also evident in Albania when, in the aftermath of the fall of communism, a great many 'boat people' crossed the Adriatic looking for a better life in Italy. Western forces, as part of *Operation Alba*, were sent into Albania to help restore some sort of order and to halt the exodus.[14] Western troops have also been involved in expeditionary operations to the coasts of Haiti, East Timor, Somalia and, in tsunami relief, all across Asia. Moreover, if Western states continue to take it upon themselves to deal with the war-ravaged (Bosnia, Kosovo) and rapacious (Iraq) countries of the world, then they will have to transport any heavy equipment by sea. Virtually all of the military operations undertaken by the world's powers in recent years have involved troops being put ashore from naval vessels.

Putting troops ashore from naval vessels, of course, might not always be accomplished in an unopposed fashion. Such troops and their transports need to be protected from 'enemy' action. Some ships will be required fairly close inshore to provide local tactical air defence. Larger ships will be needed to provide fire support and operational air defence. Aircraft from aircraft carriers (usually) will be necessary to provide air defence and air cover. And for these aircraft to be used effectively, the carriers will have to operate reasonably close to shore so that their aircraft spend less time transiting to and from the carrier, and can thus use more of what fuel they have over the target areas.[15]

The point here, of course, is that major naval units are being dragged towards littoral areas *when they were not really designed to be there*. The naval architects of the 1970s and 1980s designed the ships that are in operation today for their various roles in open waters, and did not foresee the current vogue for littoral operations. The major naval powers are now having to send their ships to operate in areas that put them at a disadvantage in relation to much weaker naval powers. There is scope for the asymmetric adversary to create significant tactical, operational and, indeed, strategic advantage given the new roles being undertaken by powerful Western navies.

Such asymmetric adversaries will not have navies to match those of the West. They will, of necessity, be utilizing systems to attack the strong navies that are not mirror images of those employed by their opponents: their means will be *very different*. In the littoral, asymmetric adversaries will generate specific advantages *vis-à-vis* large vessels by exposing those vessels to specific threats: from shore-based fire, from small submarines, from mines, from fast inshore attack craft, and from terrorist action. *These are the threats that are perceived by Western naval personnel to represent the asymmetric challenge relevant to them.*[16]

Shore-based fire

Shore batteries have always been a menace to naval vessels. Ever since the invention of the cannon, warships have been wary of approaching enemy coastlines lest they come under fire. For such fire is normally coming from shore batteries housing bigger guns than ships could safely mount, from more stable platforms than those at sea, and often from sites camouflaged on land against a target out at sea that has no hiding place. Shore positions, moreover, can be protected with earthworks, with stone or with concrete; a ship has no such advantages. The accepted wisdom was that ships stood little chance if they came within range of shore batteries. As the great naval strategist Alfred Thayer Mahan put it, 'ships are unequally matched against forts'.[17]

And the problem still exists today. While weaker state adversaries will probably lack an air force or a navy worth the name, they can, if a more powerful opponent's ships appear offshore, utilize the threat of guns of various calibres and of anti-ship missiles. Large ships operating in the littoral today still face danger from shore-based batteries. These positions will be hidden for the most part, and can be several miles inland and often behind hills. Forward observers can be employed to direct fire, and these can either be near the shore itself or on coastal craft such as 'innocent' fishing vessels.[18]

Today's Western warships have little means of defence against shore-based fire. The very *difference* of this threat means that today's warships were not designed to cope with it; it is, to naval strategists, an asymmetric threat. The problems begin with the fact that closer inshore there tends to be less manoeuvring room for ships. Taking drastic avoiding action is difficult when there may be hidden sandbanks, small islands and rocks, and a host of shipping traffic sailing past. Modern warships also do not have the protection of armour, since recent ship design philosophies have been all about saving weight (ships' defences these days are active – radars and anti-missile missiles – and no longer passive – armour and torpedo bulges). Warships today are also armed with fewer guns than their forebears, since from the 1960s onwards it was presumed that ships no longer needed guns; missiles would provide all the ordnance a ship would need. In the missile age, ships would not get close enough to each other to fire their guns, and they would not be needed to bombard shorelines since warships had no business being near shorelines. A small gun might be needed for various reasons to frighten some maritime transgressor with a 'shot across the bows', but any more guns meant greater deck strengthening, more weight and thus more expense for no real, it seemed, purpose.

We have seen how weak states will seek to acquire mobile surface-to-air missile (SAM) systems or MANPADS. They will also, if they have a coastline, be looking to obtain Anti-Ship Cruise Missiles (ASCMs). These, like the larger SAMs, can be mobile (vehicle-mounted) and thus difficult to detect. A missile costing some hundreds of thousands of dollars can be launched at ships worth hundreds of millions of dollars. And defending against these ASCMs is especially difficult in the littoral. Since most major Western warships were designed to operate out at sea in 'blue waters,' their anti-missile systems were also designed to operate in a blue-water environment. In the open oceans, missiles would be launched against their targets from many miles distant in order to protect the firing vessel. The radars of the targeted vessels would then look out across a flat expanse of ocean and pick up the incoming missile signatures fairly quickly, providing lots of time, in theory, for countermeasures to be enacted. These would include the use of anti-missile missiles and electronic countermeasures (ECMs) that would interfere with an ASCM's radar guidance or infra-red homing.[19]

Missiles fired from land, though, create a distinct problem for warships operating in the littoral. The firer would be concealed, and thus would not need distance as protection. With the shorter ranges involved, there is less time for targets to react and to employ countermeasures. Moreover, the missiles will be difficult to pick up quickly with the target ship's radar, as the radar beams would be interfered with by land clutter – hills, woods, offshore islands, etc.[20] The missiles will be 'acquired' only when over open sea (and even here there will be interfering clutter from the amount of shipping traffic close inshore). Again, this lack of early warning will slow down the rate at which anti-missile missiles can acquire the incoming missile. Additionally, the asymmetric opponent firing the ASCMs may employ forward observers who can actually remotely pilot the missile, since the target would often be visible from the shore or from a fishing boat. This type of piloting would negate any ECM that ships might employ.[21]

The most prominent example of an ASCM in the hands of a weak state (Iran significantly) is the Chinese-made Silkworm missile that has a range of some 95 km. The Chinese themselves are investing heavily in ASCMs. As a relatively 'weak' state itself, China is looking to systems that will even up any possible future confrontation with the US. One of its principal goals in such a conflict would be to hit 'that supreme icon of American wealth and power, the aircraft carrier'.[22] If such an incident were to occur, it could make the Americans hesitate and think twice about further military involvement in East Asia. Here again is evident the psychology of weaker players. In any conflict with the US, the Chinese are aware that, in the current era, aiming to win cannot be the *sine qua non*. Rather, the aim should be to invest in creating maximum impact that can lead to the achievement of strategic objectives. One fairly cheap missile against the right target, in the right context, can have the requisite result in keeping US vessels out of what the Chinese would see as their 'back yard'. As Robert Kaplan puts it, 'The effect of a single Chinese cruise missile's hitting a US carrier, even if it did not sink the ship, would be politically and psychologically catastrophic, akin to Al Qaeda's attacks on the Twin Towers.'[23]

Thus the prevalence of ASCMs can appear to mean the end of 'gunboat diplomacy'. Powerful navies may think twice about despatching their largest ships to provide international signalling in terms of registering displeasure or in terms of providing a threat when ASCMs are around. The next time a US carrier is sent down the Taiwan Strait to send a sabre-rattling message to Beijing, it could prove to be its last voyage.

Being sent into littoral areas will certainly create stresses for ships' captains. Given the short engagement ranges involved, any ship that comes under fire from the shore may leave its captain with only a few seconds to react. Mistakes can easily be made. Results may include not only the loss of their own vessel but also the loss of non-combatant ships or aircraft. Such a mistake was made by the captain of the state-of-the-art Aegis-Class cruiser USS *Vincennes* in 1988. Operating – uncharacteristically for a Cold War US cruiser – in the closed waters of the Persian Gulf during the Iran–Iraq war, the ship mistook the radar reflection of an Iranian Airbus flying in the vicinity for an inbound attack aircraft. In the heat of the moment a swift decision had to be made, and the wrong option was chosen; the airliner was shot down.[24] The strategic consequences of this event were profound, and even today adversely effect Iran–US relations. Commanders in similar situations, however, may not react quickly enough. In a 'war of choice', where casualties and collateral damage have to be avoided, the captain of a ship may wait too long for confirmation that the object coming very fast toward his or her vessel is actually a threat.

Shore-based fire was a distinct headache for the naval contingent of Coalition forces in the First Gulf War. Many Coalition warships, including the de-mothballed battleship USS *Missouri*, with its 16-inch guns, went to the northern Gulf to provide cover for a proposed sea-borne landing by US Marines. An Iraqi Silkworm fired at the fleet was brought down by a missile from a British ship; the first, and so far only, time that any anti-ship missile has been destroyed by another missile.[25] Indeed, the threat of Silkworms later forced a withdrawal of Coalition naval forces from the northern Gulf, and was subsequently to severely circumscribe naval operations in the Second Gulf War.[26]

Response to shore-based fire

The obvious advice given in order to avoid shore-based fire, and that most heeded throughout the history of naval warfare, is to stay away from the shore. But with the fashion for expeditionary operations, Western warships will of necessity be drawn into the littoral, despite the dangers.

One move that can be made is to provide current ships with additional firepower in the form of naval guns that can bombard shores. The suppressive fire they generate can thwart certain attacks. Naval gunfire would be particularly effective against unprotected personnel manning missiles or guns. Thus there needs to be a move away from the idea that modern warships need arm themselves only with missiles; missiles as currently fitted to warships cannot provide suppressive fire against targets on land.[27]

Shore batteries can also be dealt with by SF. They can move in and find any positions that might be hidden from sea-level or aerial observation. The SF can then call in air strikes. The use of air power without SF providing accurate target indication might prove fruitless, and having aircraft loitering over littoral combat zones awaiting targets of opportunity is a dangerous option. The SF, of course, could destroy such sites themselves, but SF work best in their true role – reconnaissance – in which they do not give away the fact that they are operating close by. Getting the SF ashore clandestinely in the first place is another problem. It was less so in years past, when the likes of the US and British navies employed small diesel submarines. Their shallow draught meant that they could get close inshore. Nowadays, however, all of both navies' submarines are nuclear, and therefore much larger and with deeper drafts (see section on submarines). They thus have to drop their SF further out to sea and a long way from the nearest beach.[28]

The use of Airborne Early Warning Aircraft (AWAC) operating above the littoral battle space could, through their sophisticated sensors, provide early warning for ships of missiles being launched from land. Whether they can provide enough warning, though, is perhaps debatable. If a Silkworm moving at more than the speed of sound is launched from a mile inland, and its target is a ship 5 miles offshore, then the ranges may be just too short for any warning from AWACs to make a real difference.

Of course, a totally new species of ship could be built that is specifically designed to operate in the littoral. Operations in the littoral require warships that are small enough and nimble enough to avoid the various perils that are found there. The new type of vessel that is now on the drawing boards of major Western navies is called the Littoral Combat Ship (LCS).[29] This class of ship is designed to have a shallow draught, so as to operate close inshore, and to be small, light and fast (40–50 knots). Such qualities are necessary in order to evade attacks – including from shore-based fire – and to manoeuvre in tight sea channels and move quickly between different operational areas. The LCS's small size means that it can hide among islets and present a lower radar cross-section to missiles. Its state-of-the-art engines would produce lower acoustic and infra-red signatures to any potential enemy (including missile-firers on land). The plans also call for LCSs to be heavily armed with anti-missile missiles and with guns (such as the Phalanx system, which can shoot down incoming missiles).[30] These LCSs could employ indigenous UAVs which, with on-board radar, would provide an 'eyes-in-the-sky' warning of approaching missiles. The UAVs would also provide more sophisticated radar images than those available from a ship at sea level. Finally, the LCSs should also be inexpensive. Given the risks involved in littoral operations, losses are inevitable: a degree of 'expendability' is called for.[31]

LCSs do seem to be the way forward in terms of having navies capable of operating effectively in the littoral. They are being moved from the drawing board to shipyard stocks very quickly compared to the speed of normal naval acquisition programmes, an indication of how much these vessels are needed.[32] It does take a degree of commitment, though, to produce a whole new class of ship that is designed to operate in an area that has been off limits for much of the careers of many officers in the US and other Western navies. The die, however, seems to have been cast, and both the US and British navies will shortly be commissioning littoral ships.[33]

Submarines

Submarines pose another asymmetric threat to Western navies in littoral areas. Their danger is manifest in the form of the modern diesel-electric submarine (SSK). The sense of *difference* stressed by naval strategists lies in the fact that SSKs no longer serve in the US Navy or Royal Navy.[34] There is a preference in these navies, developed from the Cold War years, for nuclear-powered boats. The US Navy was operating only nuclear submarines by the latter stages of the Cold War, while the Royal Navy had a mix of the two. Within a few years of the Cold War's end, though, even the British had dispensed with their diesel boats. The pluses of nuclear-powered vessels are obvious: they can stay submerged for months, are fast, and have great range. This makes them ideal for use in the ballistic missile (SSBN) role or in the attack role (SSN). Diesel-engined boats, on the other hand, are slow, and were always, by comparison, unable to remain long under water. Their diesels needed air to run, and thus the motors could only operate under water using battery power. These batteries would soon run down, limiting speed and time submerged (hours rather than days).[35]

There were always certain positives with SSKs, though. They were cheaper and easier to operate than nuclear boats, and were quieter and thus harder to detect with sonar. Sonar is a means of detecting and tracking objects under water by using sound. Sonar can be passive, i.e. just listening for noise (usually of the engine), or active, whereby a 'ping' (acoustic pulse) is sent out which reflects back off any target. Sonar can be mounted on surface vessels or on other submarines. But although nuclear boats are more vulnerable to sonar, given their 'noise', the navies of the US and the UK came to prefer them because, given their range and speed, they could always find a lot of deep ocean to lose themselves in.[36]

Recent years, however, have witnessed technological advances in terms of diesel submarine technology that have enhanced the potency of SSKs. First, battery power has been increased. Modern SSKs are thus now faster, and can stay submerged for several days. They have also become even stealthier, benefiting from new engine and propeller technology that has made them quieter.[37] Add to these improvements the fact that they are quite cheap to build, and the SSK becomes very attractive to those weak states who wish to control their own coastal waters. Russian Kilo-Class SSKs have been bought by China and Iran, and several Asian states have obtained new Dutch, Swedish and German diesel boats. North Korea also has nearly two dozen diesel attack submarines and several smaller, coastal infiltration submarines.[38]

These SSKs can be tremendously effective in littoral areas. Being smaller than the bulky nuclear submarines, they can more easily operate in shallow coastal waters. Indeed, their stealth factor is increased by the fact that sonar's effectiveness is degraded in these waters. Reasons for this include the fact that in shallows sonar signals can bounce off the bottom and thus send a confused series of echoes back to the operators aboard a ship or another submarine. Sonar pulses will also be affected by the amount of general clutter in the littoral. There will be more seaweed, more shipping traffic, more wrecks on the bottom, and more general ambient noise interfering with clear signals.[39] Additionally, sonar beams are reflected and refracted by the boundaries between the different layers of water that are more prevalent in coastal waters. This phenomenon is especially noticeable where there is little storm activity (in the Persian Gulf, for instance) and thus little mixing of warm- and cold-water layers.[40] The presence in littorals of strong currents and fresh-water run-off from rivers also creates confused layers of salinity which again degrade sonar effectiveness. An SSK operating in the littoral can be very hard to find.[41]

The US Navy would thus, for instance, have trouble detecting Chinese submarines in the South China, East China and Yellow Seas given the presence there of uneven depth conditions, high levels of background noise, strong currents and shifting thermal layers.[42] Moreover, dealing with the confusion of the littoral is not something that Western naval powers have normally trained their sonar operators to do. Previously, in the Cold War, the Soviet SSBNs would be out in the uncluttered open oceans, and so NATO sonar operators were given the requisite training to deal with such an environment. They would not really need to look for submarines in inshore waters; no SSBN or SSN would lurk there.

What is more, even if an 'enemy' submarine could be located in the littoral, normal ASW weapons will not function to their best advantage in such an environment. ASW torpedoes, for instance, will tend to head for the nearest sonar contact. In the wide blue depths this would doubtless be a submarine; in the littoral it tends to be the sea floor or any of the other myriad flotsam in the area. The other ASW method – of using depth charges – is an inexact science, and in shallow waters, massive underwater explosions can crack the hulls of the ships that fired the depth charges in the first place.[43]

Indeed, not only is it more difficult for these SSKs to be detected and for them to be sunk in the littoral, but the characteristics of such waters actually enhance the SSKs' *offensive* capabilities. It becomes hard for surface ships to protect themselves, given that any incoming torpedoes fired from submarines will be difficult to pick up on sensors, again because of the coastal clutter. The lack of manoeuvring room close inshore will also hinder evasive tactics. Additionally, any sub-hunting being done by Western warships in the littoral will be under-taken within range of shore-based fire. Given this threat, such ships will want to be operating at a certain rate of knots. Sonar, however, does not operate optimally when its host vessel is moving at speed. Sub-hunting vessels can thus become easy targets from land if they are moving at a leisurely pace offshore. Employing helicopters to trail sonar buoys is also problematic if those helicopters are having to face the same threat of fire from the shore.

Thus, in the current era, there is a combination of powerful navies being dragged into littoral waters where they may have to face the asymmetric threat of better SSKs in an environment which enhances the SSKs' capabilities while degrading those of their notionally more powerful opponents. 'Goliath', as one analyst puts it, is certainly in danger in the twenty-first century of becoming the 'hunted'.[44]

Response to the threat from SSKs

Since the detection of very quiet submarines is difficult in the littoral, new sonar systems will be required to find and track them.[45] And sonar operators must be taught new techniques. While they may have been, and still are, very adroit in seeking out Russian submarines in the Atlantic or the Pacific, overall they lack the experience of looking for different types of submarine in different environments.[46] Indeed, navies might consider putting sonar to one side altogether and look to detect SSKs through the use of lasers, temperature-measuring devices, or even by tracking the bioluminescence of any vehicle that is under water.[47] And once detected, better torpedoes are required that can seek out and destroy SSKs in littoral waters.[48]

In terms of defensive techniques, the powerful navies need to consider reducing their underwater signature so as to lessen their vulnerability to attack. Again, there is a need to look at how the LCSs – designed to be smaller, more agile, with quieter engines and with an increased level of high-tech defensive measures – can thwart torpedoes launched from SSKs.

We now, though, have a concept – the LCS – which has to deal with shore-based fire *and* be an ASW vessel. It would, of course, be prohibitively expensive to build a whole new class of ship and then have individual variants dedicated to only one role, e.g. ASW. The idea with the LCS, though, is to build in the capacity to mix and match capabilities. Using one basic platform (the hull), different bolt-on modules are slated to be added in order to create a vessel that is, for instance, devoted to ASW, to Mine Counter-Measures (MCM), or to Anti-Surface Warfare (ASuW), etc. Such modules could be easily removed to change the nature of the vessel. The LCS would thus not be built with just one task in mind. The flexibility garnered from such 'modularization' is perceived as a means both of saving costs and of creating highly capable craft for a new task set.[49]

Again, though, the problem is where the balance is to lie. As one senior American officer put it, 'Our assessments indicate a widening ASW capabilities gap and the need to counter advanced non-nuclear [i.e. SSK] in the littoral, but not forgetting the open-ocean submarine threat as well.'[50] A small vessel suited to the littoral and with equipment suited to the detection of submarines in the littoral may not be the tool of choice when it comes to looking for SSBNs in the Atlantic or the Pacific. And thought still needs to be put into detecting such vessels; they, after all, represent perhaps the *real* danger to the Western powers. This danger may not manifest itself today or tomorrow, but the capacity has always to be retained to maintain a watching brief over Russian and possibly, down the road, Chinese SSBNs.

Mines

Sea mines are a wonderful asymmetric instrument. They are cheap, involve no great technology or sophistication, can be planted very easily, and do not need maintaining. They can inflict great damage on, disable or even sink large, sophisticated vessels. They do not, moreover, even have to strike any targets to produce results. Merely the knowledge that they are out there will give pause to and degrade the effectiveness of naval operations by strong powers.

Mines have been a danger to shipping since the US Civil War and have always been used more by the weak than by the powerful. As a favoured tool of the weak, of course, their use has always been considered to be 'cheating'. Setting the tone as far back as the 1860s, the British, as the supreme naval power, considered mines (along with a host of other naval 'asymmetric' devices) to be 'underhand'.[51] And to many Western navies today they are still a version of 'not fighting fair', as they are forced to reconsider the threat from mines given the current penchant for littoral operations. For it is in inshore waters that mines are most effective. Out in the oceans it is well nigh pointless to sow mines, since the chances of a ship striking one there are astronomically small. Mines are much more effective in areas where it is known that ships will be moving, such as in narrow channels between land masses, in front of possible landing beaches, or in the entrances to ports.

There are various types of mine. The familiar 'dumb iron' variety (basically a large ball of explosive with prongs for detonators) will either float on the surface or be held just below by a tether to the sea floor. These will explode when one of their prongs is struck. More sophisticated, 'influence' mines will be set off acoustically (by the noise of a passing ship), by magnetic interference (from a ship's magnetic field), or by a vessel's pressure wave as it moves by.

In the past, mines have proved their worth to weak players. During the Russo–Japanese War in 1904–5, for instance, three battleships and fifteen other major vessels were lost to mines in and around Port Arthur (a debacle that led the British to consider the use of mines themselves).[52] On a single day in the First World War, one French and two British battleships were sunk by Turkish mines as they tried to force their way through the Dardenelles in 1915.[53] In the Second World War, mines brought about serious merchant marine losses to the British,[54] and Allied mines were actually a 'crucial factor' in bringing to an end the war with Japan.[55] In the Korean War in 1952, the mining of Wonsan harbour by the North Koreans delayed for a week an amphibious landing by US Marines and led to 'humiliation' for the US Navy.[56]

By the time the Cold War had fully developed, however, mines were very much a back-burner issue for the US Navy. Since this navy was one that looked to be controlling SLOCs and operating against Soviet submarines in deep waters, the general impression was that they would be unlikely to face any mine threat. Thus the US Navy put hardly any investment into Mine Counter-Measures (MCM) vessels; they would simply not be needed. And if they were, then NATO allies could take up the challenge. Despite this insouciance, the fact remains that fourteen out of the seventeen US Navy warships that have been disabled or damaged as the result of enemy action since the end of the Second World War have been the victim of mines.[57]

Other, smaller, navies in the West did invest quite heavily in mine-sweeping and mine-hunting technology.[58] Most European navies, faced with operating in narrow waterways such as the Skagerrak and the English Channel, had many MCM vessels in their fleets. These ships were, however, not the most romantic to command or to serve on. They were small, squat and slow. They needed to be small and squat in order to generate low underwater signatures (acoustic, magnetic and pressure wave) in order to counter influence mines and be able to withstand large underwater explosions. They were slow, of course, because they were small and squat; but they were also slow because they used small, and thus quiet, propellers. The lumbering nature of these craft did not really matter in the Cold War, however, as they only had to operate in European home waters.

The danger of mines finally came to impinge on US Navy consciousness in the so-called Tanker War of 1987–8.[59] Here, as oil tankers ran the gauntlet of the Persian Gulf war zone during the Iran–Iraq conflict of 1980–8, the US became concerned about the threat to the world's oil supplies. *Operation Earnest Will* was set in motion, and US warships were sent to the Gulf to protect Kuwaiti oil tankers, re-flagged as American vessels. But the real danger to the tankers came not from the expected quarter of missiles or from air attack; it lay rather in the threat from mines. Given the lack of sea room in the Gulf and the fact that there are only so many channels a ship can use, especially in the Straits of Hormuz at its exit, the situation was ripe for the use of mines. Several tankers struck those sown by Iranian forces, as did the frigate USS *Samuel B. Roberts* in 1988. The $100m worth of damage caused came from a mine based on First World War technology.[60] The problem was then ameliorated to some degree by the formation of convoys of tankers with US warships riding shotgun. The nub here was that it was one of the tankers that actually had to head these convoys and act as crude minesweepers in order to protect the smaller US warships that trailed behind. Thus, while the US sent frigates and destroyers to protect tankers from air attacks that never materialized, what it really needed to send were MCM ships. The US Navy, however, had basically none to send. Help came eventually from European navies, which agreed to operate their minesweepers in the Gulf.[61] Such vessels, of course, given their speed, took a very long time to arrive on station from European waters. This is always a problem with dedicated MCM vessels; they cannot move at the pace of other warships. They can be carried to distant operational zones on the backs of civilian heavy-lift ships, but this is a less than ideal solution.[62]

With the post-Cold War turn to more expeditionary operations and the need to get troops into position from the sea, Western warships supporting such landings clearly have to expose themselves to mines. In the First Gulf War in 1990, for instance, US naval planners conceived of an amphibious landing in Kuwait as part of the plan to free the country of Saddam's forces. To European naval personnel, the plan was problematic, given the seeming neglect of the mine threat.[63] The main issue was that there was no appreciation of the time required to clear minefields by the slow and lumbering MCM vessels. As Charles Koburger puts it, 'under war-conditions a well-designed minefield is substantially impossible to clear within any reasonable period of time'.[64] And this task, moreover, would have to be carried out within sight of the shore, meaning the loss of surprise *and* exposure to the danger of shore batteries.[65]

The First Gulf War amphibious assault plan was eventually scrapped.[66] But Coalition vessels still struck some of the 1,300 mines that the Iraqis had sown in the northern Gulf. On the same day in February 1991, the helicopter carrier USS *Tripoli* and the cruiser USS *Princeton* both hit mines as the ground war in Iraq began. A few days later the USS *Paul F. Foster* ran into a mine, but it did not explode. These incidents had a profound effect on US naval operations.[67] Here again were multi-million-dollar warships being threatened and in some cases rendered unserviceable by mines costing no more than a few thousand dollars. These Iraqi minefields took months to eventually clear.[68]

In the Second Gulf War mines were again a major fear. This time, however, less thought went into their laying on the part of the Iraqis, and more thought went into their clearance on the part of the Coalition. Some sixty-eight mines were swept up prior to troops moving ashore near Basra.[69]

The attraction of mines for use in littoral waters by the asymmetric adversary is obvious. Some states or sub-state actors who cannot afford their own large naval vessels will turn to mines as a very efficient means of preventing ingress into their coastal waters or simply of causing loss of life. Moored mines can be bought for as little as $1,500.[70] They require no great technology to lay, being merely thrown over the side of any ship. They can also remain effective for years.[71] Influence mines can be tethered or laid on the sea floor and will, again, prove very hard to find with sonar, because of the debris on the bottom and the prevalence, again, in littorals of strong currents, seaweed, flotsam, breaking waves, and the generally bad acoustic conditions.[72] Influence mines are also more effective in shallow waters, since they can detect their prey more easily. And when 'dumb iron' contact mines are placed alongside influence mines, it becomes doubly difficult to clear them, requiring both minesweepers and minehunters (which are different vessels) to be operating alongside each other. The mines, moreover, will not just be able to inflict damage on the vessels of far stronger naval powers; they will also buy that crucial advantage that the asymmetric adversary is looking for: time. Operations that are slow are operations that can be called more into question.

Mines can prove very attractive to a weak adversary. Strong navies have to think very carefully about undertaking amphibious operations if there are mines laid in any quantity. In fact, their presence can be a complete 'show-stopper'.[73] No navy can clear them easily, and any fleet commander will have to be patient and wait for the slow, cumbersome specialist ships to do their slow, cumbersome task. And the presence of mines will, of course, preclude any surprise attack from the sea; it is simply too dangerous to go in unannounced without sending in the blindingly obvious MCM vessels first.

Mines, what is more, are becoming more sophisticated. The very fact that there is a general movement of naval power from the open ocean to inshore waters has created a new market for sea mines; and when new markets are created, then so is the incentive to invest in the production of better and more sophisticated models. There is thus 'something of a race . . . developing between the increasing intelligence of mines on the one hand and the effectiveness of mine countermeasures on the other'.[74]

Response to the threat from mines

One of the main problems in raising awareness in Western navies of the mine threat is the fact that mine clearing has always been looked upon by mainstream naval officers as something of a Cinderella activity carried out by funny little craft that no officer with any vestige of self-respect would ever want to serve on. This mind-set has to be reviewed. Mine clearing is a fundamental part of expeditionary operations, and therefore of naval operations today. Thus changing mental attitudes is the first response that needs to be made.

In more technical terms, MCM vessels operating in the littoral require better sonar systems designed specifically to locate mines amongst sea-floor clutter. There is a requirement to make greater use of remote, unmanned MCM vehicles that can be carried on large ships and launched on site to search for mines. These can be carried on any vessel, and go some way to obviating the need for dedicated MCM vessels.[75] The use of remote vehicles means that a mine clearance operation should involve only a command ship rather than lots of small vessels. In fact, the US Navy did deploy for the first time in the Second Gulf War its new Naval Special Clearance Team, which utilized unmanned vehicles.[76]

Such ships, however configured, are still going to be exposed to view and to fire from the shore. To create stealthier mine detection, so that the threat from mines can be assessed adequately without the dangers of exposure, searches for minefields can be carried out more by submarines.[77] Such a capability will soon come in the form of small, remote vehicles (Unmanned Undersea Vehicles (UUVs)) designed to be launched and recovered from a submarine's torpedo tubes. Such vehicles will carry out forward reconnaissance and relay details of the mine threat back both to the submarine and to other sites.[78]

The characteristics of MCM vessels also have to be reviewed. As these characteristics stand, they do not fit in with a modern navy and its current missions. This issue is already being addressed. Much of the thinking now is to incorporate MCM technology on platforms that already do other jobs. And MCM equipment will be introduced on the new LCS platforms when they appear as a module or suite, just like that for ASW equipment. Thus the dedicated MCM ship would be a thing of the past.[79]

We must always be aware, nevertheless, that, as with other forms of asymmetric warfare, where the big players make advances, the weaker will always themselves be able to draw on better tools. As MCM improves, again, so will the mines themselves. They may yet become complete 'show-stoppers'. As the head of the US Navy's mine countermeasures put it, 'the widespread availability of highly sophisticated naval mines gives cause for concern about future operations.'[80]

Fast inshore attack craft

Operations in the littoral expose large surface units to attack from another asymmetric quarter: fast inshore attack craft (FIACs). Such craft can include jet-skis, rigid inflatables and power boats. These, given their limited range, will naturally work close to shore. FIACs can carry armaments ranging from machine guns, through RPGs, to guided missiles. Weak state actors, knowing that it is fairly pointless to spend huge sums on large surface vessels which would only provide easy targets for more powerful navies and air forces, will invest in FIACs to provide naval defence close inshore. Terrorist groups will also use FIACs. The Tamil Tigers, in Sri Lanka, for instance, had their own navy composed of FIACs.[81]

FIACs pose severe problems for Western naval vessels. In fact, in littoral waters having a large number of FIACs is far more effective than having smaller numbers of bigger warships. First of all, the larger FIACs can carry the same missiles as any warship would while working from a platform that is far harder, given its size and speed, to counter. Not only is the fast-moving FIAC very difficult to hit with defensive fire, but it is actually very difficult to detect in the first place. It would be tricky enough to pick them out on the open ocean, but put them in the littoral amongst the radar clutter of small islands, other merchant ships and inshore vessels, and detecting them becomes especially problematic. They can even hide from the naked eye by operating out of sight in the lee of other ships. Moreover, in the confused environment of the littoral it is often impossible to determine whether a FIAC is hostile if it is displaying no obvious armaments.

While it is true that individual FIACs may not pose too many problems for an alert crew, what if there is a swarm of small boats coming at a ship from all directions? And what if such attacks are combined with fire from several points on the nearby shore (including missiles)? And what if all this is happening while the ship is searching for a submarine and avoiding a torpedo attack inside a minefield? All these are possible simultaneously in the littoral. Modern warships were not designed to cope with such threat overloads. They could be overwhelmed.

Such a situation was evident with the USS *Vincennes* in the Persian Gulf in 1988. Its crew shot down the airliner while coming under attack from two Iranian speedboats. Despite being an Aegis-Class cruiser – 'the most technically advanced of all the surface ships of the electronic era' – it did not, as most ships of that era did not, carry enough deck guns to ward off these speedboats. The vessel had to be constantly manoeuvring to escape them. In such a fraught situation the captain was having to take his decision about firing at the Iranian Airbus.[82]

Responding to the threat from FIACs

The usual defence measures for large naval vessels come in the form of missiles that home in on enemy aircraft, missiles or ships. In the major conflict environment in which Cold War naval vessels were designed to operate, the philosophy was that 'if they are out there they are hostile'. Such a philosophy is evident, for instance, in the way in which the American Harpoon (and other) anti-ship missile functions. In the battle scenario, if it misses its target, it will look to acquire another one in the belief that anything in that general area is 'the enemy'. This blue-water thinking has to be thought through in the littoral against targets such as FIACs.[83] If one target is missed, a missile might then home in on a passing supertanker or a 'friendly' vessel rather than another FIAC. Indeed, the likelihood of a large missile like a Harpoon or even a smaller missile fired from an aircraft actually hitting an agile speedboat is fairly slim.[84] What are needed against such craft are guns of many different calibres that can engage with some discrimination at varying distances.[85] And even then, firing off many rounds in the compressed littoral environment may result in accidental strikes against friendly or bystander vessels. Such actions become unconscionable outside major combat operations. The 'war-of-choice' scenario limits the defensive measures that can be taken. And again, the asymmetric warrior will be playing on this need to be cautious, playing on the doubts that Western naval personnel will inevitably display.

One counter that the powers could employ would be the use of more high-speed patrol boats which would buzz around the large, expensive vessels as protection. These patrol boats lack the robustness to be effective out in the open oceans, but there the big ships would be safe anyway. These smaller boats are especially useful when the larger units are at anchor or in port. Some vessels may in future carry their own fast patrol boats and deploy them when they come close inshore or are at anchor.[86] Helicopters may perform the same function, but it would be difficult to have them constantly on station around ships. Again, with the LCSs in mind, one thought is to have a module that enables many short-range guns to be fitted so that this vessel could then provide protection for other LCSs in the vicinity as a type of 'gun-ship'.[87]

Terrorist action

It is all too apparent that Western naval units face a threat from terrorists when in port or anchored just offshore. The very sophistication and expense of these vessels and their symbolism as icons of national pride naturally draw attack. And these warships, of course, were never designed to ward off terrorists.

In October 2000, the Arleigh Burke-Class destroyer USS *Cole* was the target of a suicide attack in Aden harbour. As the ship rode at anchor offshore waiting for a fuel tender, two men in an inflatable dinghy came alongside pretending to be part of the refuelling team. The bomb that these Al Qaeda operatives detonated killed seventeen sailors and injured forty-two. The ship was put out of action for 18 months, and its repair costs were $170 m.[88] Here was the terrorist asymmetric warrior taking on the might of the US Navy and 'winning'.

The attack on USS *Cole* showed that the terrorist would and could target Western naval vessels. It was not, however, as if such terrorist action had not been considered. Before the USS *Cole* incident, the US Navy, like other Western navies, had looked at the threat scenarios and drawn the conclusion that the main concern was the possible planting of bombs near vessels as they were tied alongside piers.[89] Thus security experts concentrated on keeping ships out of danger when alongside both at home and abroad. Indeed, in the two years prior to the USS *Cole* bombing, US intelligence had foiled at least two terrorist plots against US ships visiting harbours in the Middle East. Away from the quayside, though, ships were presumed to be safe from terrorist action. Thus the captain of USS *Cole* received no official reprimand after the attack, since it was generally thought that the only precaution that needed to be taken was that the ship should be out in the harbour roads.[90]

Small 'suicide planes' packed with explosives are considered to be a possible threat to Western warships in foreign harbours or roads. The Tamil Tigers, as well as suicide boats, also once had their own suicide air squadron using small aircraft.[91]

Responding to the terrorist at sea

Since the USS *Cole* incident the US Navy has begun to increase ship security in and around harbours against the terrorist threat. The first measure is obviously a generic one, in terms of being proactive in keeping any likely terrorist opponents under pressure by various means, so that they do not have the luxury of careful planning (see chapter 2). The second measure is to try and ensure that host ports around the world increase their own security. The third measure is to create 'no-go' areas around ships at anchor. This would consist of establishing three rings of defence. The first, the outer ring, would be an 'assessment zone', and would involve increasing the state of alert on board ship so that security awareness is heightened. Some of the ship's small boats would be held at readiness to investigate potential terrorist attacks. The second ring would involve a 'warning zone' within about 1 km of the ship. Loudspeakers would be on hand to give warnings, while powerful searchlights would be available to illuminate nearby small craft at night. Within about 200 metres there would be the final 'threat zone'. Baton rounds and non-lethal shot-guns would be employed initially against any encroaching craft, and their use would prevent unnecessary loss of life. If such measures failed, then obviously lethal force would be the next step. A boom can also be used around a warship at anchor, to act as a physical barrier against the approach of small boats.[92]

These measures, however, have to take into account the fact that any harbour would be, again, cluttered. Fishing boats, lighters, small trading vessels and even tourist craft will populate any harbour. Great care needs to be taken not to overreact to what may be com-pletely innocent approaches; sinking a Greenpeace inflatable is not the same as sinking one sent by Al Qaeda.[93] What also needs to be remembered is that often the major surface vessels of any Western navy will be in harbours on 'goodwill' missions that serve diplomatic ends.[94] They are 'icons' and do represent nations. It is not, of course, very diplomatic to turn up as some floating fortress with guns bris-tling and with an aggressive attitude to any craft that gets too close. This is especially important for some of the smaller Western navies that use their ships more as tools of diplomacy than does the US. The Royal Navy, for instance, tends to be wary of too much 'force protec-tion'. But it has also looked to increase the presence of armed crew on deck when at anchor or in port. Royal Navy submariners are, for instance, now being sent to attend the Close Range Gunnery School, something they had never done up until the USS *Cole* incident.[95]

Conclusion

The role of Western navies is changing. Open-ocean operations against the Soviet foe have, in large part, been replaced by operations of an expeditionary nature that draw vessels into the littoral. The problem, of course, is that Western navies still have ships designed for their former role, and it is difficult for these to take on the new one. Ships fit for purpose are being built, but sophisticated naval vessels cannot be replaced overnight. For many years to come there will be classes of warship operating in the littoral that are ill-suited to its peculiar challenges. And challenges there are. The littoral is one area that Western navies fear to enter, given the number of 'anti-access' weapons deployed against them. Yet they must; otherwise they risk becoming irrelevant. Supporting expeditionary operations is now their primary function.

What is of most concern about the littoral is the *number* of different problems commanders have to consider as they draw inshore. To begin with, there is the strain simply of having to navigate in the complex littoral environment. Add then the myriad threats which may appear singly or indeed all at once. A vessel may come under simultaneous attack from torpedoes, missiles and FIACs, and to top it all, this may be occurring in a narrow channel where mines could be sown. Such threats, moreover, may occur in a combat environment characterized by the limitations of a 'war of choice' wherein collateral damage must be kept to a minimum and defensive fire must avoid hitting surrounding merchant vessels, fishing smacks or even built-up areas on shore. 'Friendly' vessels will also be at risk in the confusion of littoral engagements. Operations in the littoral are, to say the least, challenging.

Weak state actors around the world can see the difficulties they can cause in the littoral for such powerful navies as that of the United States. China, for instance, buys ex-Russian aircraft carriers, but then proceeds to tie them up in ports and use them as floating casinos.[96] It does this because such carriers are no actual use against a US Navy that cannot be challenged with such symmetrical systems. What China is doing in terms of increasing its naval power is focusing on those systems that will prove effective – missiles and submarines.[97]

The LCS is obviously a way forward. The LCS programme is being developed very quickly compared to normal acquisition programmes, underscoring the current need for these ships.[98] Modularity means that an LCS can change from being, say, a minehunter to a mine-sweeper quite easily within a day. Prior to the eventual introduction of LCSs, older ships will make use of remote vehicles that can perform some of the necessary tasks common in the littoral. They will have on board the likes of UAVs, Unmanned Undersea Vehicles (UUVs), and Unmanned Surface Vehicles (USVs). However, both solutions –

the LCS and new equipment on conventional ships – raise something of a problem in having to find extra trained personnel. This is especially true with LCSs. While this idea of modularity looks very good on paper, it tends to leave out the taxing issue of finding trained crews. If the vessel changes its suite, it has also to change its crew to one skilled in ASW, ASuW or whatever. If an LCS becomes a minehunter, having been an ASW vessel, then what happens to the ASW crew? They now have no ship. And if it is decided that a minehunter is needed, then is there a minehunter crew just sitting around waiting to marry up to the vessel? The human element surrounding the introduction of modular LCSs needs careful thought.

As ever where adapting to asymmetric adversaries is concerned, there exists something of a quandary. There is, in all the drive to have naval units better able to deal with the littoral environment, an understanding that open-ocean warfare is by no means consigned to history. Some of this sentiment is derived from a blimpish attitude that wants to keep to the old ways: admirals of today did not reach the top knowing about LCSs and littoral warfare; rather, their expertise is based on knowledge of carriers, frigates, destroyers and *their* operational modalities. As Lewis Page points out, 'Given the obvious reluctance of anyone to admit that he has wasted his time, high-ranking officers will always advocate [the use of such vessels].'[99] A more measured view, however, maintains that something of the past must be retained in order to avoid the 'all-eggs-in-one-basket' philosophy.[100] As one senior British officer involved in future ship development put it, 'while our operational focus today is on the littoral, we can't afford to forget about bluewater'.[101] If some state like China does quickly develop an SSBN fleet, then something has to be there to counter it. Another big problem, of course, is that ships built for the littoral may prove to be of little use out at sea. Is a LCS a suitable vessel for escorting carriers or sub-hunting in an Atlantic gale?

And finally, what of the big carriers? As icons, and as the sea-going equivalent of the Twin Towers, they are the ultimate symbol of military might, and will attract all sorts of asymmetric attacks in future years. This being so, will there come a point where they simply become too expensive and too vulnerable to be risked anywhere at sea?

6 ASYMMETRY AND LAND POWER

Introduction

The major wars that dominated the first half of the twentieth century and the threat of war that dominated its second half have produced Western armies that are designed, and designed very well, to conduct high-intensity warfare. By the Cold War's end, technology had produced advances that allowed for the creation of a very effective combination of efficient command and control, enormous firepower and acute precision. The aim of this combination, when fielded in sufficient numbers of platforms and personnel, would be to ensure victory through domination of the land battle space. For through domination comes the ability of commanders to impose their plan and their way of fighting on their enemy. Through domination any military can generate a concentration of force at a certain point or points of its own choosing to press at an enemy's 'centre of gravity'; i.e. the hub, as Clausewitz tells us, 'of all power and movement, on which everything depends'.[1] A protagonist, so the theory runs, who is allowed to apply enough force in the right places and at the right time will bring about the capitulation of its enemy.

Where today's land combat is concerned, the goal would be to apply force mainly through the use of armour. There would also be a profundity of combat support from artillery and aircraft (close air support (CAS)), and combat service support, principally in the form of a very efficient logistics system. The chief element, though, is definitely the tank. The tank is seen to be the 'Queen of the Battlefield'.[2] It is designed to have a level of armour that provides adequate

protection, a size of main armament that generates sufficient destructive power, and a power of engine that ensures enough speed around
the battlefield. Getting the balance right between survivability,
lethality and mobility has exercised tank designers – conscious of the
trade-offs involved – for decades.[3] The West's tanks today are typified
by the US M1 Abrams and the British Challenger II. The configura-
tions of these main battle tanks (MBTs) demonstrate that the chief
characteristic that has won out in the trade-offs is that of survivability: these tanks are very well armoured, and thus heavy. The M1
comes in at a basic 63 tonnes, and the Challenger at 68.

These MBTs, their fire support and their service support were all
designed to operate against a specific enemy – the Soviets – in a specific environment – the North German plain. For here would be not
only the 'good tank country' of flat, rolling fields, but also the good
roads and the bridges strong enough to take the weight of heavy
armour. In this environment, tanks, supported by missile-carrying
helicopters, could (it was hoped!) both operate and engage enemy
armour effectively. Such engagements were designed principally to be
at long range: if NATO tanks could fire at and destroy Soviet tanks
at distances beyond the effective ranges of their opponents, then
victory seemed assured. And if targets could be pointed out with
accuracy by high-tech systems such as reconnaissance planes, satellites and even, at the Cold War's end, by UAVs, then so much the
better. By the late 1980s, the process of finding, fixing and destroying
the enemy at great distance had become very sophisticated indeed.
Of course, on occasion, actual troops would have to expose themselves and close with the enemy. These troops would be carried to the
front line in vehicles – armoured personnel carriers (APCs) – that
could keep up with the tanks and have enough battlefield protection
for their human cargoes. Examples would be the US Bradley and the
British Warrior. These infantry, 'debussing' from their APCs several
hundred yards short of their target and under cover from tank fire,
would assault enemy positions. They would provide the *coup de grâce*,
clearing positions of enemy infantry.

Both Gulf Wars provided the perfect battleground for US and
British land power. Time was made available for the heavy armoured
vehicles to be transported to the theatre by ship (their weight proscrib-
ing movement by air) and to be put into position. The Coalition
armour could then operate as it was designed to, and on terrain that
was similar to the North German plain (and then some). In the desert
there were no obstacles to tanks gathering and manoeuvring into wide
echelons and presenting a fearsome line of assault to Iraqi positions.

Command and control were made easier as commanders, given flat desert and clear air, had relatively unhindered communications and excellent views of the battlefield. Visual intelligence (VISINT) was excellent. Technical intelligence-gathering assets (TECHINT) worked to their maximum potential, and air assets were, for the most part, easily able to engage targets in support of armoured thrusts. There was little cover available to Iraqi armour. Such Iraqi armour and fixed positions that survived air strikes were picked off at great distances by the superior range of US and British tank guns. The principal task of Coalition infantry seemed merely to take the surrender of Iraqi soldiers whose fighting spirit and morale had already been shattered by artillery and aerial bombardment. Western land power functioned as it was designed to. It all worked splendidly.[4]

But the enemy also played into the Coalition's hands. Today, we should not expect asymmetric adversaries – be they state or sub-state – to play into anyone's hands. The Gulf Wars are likely to prove the last hurrah for what we might call 'normal' land warfighting. The Iraqis, with all their power in terms of armour and artillery, were no match for the *truly* powerful. The lessons are there; if you want to take on Western land forces, you must do so in places and in ways that negate their capabilities. The battlefield must be leveled, and the powerful must be brought down to the level of the smaller opponent. And once the battlefield has been levelled, the smaller adversary can then seek to create occasional tactical successes that will, hopefully, meld together to become operational and strategic advantages.

In the search for such tactical successes, the weaker protagonist will adopt what in land warfare terms are considered to be asymmetric techniques. The smaller adversary will attempt to draw Western land forces into battle spaces that cannot easily be controlled, where plans can easily be sent awry, where technological prowess is negated, where the fighting potential of armour is undermined, where the use of firepower is restricted, and where logistics supply is problematic. In the current era, these battle spaces will be principally in the 'complex terrain' of urban environments and hilly regions. The asymmetric adversary will also attempt to strike at land forces where they are most vulnerable: in their rear echelons.

Urban environment

For a long time the admonition has been there that armies should avoid fighting in built-up areas. A very long time ago Sun Tzu was writing that 'The worst policy is to attack cities. Attack cities only when there is no alternative.'[5] This is as true today as it was in Sun's time. The fact is, though, that there is often no alternative to attacking cities. They are the seats of power and administration, and any army wishing to control a territory will need to control its cities.

In the distant and not so distant past, attacks on cities traditionally took the form of sieges (e.g. Leningrad, 1941–4), or quick assaults that resulted in the destruction of much of the city itself (e.g. Stalingrad and Hue). Today, though, in our impatient and casualty-conscious times, if invasive military action is to be taken by Western forces in our 'wars of choice,' then cities and towns have to be occupied quickly, while keeping suffering and damage to a minimum. The option of a long drawn-out siege is thus one denied, as is the option of taking the city quickly through the use of overwhelming – and thus destructive – force. The approach, for instance, of the Russians in their 1994 operation to take Grozny cannot be countenanced by Western forces given the civilian casualties that resulted (see below).

For the asymmetric adversary, these self-imposed limitations placed on the use of Western military power in urban areas, along with other factors that act as force multipliers for the weaker protagonist, offer the possibility to level the battlefield with more powerful opponents to a significant degree. Built-up areas, indeed, can act as the 'great equalizer'.[6]

To explain why cities can act as such a leveller, we must obviously begin with the fact that because a city will, likely as not, have significant numbers of civilians within its structures, then the normal go-to weapons systems of Western forces (artillery and airpower[7]) are, to a large degree, inappropriate; they are not capable of displaying enough discrimination. Such weapons were designed to operate in the free-fire zones of a conventional battlefield where anyone 'out there' would be the 'bad guys'.[8] Thus powerful militaries can bring to the urban environment whatever weapons they like; but will they be able to use them? Heavy civilian losses would be unconscionable in 'wars of choice'. And cities will always have a fair proportion of their normal populations remaining behind no matter how much they may be encouraged to leave prior to any offensive (as seen recently in Fallujah in Iraq). This is because there will always be those people who want to stay to protect their property from looters or who have nowhere else to go. The fact that civilians remain will also provide good cover for asymmetric adversaries as they, devoid of uniforms, can blend in with the local population.[9]

The civilian inhabitants, moreover, are not just something that gets in the way; they have to be dealt with. If Western troops have to go into urban areas, then they have to go in with the sense that they must actively 'look after' the civilian population.[10] Fighting in urban areas carries the added baggage that if you 'take over' a city, or even parts of it, you then become responsible for that city *and* its inhabitants. You have to take on such tasks as repairing the water and power grids and assume the role of the local police force, 'and every other process for running a modern society' – with all that entails.[11] As one analyst put it, if troops do not take on the role of the state, then they can, to the local population, 'very soon become the enemy'.[12]

Ironically, whereas the weapons of the powerful can be seen to have their limitations in the urban war zone, the weapons of the weak are actually given added lethality. The principal tools for the urban asymmetric warrior today are explosives and the ubiquitous anti-tank rocket launcher – the RPG-7 (and variants). Both of these can be obtained fairly easily, and both can, and have, proved effective against the armour that the West has.[13] In fact, 'the biggest single Iraqi threat to US armoured forces' in the Second Gulf War was the venerable RPG-7.[14] It is a threat principally because those armed with this simple weapon can score easy hits given their ability, using the cover available in the urban sprawl, to close with their enemy. Today's armour is designed to deal with an opponent who should be more than 1,000 metres away, not less than 100 or even 10. While powerful Western militaries have put great effort into finding their enemy from a great distance so that they can then be fixed and destroyed from a great distance, in the urban environment the enemy often cannot be found until they appear a few metres away, making use of the generous degree of close-in cover available. This cover can provide protection from both VISINT and high-technology sensors.[15]

Asymmetric adversaries in the cityscape can close, moreover, using three dimensions. They can appear from around corners, from the front or the rear, from very high buildings, and from basement cellars or sewers. They have the capability to strike tanks and other vehicles at their weak points (such as their thin overhead and belly armour, or their rear engine grills). Additionally, the asymmetric enemy will normally know the city better than their opponents. They will know the back streets, the 'rat runs' and the sewer system. They will know the ground, and they will move around easily. The stronger interloper very rarely knows the ground so well. Having all the advantages of satellite imagery, UAV pictures, the latest maps, and all the ground appreciations one would wish for, is not *really* going to provide situational awareness. There will always be doubt as to who is in the next room, what is in the building across the street, or even the best way of going from A to B.

The 'Queen of the Battlefield' is, moreover, out of its depth in many ways in built-up areas. The tank is 'ill-designed for urban combat'.[16] Armour is constrained: there can be no wide waves and supporting echelons of attack, only linear approaches consisting of long columns channelled down roads. Few tanks are then in a position to bring their guns to bear on the enemy. Forced to use the roads, tanks have to take predictable routes, and the enemy then has the information advantage – they will know the directions of approach. Tanks will also be hampered by the crews' limited fields of view provided by their small observation ports; enemies will be difficult to spot. And even if the enemy can be seen, the tank's main armament often cannot be elevated enough or depressed enough to engage targets in high buildings or in basements. The gun may also be unable to traverse fully, given the proximity of buildings. Additionally, the gun will take time to come to bear on targets, and the nimble asymmetric opponent, who will probably be on foot, will not be hanging around waiting to be hit. A tank's sensor-to-shooter time is generally not short enough in the urban environment. Indeed, under attack in a city, the tank can be a stranded leviathan; unable to manoeuvre effectively, unable to defend itself properly, and acting as nothing more than a 'death trap' to its crew.[17] Its enemies, moreover, do not have to destroy it; they can merely render it useless through the damaging of its tracks or its road wheels. And once stranded, its bulk can block roads and leave other armoured vehicles as easy static targets.

This is not to say that the tank cannot be used in urban combat, but it has to be used wisely. To operate well in cities, the tank needs to be protected through the use of dismounted infantry support. Troops have to operate on foot alongside tanks and forsake the cover of their APCs. They have to act as the eyes and ears of the tank crew and engage the close-in enemy far more quickly than can those inside the tank. Here the human element provides a far shorter sensor-to-shooter time. There is something ironic about infantry protecting the tank, but that is the way of urban warfare. The nub here is that the infantry, in our casualty-conscious times, are more exposed to fire here than in other battlefield environments. They are having to deal with an enemy who has the capacity to surprise them through the use of the wide variety of cover available. Troops, because of the need for discrimination, will often not have their usual support from heavy weapons – mortars and artillery. Fighting will be at close quarters, with grenades and bayonets to the fore. And in the confused environment, 'friendly fire' incidents will be common. It will be messy, a world removed from the clinical fighting for which Western armies have been striving for many years. And because it will be messy, casualties will be heavy. As one analyst notes, 'Recent exercises by the US Marine Corps have suggested that against skilled urban defenders, even well-trained attackers might expect little better than a 1:1 loss ratio.'[18] Put another way, there could be a 30–40 per cent casualty rate among forces assaulting a defended city.[19] This is bad enough in itself, but such losses can then bring about severe morale problems among those who are not casualties. Powerful armies with all their high-tech kit are not supposed to be subject to high losses; it is a shock. Troops, brought up on the 'can-do' idea that they are powerful and should easily deal with an enemy who is weak, can have their confidence shattered and become prey to doubt. Morale, indeed, will also be affected by the fact that the evacuation of casualties will be difficult. Ingress into and egress from the urban battlefront will be problematic for both vehicles (too much debris around) and helicopters (vulnerable to ground fire). Medical staff will have trouble getting in and getting their casualties out. Any delay may mean that troops will be watching friends bleed to death around them. The effects can be profound.

Besides medical staff, other support troops such as logisticians will also have trouble moving around and can become victims of the confused battlefield environment. They will have difficulty knowing where the front line is, where they are needed, and how to move around in a strange city which may have routes blocked by debris, where the enemy may be all around them, and where their vehicles may be unable to operate (see below). Part of the issue here is that support services – like medical and logistics – will be required to be *more active* given the nature of the fighting, which is not just high on casualties but also high on such as ammunition expenditure. For in the urban environment, given the amount of cover available, soldiers prefer to let ordnance act as a means of making sure that a position is clear of the enemy – 'reconnaissance by fire' – rather than physically checking rooms or buildings. With such an approach, ammunition re-supply is vital. Logistic troops, moreover, must be prepared to take in weighty supplies like ammunition and water by hand.[20] Heavy expenditure and slow re-supply are not a pleasing combination.

The medical and logistics requirements add to the number of troops needed in urban operations. There is already a general requirement for a greater number of troops to be committed to built-up areas, since ground has to be assaulted and cleared in three dimensions rather than one. And once cleared, buildings, high-rise structures and sewers all have to be held against an enemy who could attempt to reoccupy them from any direction. Many troops have then to be left behind on guard duty. Other troops will be required to deal with the civilian population and to ensure that essential services work.[21] Thus, in many ways and to a greater degree than in any other operational environment, the urban battlefield 'soaks up manpower like a sponge'.[22]

Having all these troops in a compressed battle picture raises another problem: command and control. The urban environment is one that lends itself to chaos and confusion and makes command and control uniquely difficult. Besides the fact that radios often will not work properly in built-up areas (buildings block signals), the urban battle space is plagued by the fact that force elements have no real idea where they are in relation to other elements.[23] The ideal in 'normal' urban fighting is to have multiple and mutually supporting axes of advance. But if some units move forward too much, or fall behind the movements of other units, then mutual support, and thus combat potential, will be lost. Elements can then be picked off piecemeal by a clever adversary. Momentum can quickly be lost as power is dissipated in small-scale, non-linear engagements. And once momentum goes, then morale, already possibly fragile from the number of casualties, can go with it. Thus urban warfare can be markedly 'disintegrative'. Order and purpose can break down as unit cohesion, unity of purpose and morale all come under pressure.[24] The great attribute in such situations is leadership. This point is important and will be returned to later.

There are several recent examples of the ways in which asymmetric adversaries in urban terrain have produced significant strategic effects on much more powerful foes.

Mogadishu

The vagaries of post-Cold War operations in built-up areas came to general attention after what became known as the 'Black Hawk Down' episode in 1993. US troops, working under a UN mandate to establish peace and security in Somalia, tried to seize some recalcitrant warlords in the capital, Mogadishu. The mission went awry for a number of reasons. First, the several dozen Rangers who were to take part in the raid were not familiar with the layout of the city, despite their having being in-country for several months. Familiarization patrolling of the city had been kept to a minimum because it was politically expedient to reduce the possibility of US casualties. In large part this was due to political diktat from Washington demanding that casualties be kept to a minimum.[25] Troops were kept in barracks for the most part. Thus, when the Rangers were called into action in Mogadishu, and their column of vehicles attempted to find its way to a rendezvous point with US Special Forces (who had already seized some Somali clan leaders), they became lost in the urban sprawl.[26] All the satellite photos and all the latest maps were no substitute for what was really necessary: knowing the ground through personal evaluation. Other technological assistance in the form of helicopters operating above the area also failed to provide adequate guidance.[27] Lost, in light vehicles, coming under fire from irate local inhabitants, and with their support helicopters being shot down, the Rangers had to be extracted by other US troops.[28] These had to come from a base at Mogadishu airport using APCs borrowed from a UN detachment of Malaysian forces.

The loss of the eighteen men in this operation meant that orders went out from Washington (via congressional pressure) that US soldiers were henceforward to be kept off the streets of Mogadishu, and to be withdrawn completely some weeks later. This 'minor engagement'[29] and the pull-out that followed had strategic effect; in fact, according to Mark Bowden, it 'changed the world'.[30] It not only compromised the success of the UN mission in Somalia; it also created a general US 'hands-off' attitude to the continent of Africa as a whole. This led ultimately to a lack of US assistance to stem the tragedy in Rwanda the following year, in 1994.[31]

Mogadishu also raised the thorny issue of leadership in complex terrain. For what caused no little problem in the general mayhem surrounding the clashes between the Rangers, the Special Forces and the Somali irregulars was the seeming lack of proper command and control on the American side. This came about principally because officers on the ground and in touch with the combat realities were constrained in issuing orders because they knew that other, more senior officers were observing the situation through the wonders brought about by the moves towards Network Centric Warfare (NCW) (or Network Enabled Capabilities (NEC)). These officers would be watching either in helicopters above or via video links in Mogadishu.[32] Such senior officers would come to their own conclusions and would proffer their own 'advice'. And when a senior officer provides 'advice', more junior ranks tend to equate it to an order. But these distant commanders could have no real feel for the situation and could not have all the facts to hand. As Cordesman puts it, 'Real-time information can provoke real-time micromanagement.'[33] This was something that had been warned about in Vietnam, where senior officers in helicopters would be telling platoon commanders on the ground what to do.[34] And now, with IT providing video links to all and sundry, the problem has become worse. The main difficulty that emerges here is that when decision making is not left to those on the ground, then command and control in general can become laborious and slow. 'Leaders', as Martin Libicki says, 'who grow up expecting an omnipotent boss to be watching over their shoulders every minute can scarcely be expected to exercise much initiative.'[35]

The problem here – and it is a problem that powerful Western militaries are prone to when facing asymmetric adversaries – is that commanders on the ground need to make swift decisions. Asymmetric opponents gain much of their relative advantage from their agility and flexibility. Their small size and lack of infrastructure mean that they move quickly, act spontaneously, change courses of action adroitly, invoke surprise, and generally think and act at a pace that large, ponderous forces cannot match. Battles with asymmetric adversaries in a land environment which favours them will be fluid and will take place in a 'disintegrative' environment. In such a situation an immense advantage for the stronger power would accrue if its commanders could go at least some way to match their asymmetric adversaries by speeding up their own decision-making processes and thus response times. And the best decisions will come from those junior leaders who are on the ground and who can get a full three-dimensional 'flavour' of the battle, rather than the kind of one-dimensional 'picture' that is available to remote senior officers. Leaders in the field who can think quickly and give timely, suitable orders are the ones who will cope best with nimble opponents. Anything that gets in the way and slows down the decision-making cycle at lower levels will compromise on-the-ground responses. Such tardiness can be created by higher-level interference. Many officers on the ground are now tempted to *wait* for orders from above, rather than acting instinctively.

Grozny

Although this book is concerned with the actions of Western armies fighting their 'wars of choice', the Russian army's operation in Grozny (December–January, 1994–5) bears some examination here. The assault on the capital of the breakaway republic of Chechnya is seen as 'an example of how not to conduct military operations in a city'.[36] The debacle began with the fact that the Russian army itself was given so little preparation time (11 days warning) by political masters impatient to end the Chechen secession. The result was that not only were the assault troops ill-prepared for urban combat, but also that the force assembled consisted of an ersatz collection of *ad hoc* units and sub-units: troops were unfamiliar with each other. Among the forces gathered, moreover, the general level of training was poor, and nonexistent when it came to urban warfare drills. Add to all this the fact that, despite Russian doctrine calling for urban operations to be conducted with a 6:1 favourable force ratio, the size of the actual assault group fell well below this figure.[37]

As Russian armour moved towards Grozny city centre in long columns of march, the lightly armed Chechen defenders used high buildings and basements as firing points. They would destroy lead and tail vehicles to restrict the movement of those in the middle. Individual vehicles would then be picked off at leisure. One brigade lost 20 of its 26 tanks and 102 of its 120 APCs – mostly to RPG fire.[38] Losses were compounded by the fact that soldiers, brought up on the idea of the invincibility of their armour and its protective properties, were not willing to dismount and deal with their Chechen enemy. Russian soldiers died in their vehicles in their hundreds. In the end, having failed with armoured assaults, it was left to artillery and air raids to pound the city into submission. By the time opposition was eventually subdued, Grozny 'resembled war-ravaged Berlin'.[39] One interesting fact was the effective use of flame-throwers, which were (and still are) seen as one of the 'must-have' weapons for urban campaigns.[40]

Iraq

Just before the Second Gulf War, much was made of Saddam's perceived desire to bring US and British forces to battle in the urban environment.[41] Having witnessed the destruction of his forces in the First Gulf War through the ability of Coalition forces to engage and destroy Iraqi armour in the open desert, Saddam was supposed to have seen the writing on the wall: the only way to take on Western armies was to force them to fight in complex terrain. But Saddam, for whatever reasons, did not make use of urban areas. Coalition forces were able to engage the Iraqi army for the most part, again, where their technological edge could be brought easily to bear. During the war itself it was Saddam's irregulars, the Fedayeen, attacking in built-up areas who posed the greatest threat to US forces. Nine M1 Abrams tanks were lost to Fedayeen RPG fire.[42]

In post-invasion Iraq, opposition groups within the country began to make good use of the urban environment in their conflict with the 'occupation' forces. Such urban conflict, post-actual hostilities, always needs to be handled with some delicacy. Again, the constraints are obvious. The town of Fallujah, for instance, saw two assaults by US Marines (in April and November 2004), again undertaken through political pressure to act in haste.[43] The first, unsuccessful attack left much bitterness within Iraq, given the clumsy way in which it was handled. Indeed, there are those who perceive that this assault actually 'triggered the bloody insurgency still sweeping Iraq'.[44] The second assault was more successful, in that insurgents were cleared from the city, but the methods used may be seen as largely counterproductive. This was understood by some beforehand. According to one prominent US Marine Corps analyst, this second assault on Fallujah was bound to have negative consequences: 'We know', he said, 'we're going to create more insurgents'.[45] For US troops in this assault, 'whenever they were challenged . . . replied with overwhelming power using tank rounds . . . and even air strikes to pound suspected militant positions'.[46] With such techniques and the 'excessive' force levels applied in areas where many civilians remained, widespread antipathy was engendered. Much of this was spread via Arab media outlets which broadcast far more images of the destruction in Fallujah than did those in the West.[47] Iraqis and the Arab world in general were far more conscious of the results of the use of, as they saw it, excessive force in urban areas. Fallujah made it much harder for US troops all over the 'Sunni Triangle' to adopt a viable hearts-and-minds policy. This was especially the case in Fallujah itself: US forces faced a challenge in winning back 'the confidence of the people whose city they [had] just destroyed'.[48] When fighting in urban terrain in counter-insurgency campaigns is not conducted as clinically as it might be, then it can have immeasurable strategic consequences.

Hilly terrain

As the one-time Chair of the Joint Chiefs, Gen. Colin Powell, once famously remarked, 'We do deserts; we don't do mountains.'[49] His comment about what US armed forces were capable of doing was a reaction to the pressure he was coming under, in the early 1990s and from a variety of quarters, to send US troops to Bosnia.[50] Powell feared that combat operations in Bosnia would have presented far greater difficulties than did those in the First Gulf War of 1990–1. For Bosnia had none of the topographical advantages provided by the terrain in Iraq that had worked so profoundly to the advantage of Western military technology. Operations in the hills of Bosnia would have created numerous problems for any army, let alone one so wedded to the use of heavy armour as US forces had become by the early 1990s.[51]

The principal disadvantage in hilly terrain, as in the urban environment, is that manoeuvre is restricted. Armour does not 'do' mountains. It does not go up steep hills, or down steep valley sides. In such terrain roads are used. Thus, again, there can be no wide echelons of attacking armour; only long columns of march forced to use the road network. Even then the only roads that can be used are those with bridges (and there are many in hilly terrain) that can take the weight of heavy tanks. Many bridges in Bosnia, for instance, would not take a 20-tonne APC, never mind a 70-tonne tank. A tank's 'mobility' is thus not just about how fast it can go; it is also about *where* it can go.[52] Armour and other vehicles are therefore channelled; lines of attack are obvious and limited, and can be defended by a handful of the adversary. As in the urban environment, all an opponent has to do is to destroy, say, the lead vehicle of a column on a valley road, and then the whole road is blocked. Indeed, an asymmetric opponent could simply blow up certain valley roads, and then there is no way forward at all. UN armoured formations discovered this inconvenient fact in Bosnia in 1992–3. One may have the best tanks and armoured vehicles in the world, but even they will not be able to operate without roads and without strong bridges in hilly terrain. Indeed, in Bosnia in 1992–3 and with roads destroyed, British Army engineers had to build their own 50 km-long road through the Herzegovinian mountains to secure access for UN vehicles into central Bosnia.[53]

Moreover, in places like Bosnia, the hills are covered for the most part by trees. Woods (and likewise jungle) hinder the movement of vehicles, and can offer good opportunities for asymmetric adversaries to use camouflage and concealment measures.[54] Opponents are not exposed as they would be on open plains or in the desert; VISINT is limited. Tree foliage, moreover, can hide positions and vehicles not only from VISINT, but also from aerial observation by infra-red sensors. Leaves blur the heat signatures of both engines and people. And if the enemy cannot be detected, he cannot be destroyed, no matter how sophisticated the weapons system employed. The cover provided by trees and foliage also allows opponents, as in the urban

The asymmetric warrior will always be trying to level the battlefield. In the land environment he can do this by ensuring that combat takes place on terrain that negates the strengths of his powerful opponent while enhancing his own. Thus we should expect to see more engagements in the future in urban areas and on hilly terrain. We should also expect to see armies having to face an enemy who will not conveniently be 'to the front'. Attacks will be seen more in rear areas. And it is because future conflict scenarios are more likely to involve complex terrain, and more likely to involve attacks on support forces, that the armies of the Western states need to ensure that they are ready. Responses need to be made.

Response to the asymmetric adversary on land

The changes that Western ground forces need to make to ensure better fighting potential against the asymmetric adversary in complex terrain and in rear areas are, for the most part, generic.

It is obvious, first of all, that more training is needed to conduct operations to greater effect in complex terrain. Steps are being taken, particularly in the US military, to ensure that troops are better able to deal with urban combat. There are now longer training stints spent at better facilities. These new facilities make use of actual mock 'towns', rather than the mock 'villages' of Cold War vintage.[67] The new techniques being taught are designed to reduce the horrendous casualty rates that urban operations normally produce: down, it is suggested, from the 40 per cent mark to a more manageable 10 per cent. Increased effort is also going into ensuring that troops, using night-vision devices, can operate in the dark in urban areas and thus dominate night combat.[68]

And if support troops are now going to be in the firing line far more than in the past, then it seems that they must be more capable of acting like front-line troops. This patently means that training regimes need to be altered in order to produce rear echelon troops who are double-hatted. Some armies, notably the British, see it as a given that support troops have to act as infantry on occasion.[69] However, it becomes more of an issue for US forces. One of the problems is, of course, that the more time spent on giving extra training to support forces, the less time those forces spend on actual operations. The military is then getting less for its investment in personnel.

This problem is exacerbated by the fact that front-line troops and rear-echelon troops are already becoming less and less interchangeable. This is happening as the technology that is part and parcel of any modern military force – be it in the front or rear areas – becomes more and more sophisticated. More and more time then needs to be devoted to training soldiers so that they can operate and, if necessary, fix their *own* equipment. Less time is then available to be taught to do, what is, in essence, someone else's job.[70]

Of course, it is not just the training of the human element that can be improved; vehicles obviously still have a place in complex terrain. But they need to be fit for purpose. Hilly terrain especially requires vehicles that are lighter and can move off road, and which are not so heavy as to collapse flimsy bridges. And if tanks and other armoured vehicles are to be used in urban engagements, then they need to have greater protection. Increased belly armour will be useful against mines, and increased overhead and rear armour is needed especially against RPG fire.[71] This protection can come in the shape of extra slabs of appliqué or of reactive armour.[72] The problem with reactive armour is that it was designed to be used on tanks operating on open battlefields, and not with supporting infantry moving alongside as can occur in the urban scenario. Casualties will result among surrounding infantry if reactive armour is deployed.[73] Putting metal meshes or grills around vehicles so that any RPG-like round will explode away from the vehicle side will help.[74] The British Army first used this method in the early 1970s in Northern Ireland.[75]

The problem with adding extra armour to any tank is that it then becomes even heavier. There are plans now in many Western armies to move away from reliance on the tank (*c.*65 tonnes) towards employing lighter, wheeled armoured vehicles (16–18 tonnes).[76] These have the advantage of being air-transportable, and therefore can arrive in operational zones far more quickly than tanks, which have to come, almost exclusively, by sea. These wheeled vehicles are also more mobile around complex terrain and require less maintenance than tracked armour.[77] The issue here is obviously that they are not as well protected as tanks.[78] As ever with armoured vehicle design, there is some robbing of Peter to pay Paul. The deployment of the American vehicle – the Future Combat System (FCS) – has been delayed because it is realized that it will not have enough armour to deal with the urban combat environment in Iraq. Stick more armour on, though, and it goes above 18 tonnes and cannot be carried, as desired, in the air transportation work-horse, the C-130 Hercules.[79]

The opposite solution to adding more armour to vehicles is to take it off. When armour is added to any vehicle, the tendency is to restrict fields of view – with armoured vehicles you cannot have armour *and* windows! Steps have to be taken to increase the degree of visibility. This process can range from the opening of hatches and having heads sticking out (actually, normal procedure in urban combat) to having all the sides removed from light vehicles. If such a vehicle has all its protection stripped away, then fields of view, and of fire, are considerably enhanced for those inside. The idea here is that those using weapons such as RPGs will operate from very short ranges and will usually have to move out into the open to fire.[80] Thus actual *protection* for some vehicles can result from the fact that such firers can be seen and engaged very quickly. Manoeuvrable, small-calibre weapons can be brought to bear on them before they can fire. And actually hitting them is not so much the issue; if bullets are flying around their heads, then their aim will suffer. This stripping-down procedure works best, of course, in post-major combat scenarios in the urban setting where occupation duties are being conducted in the counter-insurgency role.[81]

Stripping vehicles down will not be an option in many cases, but with light patrol vehicles it can be possible.[82] A drawback obviously is that vehicle crews have less protection from that other distinctive urban threat, the roadside IED (Improvised Explosive Device). Where IEDs are concerned, we may recognize an interesting difference in approach between two Western armies as they deal with this danger in Iraq. The American approach is, basically, to go for as much protection as possible. The British, however, as with some other European armies, while recognizing the benefits of protection are less zealous in this regard. They have a slightly different outlook. Their point is that in any complex terrain there will be indigenous populations. These can act as a great source of intelligence, including pointing out to Western forces *where* IEDs are located so that they can be dealt with or avoided. Civilians will only do this, of course, if some sort of rapport is generated between the occupying troops and the civilians. The British therefore take the view that if certain vehicles are stripped down as much as possible, then the troops inside are completely visible to local populations. They do not present themselves as closed-off aliens from another planet. They can wave and engage in banter as part of a general hearts-and-minds strategy. Such an approach is but one cog in a general scheme, including high-profile foot patrols, to curry favour with the indigenous people and gain vital HUMINT. If you are part of the community, so the theory runs, the community will protect you. It is risky, and will not always work, but in the long run can prove cost-effective.[83] British and Dutch troops in Iraq take this view: 'making soldiers accessible and vulnerable to their surroundings increases their security, they contend. Making them inaccessible decreases it.'[84] Of course, most of these activities will be carried out in counter-insurgency operations rather than in combat itself, but the aim in situations where the enemy is as close and as well hidden as they are in complex terrain, has always to be to gain as much HUMINT as possible to thwart their designs. This is but one example of the need, when taking on asymmetric opponents, to open out the envelope to include all manner of schemes beyond simple, naked military force.

HUMINT is vital in situations where, as in complex terrain, 'the fog of war remains to a considerable degree impenetrable even to the latest technology'.[85] Technology tends to do very well at providing battlefield intelligence where there may be actual kilometres between two symmetrical antagonists; it does less well when they are far closer and events are moving very quickly, as they often are in complex terrain.[86] Intelligence is useful only if there is time to act on it. Imagery from satellites or aircraft can be provided with enough time sensitivity on the 'normal' battlefield, where space provides time. But such intelligence becomes very 'perishable' when the enemy may be in the next bush, just around the corner, in the nearest cave, two floors up, or a few feet below in the nearest sewer. In these environments, intelligence needs to be self-generated by forward troops themselves, who can then act on it quickly themselves. Small UAVs, available down to platoon level, can provide some assistance,[87] but much can be garnered in human terms from the local mayor, the corner storekeeper, a rural shepherd, a captured enemy or the nearest street urchin. The intelligence-gathering process, when faced with asymmetric opponents on their 'home ground', rests to a large degree on the need for combat troops to realize that they must develop the idea that not everyone around them is the enemy and instead work to cultivate relationships. Front-line linguists are then needed who can talk to indigenous people. To get linguists at the sharp end of combat operations, however, is difficult to engineer. Teaching soldiers to strip and assemble their personal weapons is one thing; teaching them genitive case endings in a foreign language is quite another. Native speakers can be used, but their reliability, especially in the teeth of battle, will always be open to question. However language skills are generated, though, they must be generated.

HUMINT is also not just about the tactical. If before entering a city, for instance, there is enough understanding of the local cultural attributes, the social structures and the resident hierarchies, then troops can aim at the right centres of gravity and the line of least resistance.[88] If they know, for example, that if they destroy the local secret police headquarters in a town or city, then the rest of the population will welcome the interlopers, then so much the better. If they know that by bombing a certain dominant mountain tribe into submission, other tribes will also accept terms, then so much the better. But again, such knowledge can only accrue from much investment beforehand. The question then arises as to whether huge investment in country profiling and linguistic training will always be cost-effective. What countries do you choose? When the Soviets constituted the resident demon, it was easy, and the West was awash with Russian specialists and linguists. But who knows where the US and other Western militaries may end up next.

Technology, of course, can help. Besides UAVs, there are systems now available that can track friendly units in the urban environment and help reduce some of the evident command and control problems.[89] Weapons of greater precision will also be very useful in maintaining discrimination in urban fighting; but they have to be immediately to hand. It is no good calling in air-delivered ordnance, such as the Joint Direct Attack Munition (JDAM) – which may be very accurate but take 20 minutes or so to arrive – against positions that a clever adversary will have vacated long before.[90] The good asymmetric adversary will always be operating at pace, and will not sit still to be targeted. In terms of fire support, precision artillery strikes are perhaps more pertinent, given their generally greater speed of response. Technology in the form of robots doing some of the difficult work in complex terrain is perhaps another way forward, but they are still a long way off, despite some field trials.[91] And anyway, in the likes of the urban environment, can any robot learn to discriminate between combatant and non-combatant?

One of the chief problems with the *availability* of technology, be it in the form of robots, satellite imagery, UAVs, firepower support, etc., is that there is a great temptation to use it. This is especially true if friendly casualties are beginning to mount in any particular operation in complex terrain. But relying on technology all the time can slow down the speed of operations, and momentum will be lost. If, before going around the next corner, say, in an urban combat environment, you wait for a UAV picture, or before assaulting into a room, you call in the nearest robot or JDAM, then pace and tempo suffer. Momentum is essential in keeping asymmetric adversaries on the back foot and under pressure in complex terrain; lost momentum will mean that adversaries can escape (Tora Bora, Fallujah) or even that combat advantage can swing the other way.

This is not to suggest that technology has no place in complex terrain. It does. But more and better technology suited to purpose is needed. One of the factors here, though, that hinders development of the requisite technology is the fact that so much of it is small and relatively cheap. For whereas there are huge amounts of defence dollars at issue in providing better big-ticket items such as aircraft, ships, satellites, tanks, artillery systems and the rest, there is little profit to be made in providing better intelligence assets, small battle-field UAVs, better flame-throwers and, ultimately, a better-trained Mark One human being. This being so, the corporate incentive to be involved in developing technology for use in complex terrain is limited.[92] And when corporate interest is limited, then there will be fewer jobs at stake, and thus political interest will likewise be limited. Many senior officers, approaching retirement, also need to think about future employment prospects – like as not with some defence contractor. They will push what these contractors want them to push, i.e. the large and the costly.[93]

The ultimate result is that little research and development goes into equipment that is needed in complex terrain.[94] Allied to the lack of push from industry is the lack of pull from the military themselves. There is a whole generation of officers convinced that, since the US Army is so good at conducting the fast-moving armoured battle, why make any changes to better conduct some other form of warfare?[95] Officers whose skill sets are in one area are not going to undermine their own authority by pushing for change. As Ralph Peters puts it, 'We declare that only fools fight in cities and shut our eyes against the future.'[96]

Another response that needs to be made in order to tackle asymmetric adversaries is the development of better leadership. There are many reflective officers who are returning from Iraq and Afghanistan having 'concluded that great advantage can be achieved by outthinking rather than outequipping the enemy'.[97] But officers must be *allowed* to out-think the enemy. This is especially important in complex terrain. In complex terrain the fluidity of combat means that the battle space is far from being controlled. As Anatol Lieven describes it, 'Urban fighting shows up cruelly the shortcomings of an army used to relying on major units acting together in accordance with a rigid hierarchy of command, because . . . it tends to break down units to section [squad] and even subsection level, throwing tremendous responsibility not just on junior officers and NCOs, but on the individual soldier.'[98] Given the fluidity of combat in complex terrain, *in situ* leaders must be allowed to lead; too often they are not, especially when more senior officers have access to images of tactical engagements. As Douglas MacGregor points out, 'To be effective in the confusion of 21st century close combat, soldiers must be trained and prepared to exercise independent judgement.'[99] And as a Center for Defense Information study observed, when facing asymmetric opponents, there is a need for 'training and empowering officers to exercise more initiative'.[100] Asymmetric adversaries do things *differently*. And because they do things differently there will be no manual that will indicate every trick and feint that they will apply. To respond to such approaches, battlefield leaders must themselves be able to develop counters 'on the hoof'. They may have to take actions that are not in 'the book'. But for this to happen, an atmosphere must be created that encourages initiative and risk taking – i.e. also doing what is 'different'.

Of course, in many ways the genie is out of the bottle. UAVs and other surveillance devices and layers of command are not suddenly going to disappear so that leaders on the ground can go about their business without interference. It is too late for that. But there does need to be a realization that, when it comes to command and control against asymmetric adversaries, those best equipped to deal with the situation are those with first-hand knowledge.

Conclusion

Western land forces, like their air and maritime counterparts, are to a large degree victims of their own success. Their opponents cannot, in future, hope to match the combat potential of US ground forces and those of a number of its allies. The weak, in the action–reaction model, are having to adapt and evolve new ways of fighting. They will attempt to negate Western land power, not match it. For the weak, seeing the light will mean dragging their stronger opponents into combat in complex terrain: in urban and hilly areas and, possibly, down the line, in jungles once again.[101] And they will make sure that there will be little in the way of difference between front and rear areas; the battle space will have no firm boundaries. Asymmetric adversaries will want to make combat messy and uncontrolled. They will make it heavy on casualties, both military and civilian. And they will, of course, ensure that operations drag on, so that time is made available for operations to become unpopular domestically in the West.

The goal, then, is to try and win wars quickly. But in complex terrain, if Western armies are to win wars quickly, with little pain and with little 'mess', then they will have to do so by employing no little subtlety and artifice. The thinking of Western land forces, especially those of the United States, about the application of land power is still dominated by the sense that weight of firepower and precision ordnance will win the day. The heavy tank is still seen as the chief battle-winning tool with backing from artillery and air power and with supporting troops taxied to the front in APCs (see chapter 7). When land assets are organized in such a way, and when there are enough of them manned by well-trained personnel, then, like as not, they will always prove victorious in the end, whether combat takes place on an open plain, in a city, or on a mountainside. But will they be allowed to prosecute war in a manner that allows for it to be won with the necessary speed and with the necessary dearth of casualties? Immense combat potential is not necessarily war-winning potential against today's asymmetric adversary.

This is not to say that all heavy weapons should be thrown away. Brute firepower, though, is not enough, and it must be employed more adroitly against the asymmetric warrior. Here again the human element is of vital importance. Getting troops – human beings – to do things better, rather than constantly looking to get technology to do something better, is the way forward *in complex terrain*. Here there is a need for troops who are *better* trained than they are currently. And the leaders of such troops, rather than relying on technology to win for them, must themselves think more about how to achieve success. Moreover, they must think, quickly. In complex terrain the operational tempo does not allow time for debate, prevarication or inconstancy. Minds must be sharp enough and formations flexible enough to match the pace, the agility and the flexibility of the asymmetric adversary. If Western land forces are going to be forced into engagements on the ground of the asymmetric opponent's choosing, then they had better be ready with the requisite tools.

There is much to be said for the idea that the powerful must become more like the weak in order to match *their* capabilities. To many military minds, of course, trying to be more like one's weaker opponent is counter-intuitive. Concentrating less on technological means and more on the human element seems a backward step. We are supposed to be in an era in which technology promises to make warfare more efficient and to remove some of the danger. But war is dangerous; casualties are part of its fabric. If we in the West are going to send our troops abroad to face asymmetric adversaries in complex terrain, then we have to accept that there will be many who will not come back.

As a final point – and it is one which bears reiterating – we must also bear in mind that there is an argument that today's conflicts with asymmetric opponents may be merely a passing fad. Perhaps there will be 'big wars' in the future against the likes of China. Yes, we may end up with land power being used as it was designed to be used as on the North German plain. But even the Chinese can see which way the wind is blowing; they are just as likely to adopt measures that nullify Western military superiority, including opting to fight in complex terrain, as any other asymmetric adversary. Sun Tzu, after all, was Chinese.

7 THE US MILITARY AND ITS RESPONSE TO THE ASYMMETRIC OPPONENT

Introduction

The United States' military is the most powerful in the world, by a considerable margin. Given this fact and the frequency of its operational commitments, it is the military organization most likely to come up against opposition, which will invariably, by dint of lack of resources, be forced into asymmetric approaches. Thus it is the US armed forces that, more than all others, need to think most about how to counter asymmetric adversaries. So far, this book has indicated how the US Army, Navy and Air Force understand the problem and are introducing some changes. The intention in this chapter is to take a wider look at the debate within the US military establishment over the actual degree and nature of change required. This debate, however, generally leaves to one side a crucial factor. For one of the major problems for this military in countering asymmetric adversaries lies not so much in its reluctance to change hardware, troop numbers and doctrines; it lies, rather, in the need to change something far more deeply entrenched and much more difficult to alter: mind-sets.

As a starting point, we need to consider the great strength of the US military. This rests in its capacity to win the symmetrical wars. It can do this because it is a very large organization employing a plethora of high-tech equipment to produce significant combat potential. The US military also wins its wars by utilizing sound doctrines and by being professional, with its personnel showing skill, determination and, when called upon to do so, considerable

bravery. All these characteristics, which are required to win symmetrical wars and to win them well, were shown to their best recently
in the two Gulf Wars. The combination of 'shock and awe' was a
war-winner.

In recent years, however, there have been wars and conflicts, asymmetric in nature, in which the US military machine may be seen as
wanting and in which assets such as high-tech equipment, sound
doctrines and overwhelming firepower were not enough to ensure
completely positive results. Vietnam is one obvious example, and
more latterly, Somalia, Bosnia, Kosovo, Afghanistan and Iraq come
to mind.[1] There seems to be general agreement that all of these operations, in the light of genuine self-reflection by both civilian and
military analysts, could have been conducted better. There was something in the approach of the US military – and in particular that of
its most high-profile element, the ground forces – that appeared to be
lacking.

That something may be described as a lack of subtlety. Subtlety
seems a strange word to use when talking about the conduct of war.
But a degree of subtlety is essential when faced with asymmetric
adversaries. Subtlety was lacking in Vietnam, as rather clumsy
actions under a general policy of 'attrition' had little positive war-
winning impact. Such clumsiness did, however, result in the deaths
of hundreds of thousands of Vietnamese, and left those who survived
with an undying will – in both South and North Vietnam – to
defeat the American interloper. Attrition, as Robert Buzzanco
expresses it, 'was not only alienating the people but could not
succeed as a policy either'.[2] The means employed were built largely
around a 'slavish' reliance on technology to deliver a degree of firepower that showed 'a sense of indifference towards, or disregard
for . . . indigenous people'.[3] The same lack of subtlety was evident in
the US interventions in Grenada (1983) and Panama (1989). Gen.
Colin Powell, at one time the Chair of the Joint Chiefs, saw that the
lesson of both interventions was that whatever the level of the operation, 'Use all the force necessary, and do not apologise for going in
big if that's what it takes. Decisive force ends wars quickly.'[4] One
Cuban officer in Grenada on the wrong end of such a philosophy
observed that 'Their reaction is to destroy everything with their
planes and artillery fire and see what's left.'[5] In Panama, overwhelming force was used to secure a 'quick victory at minimum cost'.[6] In
Bosnia, the UN official, Carl Bildt, saw that in the US troops' 'mode
of operations there was very little between doing nothing and a
massive use of military force'.[7] Another analyst described the same

approach in Somalia: US troops 'found it very difficult to find a middle way between the application of massive firepower and doing nothing'.[8] In Mogadishu, US forces were perceived to have failed in their mission, because their position had become untenable after alienating a good proportion of the city's population through their heavy-handedness. 'In the end', as Mark Bowden put it, the operation there was just 'another lesson in the limits of what force can accomplish'.[9]

Something also went awry where *Operation Allied Force* in Kosovo was concerned. Here the idea that air power – technology – could win wars on its own without back-up from ground forces was undermined: troops were patently needed to produce the required degree of coercive pressure. The heavyweight US Army, however, could not deploy with sufficient speed. As European armies waited in Greece to move troops into Kosovo, there was no support from their US counterparts, since it was taking too long for them to arrive. The US Army, indeed, was 'stung by its inability to deploy rapidly into theatre during *Operation Allied Force*'.[10] The whole war in Kosovo thus dragged on for too long. In Afghanistan, the 'heaviness', again, of the Army meant that it lacked proper offensive capabilities. Much of that offensive was then taken up by air power, which proved ineffective as over-zealous targeting procedures were applied that led to excessive civilian deaths with sometimes 'disastrous' political consequences.[11] In Iraq, the lack of subtlety was, and is, eminently apparent.[12]

The perceived lack of success in places like Vietnam and Somalia, and the problems associated with Kosovo and the continuing missions in Iraq and Afghanistan, raise issues as to the way in which the US military attempts to counter asymmetric adversaries. If there is a problem and a lack of success ensues, then normally, as in any organization, changes need to be considered. The US military, and in particular its ground forces, are, of course, currently considering changes. As the head of the Office of Force Transformation, Admiral Arthur Cebrowski, saw it, the armed forces needed to change to be 'a flexible instrument of policy engagement, not simply provide a larger sheaf of thunderbolts'.[13] In essence, in order to be this 'flexible instrument', US forces would have to adopt operational modalities characterized by greater dexterity, flexibility and, to return to that original word, subtlety. Again, the thought was that they should thus, to some degree, copy the adversaries they faced and adopt some of *their* ways of warfare. But there are many factors that stand in the way of such adaptations.

Fourth generation warfare

Actually, thoughts about how better to respond to asymmetric adversaries have been around for a number of years within the US armed forces. Most of the new ideas were coming from the US Marine Corps (USMC). Back in 1989 the Marines introduced a new term to the military lexicon, one which has received a considerable airing in US military circles – 'fourth generation warfare'. It is important here to understand exactly what is meant by this phrase, given its current ubiquity and the fact that it is analogous to 'asymmetric warfare'.

The ideas emanating from the USMC carry weight in that they represent the leading edge of the debate over the need for fundamental change within the US military establishment as a whole. It is the Marines who are mostly setting the agenda and applying the pressure (although the Army is having the same debate[14]). It is they who are looking at the way in which today's asymmetric adversaries can best be countered by American military might.

Traditionally, of all the US armed forces, it is the Marines who have been most receptive to the concept of change related to what they refer to as 'small wars'. For these are the types of conflict that the Marines, a relatively light force designed to fight America's wars at the lower end of the conflict spectrum, have traditionally excelled at. From dealing with the pirates of the Barbary Coast in the early nineteenth century, through the Banana Wars of the 1920s and 1930s, and up to the Vietnam War and beyond, it is the Marines who have been doing the low-intensity conflicts and who have been thinking hard about how best to conduct them. The Army, on the other hand, has concentrated on fighting the 'big wars' and how best to fight them.[15]

Beginning in the late 1980s, as the Cold War was drawing to a close, Marine officers and analysts (led by William Lind) attached to the Corps began looking at the contemporary security situation, and realized that the US military had to become more attuned to dealing with what they called 'fourth generation warfare'.[16] Setting down their ideas in a seminal article in 1989 in the *Marine Corps Gazette*, they noted that in modern military history there had been three distinct eras, or 'generations', of warfare. The first generation – the 'Napoleonic' – came about when the political, economic and social structures within Europe had developed to such an extent that they allowed states to field mass armies. When these opposing armies clashed, they did so using lines and columns of soldiery who employed smooth-bore muskets and a few muzzle-loading cannon. Thus, in the late eighteenth and early nineteenth centuries, although there might be the social structures to put large armies into the field, there was actually insufficient industrial back-up to furnish those armies with much in the way of firepower.

The second generation of warfare could also be termed Industrial Age warfare. Here the increasing wealth of nations and the ability to engage in mass production enabled large, well-equipped armies to be deployed in the field and to be supported by copious amounts of supporting ordnance. With the likes of machine guns, breech-loading cannons, barbed wire and improved logistics, the nature of warfare changed, to reward with victory those who could produce the most firepower to crush their opponents in linear battles. Once large numbers of artillery pieces and the ammunition to go with them had made their debut on the battlefield, then warfare became a case, in the words of a French maxim of the early twentieth century, of artillery conquering while the infantry merely occupied.[17] Hence, to a large degree, firepower had replaced manpower as the cutting edge of military force. And while war of this type was seen to be characterized mostly by the static artillery duels of the First World War, the improvements of the second generation also provided the means to enhance communications through the telegraph and then radio, and to engender greater mobility through the use of railways and the nascent internal combustion engine. The battlefield thus came to belong to those who could create enough mobility to introduce the greatest amount of firepower at certain points more quickly than could an opponent. This increase in mobility, moreover, began to open the door, said the Marine analysts, that led to the third generation of warfare.

This was the period in which manoeuvre actually overcame mass: speed, co-ordination and *ideas* were the chief characteristics of the third generation. The first signs were noted in the First World War. At Riga in 1917, and in the Ludendorff offensives of 1918, German *Sturmtrupp* assaults shattered the stalemate of the trenches. The same philosophy underpinned the doctrine of *Blitzkrieg* in the Second World War. German operations and tactics were non-linear and non-attritional. Infiltration at various points using speed and panache bypassed enemy strengths and attempted to bring about, mainly through a shock effect, a collapse in the enemy's cohesion and will to fight. Thus third generation warfare relied on both mental and physical agility to ensure that the right targets were attacked with sufficient speed. Quick victories were brought about without bringing to bear the ponderous second generation forces whose mass made them cumbersome and logistically punitive. Where technology was the primary driver of the second generation of warfare, ideas were the primary driver of the third.[18] An illustration of this appears at the beginning of the Second World War when Great Britain, France and Germany all had roughly the same equipment available in the same amounts; profoundly different results, however, came about from thinking how best to use that equipment. German armoured forces easily won against the French and British in the Battle of France in 1940.

It tends to be the case (as pointed out in the *Marine Corps Gazette* article and by subsequent USMC analysts) that the favoured form of warfare of the contemporary US armed forces is that of the second generation. The linear methods and a reliance on the virtues of naked firepower still, to a large degree, dominate US military doctrine.[19] At root, what Russell Weigley once called the 'American Way of War' continues to be based, as these USMC and other analysts attest, on the second-generation virtue of overwhelming firepower to 'attrit' enemies.[20]

However, as another USMC analyst, Col. Thomas Hammes, points out, it is possible today to recognize that the US military actually employs both second and third generation techniques. In Iraq in 2003, for instance, the initial, third generation Coalition campaign of 'shock and awe', interspersed with Special Forces attempts to disrupt vital communications links and even to assassinate regime leaders, was followed by a traditional second generation US and British heavy forces push to the major cities. This push utilized heavy armour moving forward after preparatory artillery barrages and air bombardment.[21]

There now comes into the equation the original point of the USMC 1989 article. This is the contention that there now exists a new form of warfare – fourth generation warfare (4GW). The reasoning behind the assertion is that, because the US military is now so preternaturally strong, the strategies and tactics that must be adopted by future adversaries will have to be so radically different from those employed hitherto as to constitute a completely new 'generation' of warfare.

The chief aim, as Lind et al. noted, of the 4G opponent – be they state or sub-state – would be to bypass the military might of the US and go for its soft underbelly. The American will to fight would be undermined by the use of completely non-linear tactics designed to produce a 'collapse' of some sort from within. Thus, whereas the first three generations of warfare were targeted purely at military forces, 4GW looks to target both fielded forces *and* home populations, with the general aim of creating the most effects in the civilian rear. The 4G warrior will carry out a skilful assessment of the vulnerabilities of the US so that even when small amounts of force are employed, they can leverage strategic changes. As Hammes put it, 'Fourth-generation warfare uses all available networks – political, economic, social, and military – to convince the enemy's political decision makers that their strategic goals are either unachievable or too costly for the perceived benefit. It is rooted in the fundamental precept that superior political will, when properly employed, can defeat greater economic and military power.'[22] The chief exponents of 4GW (although not excluding the likes of China and Iran) would be the types of terrorists, insurgents and guerrillas clearly in evidence today in places like Iraq and Afghanistan.[23] These groups are subtle. They take advantage of their small size, lack of hierarchies, low profile, patience and flexibility, and use them to target effectively the *opposite* characteristics in stronger opponents.

In essence, 4GW contains all the elements of what is known more widely as 'asymmetric warfare'. But the idea of analysts within the US military employing the notion of a different *generation* of warfare is clear. In conceptualizing the issue as a new *form* of warfare, distinct in nature from others that have gone before, writers such as Lind and Hammes are providing an analytical lens through which to view the type of opposition that exists now 'out there', and to highlight the shortcomings of the current US military in dealing with that opposition. The point they want to make is not just that the military's structure and equipment are ill-suited to the 4GW problem, but so is its psyche. It is seen as being organized as, and with the *thinking* of, a military basically geared to conduct 2GW while attempting some elements of 3GW. 'Thunderbolts' it does well. But when opponents are using 4GW means, this military as currently configured is an inappropriate tool, both structurally and psychologically, to counter them. For the likes of Lind and Hammes the main issue is that to be truly effective against 4G adversaries, the US armed forces should adopt some of the thinking and approaches of their adversary. This powerful military should become more like its weaker opponent. It should defeat them 'by being better at their way of fighting than they are'.[24] In practice this means that US forces have to increase their own degree of flexibility, their own level of patience, and their own capacity to display subtlety. As a concomitant, of course, it must decrease its reliance on technology and the use of excessive force.

The criticisms raised by the likes of Lind and Hammes (and latterly by another with USMC links, Frank Hoffman[25]), though, are not coming from the mainstream; they are very much voices off. For it is a tall order to ask a US military that remains 'wedded to the premise that success in war is best achieved by overwhelming technological advantage' to adopt techniques that represent 'the antithesis of the high-technology, short war the Pentagon is preparing to fight'.[26]

High-technology war

Lind, Hammes and Hoffman do have a point. Technology cannot always be relied upon to improve combat effectiveness when the combat is with asymmetric opponents. It does not, as has been indicated already, provide all of the solutions all of the time. But the idea that it does runs deep. Thus, if a problem arises in engagements at the lower end of the conflict spectrum, the question raised most often does not seem to be 'how can we solve it?', but rather, 'what piece of technology is best to deal with it?' And since, in the case of the US military, there is always a great deal of technological help available, the temptation is to let that deal with the problem. This thinking is basically flawed, in that it can lead to the exclusion of *better* alternatives. The preference of TECHINT over HUMINT sources is a case in point, as is the preferential employment of air power when ground troops might do a better job. The enticement of air power is, of course, that it can be very destructive, pretty accurate and, above all, offers to save the energy and lives of ground forces. But its use may be a case of substituting the easiest way for the best way. One example from a previous counter-insurgency campaign serves to illustrate this point. The British, operating against rebels in south Arabia in the 1960s, realized the error of their ways in their use of air power: 'The most serious long-term consequence of the ready availability of air control was that it developed into a substitute for administration . . . the speed and simplicity of air attack was preferred to the more time-consuming and painstaking investigation of grievances and disputes.'[27] In this case, for the British (and it is indicative of many others in the history of counter-insurgency) the sense was inculcated that if there was a problem – an increase in road ambushes, a town taken over by rebels, etc. – then the ideal solution would be merely to let technology deal with it. Wiser heads, however, thought it better to deal with the actual cause of the problems, rather than merely with its symptoms, in order that the problem would not arise again. The 'sticking plaster' approach offered by technology, while having the allure of 'speed and simplicity', may actually make original problems markedly worse.

The 'speed and simplicity' of firepower delivered by high-tech means can only work to any degree, moreover, if there is something obvious that it can be pointed at. In places like Iraq and Afghanistan the asymmetric opponents seem not to present any 'real' targets. Even in Vietnam there were targets. And this is the difference, as Henry Kissinger notes, between Vietnam and conflicts like Iraq today. In Vietnam there were points to aim at; the Vietcong had a proper infrastructure and were reliant on logistic support, and the North Vietnamese Army had its physical assets. Nowadays, the modern asymmetric adversary seems to possess very little that can be targeted.[28] If the enemy's fielded forces appear as no more than ephemera, if they have a low profile, and if they blend in with surrounding civilians or the landscape, then that enemy cannot really be targeted and cannot be destroyed or disabled by high-tech means. The enemy may also, of course, have no leadership to target. Most modern centre-of-gravity appreciations (SPOT bombings, etc.) target leaderships: remove them, and the opposition should collapse. This was certainly the view taken in the early days of the Second Gulf War, when Saddam was the chief target.[29] But aiming for the leadership is difficult when there may be no obvious command and control nexus. If the enemy is driven more by a cause than a hierarchy, it has no command and control system that provides a vulnerability. Moreover, while one might kill individual leaders, there may always be others to take their place; that is the nature of causes that are underpinned by deeply held beliefs. Thus, while US forces may have lots of firepower and the technological means to deliver it accurately in places like Iraq, it is by no means apparent where it should all be directed.[30] If it is all directed wrongly, moreover, it can have markedly negative effects, especially if excessive force is used.

Excessive force

In previous chapters it was noted that the use of excessive force at the tactical level could have strategic consequences when dealing with asymmetric opponents. Indeed, even at the tactical level the use of force can often achieve little when faced with adversaries inspired by sufficient fervour. Aiming to kill as many of them – insurgents, terrorists – as possible can prove to be a 'meaningless exercise'.[31] There seems to be no shortage nowadays of people prepared to sell their lives cheaply in many of the world's trouble spots. Even back in Vietnam the paucity of the 'body count' approach (used as a means of expressing 'success') was understood: as the Army commander, Gen. William Westmoreland, put it, the Vietcong guerrillas were 'inclined to multiply as rapidly as you killed them'.[32] Another writer makes the point that while 'American troops killed as many as 1,000 insurgents in Fallujah and seized stocks of weapons and ammunition . . . neither guns nor dedicated fighters are scarce in Iraq'.[33] Killing the contemporary asymmetric warrior cannot be counted as an end in itself. Numbers are not their centre of gravity. And, of course, if too great a degree of force is used in attempts to kill as many of them as possible, then collateral damage is inevitable in terms of destroyed infrastructure and the deaths of innocents. Along with the antipathy this generates on the ground, there runs also the inevitable negative media attention that has effects further afield. There is, then, the sense that ill-considered actions at one level become recruiting sergeants at another. It is the old story of the use of force seemingly working well to gain individual tactical successes, while actually adding yet more bricks to the edifice of possible strategic failure.

Change and organizational health

What pressure there is encouraging the US armed forces to use less technological-based firepower and to become generally more adept at dealing with 4GW/asymmetric opponents has had little effect. This does not mean to say, however, that the Pentagon in recent years has been totally averse to the idea of change. Those changes that are taking place and those which are being considered, though, cannot all be seen as aimed at creating a leaner, smarter, subtler force. The actual process of change has been one dominated by the ideas enshrined in the RMA or the very similar ones involved in the process of 'Transformation'.[34] There is nothing here, it needs be said, that can be seen as reverse engineering at work. The RMA and Transformation are driven not by the nature of any specific opponent or threat, but rather, it seems, solely by the need to find new ways to bring more high-tech to the aid of basic military endeavours – i.e. 'normal', symmetrical war.[35] Both have 'been interpreted exclusively as a technological challenge'.[36]

Wherever one looks, there seems to be a desire to move forward in fielding better *big-ticket* technologies that are of little use in the fight against insurgents and terrorists. The Army still wants its heavy armoured divisions; but against whose tank forces are they to be used? The Air Force still wants its F-22s, yet they are designed to carry out only one particular role: air interdiction. But who is there out there to interdict?[37] F-22 acquisition, as Anthony Cordesman points out, seems to 'reflects cold war-era visions of the future'.[38] The US Navy is still emphasizing its need for more 'big' ships, rather than the smaller ones designed to deal more effectively with current threats in the littoral.[39]

It is an old refrain where change in military organizations is concerned: 'Keep things as they are, don't rock the boat.' 'Current equipment trends', as one observer puts it, 'indicate that America's military is not so much transforming its forces as pursuing a more technologically advanced means of "fighting the last war"'.[40] There is obvious support for changes that suit the big-ticket school of thought. This is evident both within the US military and without. We have seen that there is a very powerful nexus of senior commanders, defence contractors and politicians who want continued investment in high-end technologies, and not in those geared towards asymmetric/4G warfare. As Hammes points out, there are 'dozens of constituencies threatened by the shifts in budget required by 4GW'.[41] Such constituencies can and do swing debates over change.[42]

The 'lust for high technology' has also led to the creation of a whole command structure in the US military. An entrenched bureaucracy has emerged built around the use of complex technologies.[43] Thus talk of using fewer technological systems means talk of less bureaucracy and thus, crucially, of less command appointments – i.e. jobs.[44] Moreover, in a military dominated by the use of machinery, many of those in positions of responsibility have doubtless reached their exalted rank by having skill-sets linked to such machines. They will not wish to undermine those skills by suggesting that the role of technology needs to be downgraded. Turkeys seldom vote for Christmas.[45]

Here we also see one of the problems with very powerful organizations. Power is normally a function of size, and the bigger any organization is, the bigger the bureaucracy that runs it. And if, as in any organization, bureaucracy hinders change, then the bigger the organization, the less the willingness to accept change.[46] Personnel within organizations are used to doing things in a certain way, and they surround themselves with an infrastructure designed to back that way up. The way becomes set in stone, and inertia naturally results.[47] As Lind notes of the US military, 'the problem is that, typical of a Second Generation military, the US Armed Forces must bear the burden of a vast, centralized, bureaucratic command structure that has little interest in adaptation'.[48] Thus, even when a 'new' enemy appears in the form of the asymmetric warrior, it is very difficult to pull this command structure away from 2GW thinking.[49]

All this is not to suggest that there has been no movement in terms of trying to make the US military a more flexible animal that can handle other types of wars, rather than just the 'last' one (usually taken to mean the Second World War). Attempts have been made to 'lighten' the forces. In the early 2000s Defense Secretary Donald Rumsfeld, for instance, was trying to remove much of the 'heaviness' that seemed to belong to the Cold War era. Regarding the need to deal with the newer, smaller opponents, he stressed that 'business as usual won't do it', since US forces, he said, are 'ponderous, clumsy and slow'.[50] Rumsfeld scrapped, for instance, the Army's proposed (and indelicately named) Crusader heavy artillery system because its weight (40 tons plus) affected its deployability.[51]

Additionally, several post-Cold War Army Chiefs of Staff tried to create a lighter and more agile force. Generals Gordon Sullivan, Denis Reimer and, latterly, Eric Shinseki, however, made little headway in trying to make the army less reliant on heavy firepower and heavy armour.[52] Their main problem was that such attributes had actually proved their worth in the First Gulf War and later in the Second Gulf War. The US military had proved itself inordinately powerful, and as Cohen relates, such power tends to 'invite hubris'.[53] Both in terms of pride and in terms of what the organization theorists call 'individual stakes', those responsible for carrying through the victories – the mid- to high-ranking officers – were quite content to keep things as they were; turkeys and Christmas again.[54] Thus, even those at the top of the organization, even when they wanted to introduce change, were not capable of overcoming the bureaucratic inertia lower down.

So the vast majority of the changes that are taking place within the US military appear to be occurring in response to the need to preserve organizational health and not in reaction to the enemies who are 'out there' currently. Thus the threat from the asymmetric quarter is not acting as a driver for change. As Eliot Cohen laments, possibly the 'worst mistake of all' is that 'the enemy never really figured very much in the RMA debate'[55] – a point echoed by Marine officer Lt.-Gen. James Mattis, who noted that it was 'almost embarrassing intellectually' that commanders 'looked to unspecified future wars to reshape the military, rather than to the insurgents it faced in Iraq'.[56] The fact, though, is that the US military, if it is to respond effectively to the threats posed by the asymmetric/4G warrior, has to have a wider rethink relating to some of its strategies and structures. The stress on technology and on its role in delivering firepower has to be reduced.

When force is used against current asymmetric enemies, it must be used in focused packets, in limited amounts, in the right places, for the right reasons, and with an end in mind – and that end must always be strategic. The use of technology and the firepower it helps generate have to be circumscribed. One obvious message here is that if there are to be such limitations, then it means that a more patient approach is required: time has to substitute for 'speed and simplicity'. An approach geared towards the selective and limited use of force may appear to promise only the more tardy resolution of tactical problems, but it could actually lead to quicker mission accomplishment overall. If more *thought* is applied about how best to employ violence, then violence will retain its utility. 'War', as Robert Scales points out, 'is a thinking man's game. A military too acculturated to solving warfighting problems with technology alone should begin now to recognize that wars must be fought with intellect.'[57] And if ever a type of warfare needed intellect, it is the 4G/asymmetric kind.

Human input

'Intellect' comes from human input. Throughout this book there has been a general theme that when it comes to responding to asymmetric adversaries, a greater degree of this human input is required than for symmetrical, technology-dominated warfare. There are three distinct areas where such input is needed: in gaining intelligence, in the 'struggle for men's minds', and to 'out-think' the enemy.

Human intelligence

The firepower generated by high-technology systems is only ever useful against small-scale, low-profile opponents when it is guided by intelligence that is good enough to provide workable target indication. This is especially pertinent where collateral damage is a serious issue, and it is vital to make sure that only the 'bad guys' are the ones targeted. Here human intelligence (HUMINT) sources (the likes of SF, local inhabitants) will always provide the best indications, provided such sources can be trusted. There are some who say that technology itself can provide the necessary intelligence, but, as we have seen, TECHINT means can lack the level of adroitness required, and they can be fooled.[58] For powerful military organizations, the best intelligence-gathering tool where asymmetric warfare is concerned is still the human being.[59]

'The struggle for men's minds'

Any worthwhile tome on counter-insurgency operations would acknowledge that the 'enemy' is not best defeated by technological solutions or by the use of overwhelming firepower. Rather, they are defeated by political and socio-economic tools backed by focused security measures. In essence, the contest in insurgencies, as Mao understood, was for the support of the 'people' – the 'sea' in which both guerrillas and security forces operate.[60] In insurgency warfare, whichever protagonist gains the support of the people is the one who will emerge victorious. The British counter-insurgency expert and soldier Frank Kitson, in the same way, saw that any counter-insurgency campaign was principally 'a struggle for men's minds', rather than a physical battle between armed protagonists.[61] When the forces countering any insurgency make the 'people' feel safe, and when they can guarantee their security and a path to a better future, then they will gain the people's support, and ultimately they will win. If this does not happen, then the 'people' will be forced to support those that they fear – the insurgents.

The first point here is that the 'people' will only feel confident with the security provided by the proper authorities when they see that the forces of that authority are close and available. If they are, then the authority tends to be accepted as the legitimate power, and the 'people' will be attracted to that power like moths to a flame. But if that power is absent, if there are not enough troops on the ground close and available and providing protection, and if there is a security vacuum, then the axis of power will shift to those who are around – the insurgents.

On the opposite side of the security coin, the insurgents cannot be allowed to operate with impunity. They have to be put constantly under pressure by the forces of authority. Both sides of the counter-insurgency coin – gaining support and applying pressure – require, among other tactics, constant patrolling and the setting up of manned static positions. Machines cannot hold and dominate ground; troops can. Machines cannot provide security and reassurance; troops can. Helicopters flying overhead and occasional raids are not enough; boots must be on the ground. In fact, in certain recent conflict scenarios involving US forces, technology has been seen not so much as a force multiplier, but actually as a 'force crippler'. 'The prophets', says Cordesman, who called for a ' "revolution in military affairs" and focused on conventional fighting and high-technology forces as a substitute for manpower and force numbers have been proved terribly wrong.'[62] Putting more boots on the ground as a response to the need to tackle insurgents (and terrorists) requires, of course, that numbers be added to the US Army and Marine Corps. To many movers and shakers, however, technology was supposed to act in the stead of the expense of sheer numbers. To them it is heresy enough to maintain current force levels, never mind to increase them. There is, moreover, little in the way of a constituency to back any swelling of the ranks. As one analyst pointed out just a few years ago – and little has changed since – there is no 'Lockheed Aircraft Corporation or Newport News Shipbuilding associated with infantry divisions'.[63]

It is one thing, though, having enough troops; it is another to have them acting correctly. Having the capacity to neutralize the insurgents while, at the same time, being competent enough to win the 'struggle for men's minds' calls for no little skill. Here the way in which forces are used is crucial; for troops must be trained to apply measures that are geared to strategic ends, and not just the tactical. They will use force, certainly, but as just one element in a package of measures that will defeat asymmetric adversaries, be they insurgents or terrorists.

One vital force multiplier that these troops do need is intelligence. Intelligence is crucial in establishing where both violence *and* psychological operations should be targeted. There are two necessary actions here. The first is to create a general atmosphere that encourages intelligence to be given. This will involve everything from convincing the 'people' that the forces of authority represent the future, to using force wisely so that collateral damage – particularly the deaths of innocents – is avoided: i.e. don't give succour to the asymmetric warrior by alienating populations and make the same mistake as in Vietnam. There the lesson was that the 'excessive or inappropriate use of force breeds resentment and plants the seeds of future conflict'.[64] An alienated population is one that does not provide intelligence, and troops without intelligence will stumble in the dark.

The second action is to keep a human presence on the streets so that if any intelligence is available, it can be picked up. Good tactics are important here. Any civilian who wants to provide information about insurgent activities is not going to rush into a street and wave at a helicopter or stop a Humvee which is flashing past. Neither will they do anything as visible – or as dangerous – as walk up to a police station or military base. They may, though, approach a foot patrol that is passing down their street. The human presence of foot patrolling is one of the best counter-insurgency techniques: it dominates ground; it exhibits the power and control of the proper authority; and, crucially, it gives ordinary civilians a point of interface.[65] Foot patrols can also act as an important propaganda tool. Many in the Muslim world see countries like the US and the UK as, among other negatives, purveyors of the evil of globalization and as supporters of Israel. Their presence, therefore, should not be countenanced in Muslim lands. This 'strategic' negative has to be overcome. While 'mainstream' psyops can be used, they cannot really overcome the message that is heard from indigenous media sources. The best form of psyops comes from the 'tactical' plus of having representatives of such countries – its troops – on the streets of, for example, Iraqi and Afghani villages, towns and cities acting in a respectful, engaging and approachable manner. At such a low level, though, and no matter how many schools and community centres you build, inordinate care needs to be taken not to offend sensibilities. Seemingly minor issues can assume greater proportions. House searches have to be carried out very carefully and the habit, for instance, of US troops wearing sunglasses on patrol, which many cultures find reprehensible, needs to be reconsidered.[66] When eye contact is prevented, then so is contact in general. Without contact, no intelligence flows.

It is through such tactical nuances and subtle approaches that intelligence can be garnered. Of course, there is much discussion here of tactics, of actions at a very low level. But in dealing with asymmetric adversaries, good tactics are essential. Given the fact that there are so many strategic negatives for Western forces to overcome (having in many cases already lost the overarching information war), good tactics can tip the balance in certain areas and at certain times.

'Thinking' men

If conflict against the asymmetric adversary is not 'a medieval clash of the titans' but a 'thinking man's game', then human actors must be allowed to both think and then be allowed to *act* on that thinking. We have seen how the asymmetric adversary, in order to level the battlefield with stronger opponents, will be trying to invoke the element of *surprise* by taking actions that are *different* from the norm. In order to ameliorate the disadvantage that surprise creates, the capacity has always to be present to respond – to think and act – quickly; to deal with the *surprise* and the *difference*. For power can sometimes mean nothing if it cannot be brought to bear in a timely fashion. Effective action against the asymmetric warrior will often call for initiative, speed of thought, and mental agility: asymmetric opponents need to be faced by 'free-thinking, aggressive, risk-taking officers'.[67] It is only they who can generate the subtle and nuanced responses to asymmetric action.

Part of the problem for the US military in responding to the asymmetric adversary is the fact that its leaders seldom seem to be given the chance to use their own initiative. A culture of independent thinking is lacking. There is a dearth of what is known in the US military as *Auftragstaktik*, or what the British call 'mission command': the ability of *in situ* leaders to take whatever measures they see fit without having to refer to higher authorities. Indeed, as many see it, there are factors present today which are actually increasing the degree of centralizing authority.[68] We have noted that at the tactical level technical means of command and control (aerial observation, UAV videos, etc.) have stifled initiative taking. We have also seen that thinking about the best means to deal with problems in counter-insurgency campaigns, for example, has tended to be hampered by the idea that there is always some form of technology available to deal with them; alternatives have thus been limited. There is also the sense again that the bureaucracy of the US armed forces hampers independent thinking. The issue here is in large part that *big* organizations are not just bureaucratic, but because of their very size, they have to be very *ordered*. Size dictates that everyone in the organization needs to have some frame of reference in order to ensure that they are all singing from the same hymn-sheet, some form of standard operation procedures (SOPs).[69] And the US military, in this case, is one that is very reliant on the hymn-sheet of doctrine. As Martin Van Crefeld expresses it, US officers 'regard the invention of military doctrines as both an industry and a pastime'.[70] Of course, if everyone is singing from the same hymn-sheet, then there is a natural outcome such that, as Correlli Barnett notes, 'the American officer . . . display[s] undue respect for orthodox doctrine, and an unwillingness to deviate from standard procedure'.[71] Writing about West Point-educated US officers in the Second Gulf War, John Keegan saw them as having 'a doctrinaire approach so often characteristic of the products of Sparta-on-Hudson'.[72] One British commander in Iraq (whose pre-battle speech to his soldiers President George Bush pinned on his wall) even went so far as to say that in the US forces 'everyone . . . behaves the same. An almost puritanical pursuit of this ideal has . . . led to an automaton-like code of . . . behaviour.'[73]

Such behaviour, of course, makes the asymmetric opponent's mission easier. Doctrine is fine for the set-piece symmetrical battles when the powerful are in control – when they are dominating the battle space. However, when surprise is introduced and warfare begun that is 'unfair,' then personnel who look always to doctrinal solutions will be disappointed: 'familiarity with doctrine . . . is not sufficient preparation for the unexpected.'[74]

This fault has been recognized by several analysts as a hindrance: 'Doctrine must embrace a philosophy of initiative and creative thinking to counter uncertainty. The more asymmetric the opponent, the more important this is,'[75] and 'doctrine cannot predict the precise nature and form of asymmetric engagements.'[76] The Center for Defense Information in Washington also produced a long study just before September 11 that took a critical look at the capability of the US armed forces to deal with asymmetric threats. One recommendation was that there should be a move to 'quicken military forces and reform some of the small-scale contingencies – in which they are likely to face challenging asymmetric or "fourth-generation" warfare – by improving their mobility, agility, flexibility, and decision-making speed'. To this end, the report went on, 'The most important thing is to ensure that personnel policies create a force of . . . agile, initiative taking leaders,' and that there should be a system for 'training and empowering officers to exercise more initiative.'[77] Without initiative, it is very difficult to generate any kind of subtlety.

Thus it is clear that on several levels the US military has difficulty in making the requisite changes to respond effectively to the asymmetric adversary. The reliance on technology, the use of excessive force, the lack of flexibility, and the downplaying of human input, while they may be seen as 'force cripplers' where the asymmetric opponent is concerned, are factors that actually suit the bureaucratic preferences of this particular military. However, there is also a more fundamental obstacle to change where this particular military is concerned. It is one that hinders it significantly in attempts to adopt the right strategies, structures, tactics and techniques against the asymmetric opponent. For there are deeply rooted mind-sets at work that actually reinforce the desire to employ technology, to use overwhelming force, and which abjure the quality of subtlety in warfare.

The influence of culture

There are seemingly many facets of the approach of the American military to the conduct of warfare against asymmetric opponents that need to change. And we have seen that there are several reasons why the requisite adaptations are not being made. There is, though, another factor that adds its own particular influence. This aspect actually underscores several of these current reasons. Here we are talking about mind-sets. There is a mind-set at work here that will always militate against the US military, and indeed the United States in general, dealing effectively with 4G and asymmetric warriors: i.e. the general and well-entrenched American attitude to its enemies.

Here we are talking about culture. Culture 'describes an attribute or quality internal to a group . . . a fairly stable set of taken-for-granted assumptions, shared beliefs, meanings and values that form a kind of backdrop for action'.[78] There is always a reluctance in the world of political science to employ culture as a variable when trying to explain behaviour. 'Culture', as Nicholas Rengger puts it, 'is one of those terms that often prompts . . . international relations scholars to reach for their revolvers . . . It is an inevitably loose concept that defies rigour and precision and is open to endless reinterpretation. Yet its significance . . . cannot really be doubted.'[79] Ken Booth concurs; the causal effects of culture on behaviour are, he says, 'difficult to exaggerate'.[80] And it cannot really be doubted as a tool in explaining why the US military has, and will continue to have, difficulty in adopting measures that deal most efficiently with asymmetric adversaries.

The methodologies that the US military employs in its missions at all levels of warfare are inextricably linked to a general American approach to warfare. There are mind-sets involved here which are very difficult to alter. To examine these mind-sets, a careful review of the literature devoted to the American approach to warfare is required.

Historically, the US military has never been at its best against small-scale opponents. Whether the opposition be guerrillas in the Philippines in the early part of the twentieth century,[81] the Vietcong, Somali warlords or insurgents in Iraq, US forces have invariably proved less than adept at dealing with them. These were, and are, 'small wars'. It is not in the tradition of the US Army, however, to 'do' small wars. It is in their tradition to do the 'big wars'. As Deborah Avant relates, 'Police actions and unconventional wars were seen as outside the missions of a professional army.'[82] For this army was, and is, all about defending the nation against those foreign aggressors who threaten the fundamentals of American liberty and who provide a crystal-clear distinction between an 'us' and a 'them', between 'good' and 'evil'.[83] The Second World War, for instance, saw the US military doing what it did best, and the Cold War, as William Pfaff puts it, 'suited the absolutionist conceptions of the US military'.[84] It is this preference for the absolutist approach that bears some scrutiny in attempts to discover why this army is so uncomfortable in fighting 'small wars'.

To consider this aspect properly, we need to go back to the idea of American 'exceptionalism'. When the Founding Fathers established the United States, they did so on the principle that it would stand apart from the autocratic, monarchist and feudalistic regimes that to them so blighted the continent of Europe at the time.[85] As an avowedly Christian nation, America was to be something unique and unsullied.[86] And, as a liberal democracy, America was a 'good' place. What was created was something better, something different – 'exceptionally' so.[87] Of course, in order to be different and to be better, there must be an 'other' out there to act as a comparator. The term 'American' is an idea defined more by what it is not than by what it is. American identity 'is created chiefly through the reaction to the danger of what should be excluded'.[88] Thus, what was different about America, its 'goodness', could only be a function of what it stood in relation to: i.e. a general foreign 'evil'.[89]

Part of this aspect of difference was that, as a peace-loving nation, Americans should not be dirtying their hands with 'foreign entanglements'. For much of their early history Americans were 'isolationist'. But the isolationist tendency to keep American soldiers at home had to live alongside the corollary of the United States being a force for idealistic 'good'. The American was seen to be willing to go to war if the cause was perceived to be just. There has always existed an American desire to intervene abroad – Samaritan-like – and right wrongs. As Deborah Millikan put it, 'America's traditional proclivity toward isolationism is balanced by its ideology, which, at its core is interventionist in its call for individual human rights and democratic freedoms.'[90] Thus, if the Army was called into action abroad, it would be for messianic reasons: to stand up for what the American people and their exceptionalist creed held to be right and proper. The rationales, therefore, for such military interventions as did occur were always couched in religious terms, with God-like America being confronted by a Satanic 'other'.[91] As Barry Buzan and George

Segal relate, 'American power is about crusades not about messing in sordid little wars.'[92] The United States should thus be either involved in a crusading war or at peace; the concept of anything in between does not sit well with the American psyche. In such a psyche, 'War and peace remain two very separate moral spheres,'[93] where 'the American . . . either embraces war wholeheartedly or rejects it completely.'[94]

The sense of crusade is an important one to appreciate when evaluating US foreign and security policy. 'Exceptionalism' is exclusive; inherent in its tenets is 'a cultivated ignorance of other nations and a stress on the "differentness" of other peoples'.[95] Americans thus tend to create psychological, if not indeed physical, distance between what is foreign and what is American – a sentiment which reached its apotheosis with the anti-communist sentiments of the Cold War era.[96] Here, as Ken Booth put it, the Soviets were 'projected as a devil to be extirpated'.[97] Such sentiments naturally make diplomacy problematic. American diplomacy is wont to exclude the sentiment of compromise: if one is 'good', how can compromise be achieved with anyone who is opposed to American ideals? They must, by definition, be 'evil', and be seen in 'demonological terms'.[98] As Richard Payne describes it, 'Exceptionalism and its accompanying religious passions are inconsistent and largely incompatible with compromise – the essential ingredient of peaceful diplomatic efforts.' Indeed, the arts of negotiation and compromise are, in American eyes, according to Payne, 'indications of weakness, naivete, and indecisiveness'.[99] When dealing with good and evil, the only goal is victory, never accommodation: 'victory is widely seen as the ultimate determinant of what is right, just and good, defeat is tantamount to evil'.[100] Kenneth Waltz concurs; he saw that it was the British who, in their foreign affairs, had a 'predilection for compromise', while Americans had 'a passion for victory'.[101] It is thus not hard to see why analysts refer to an American propensity to move swiftly from diplomacy to the use of force, from peace to war, to send its military on 'crusades', and why violence is seen as being 'efficacious in settling disputes'.[102] 'Crusades', as Booth points out, turn the normally peace-loving Americans 'into warriors', thus making the use of violence excusable.[103] And the more violence the better, since this is the only way to deal with enemies – the other – as they have to be dealt with swiftly and absolutely.[104] Peace – the natural condition – must be restored as soon as possible. If one does go to war, then it has to be a quick win, so that 'normality', in the form of peace, is restored, and everybody can go home.[105] Thus, as Wilkinson notes, 'A get-it-over-with psychology has often colored

American military tactics . . . The American belief in dynamism and grand-slam impact, in speed for survival and winning, undermines their commitment to endurance, to "hanging in there" and "gutsing it out".[106] Lawrence Freedman has an interesting – or perhaps an unfortunate – metaphor: 'War', to the Americans, 'should be similar to the spanking of a naughty child; not a wrestling match.'[107] Thus, in his seminal work on the American 'way of war', Russell Weigley can relate that, from a very early period, the US military has sought to 'annihilate' its enemies, and has rejected strategies of 'attrition, exhaustion or erosion'.[108]

These observations are but some from a raft of literature on the subject of American culture and how it relates to US military culture. Hard-nosed political scientists may dismiss such observations of cultural norms as mere 'explanations of last resort', but they provide some explanatory power, nonetheless. It is bad science to ignore variables: 'Decision-making by individuals and groups . . . is affected and sometimes actually dictated by their being part of a distinct societal-national environment, culture and experience.'[109] Of course, as with any cultural attribute, such norms that effect behaviour are not universal. They will not be employed by every individual or by every particular grouping. They will not be in evidence *every* time the US military goes into action. These attributes can be seen, though, to represent a dominant mind-set that does influence behaviour.

There is also the self-reinforcing aspect provided by the development of the US military after the Second World War. It came to be of such a size and shape, and to have the wherewithal to develop such enormous amounts of 'annihilatory' firepower, that its structure then marched in lock-step with extant cultural traits. With the default setting to solve military problems quickly and with the technology available that offered to do this, then the scene was pretty much set. Yes, the Gulf Wars could be won easily, but if anything required a degree of patience and caution, then problems arose and continue to arise. If we accept that a degree of subtlety and nuance is called for in dealing with asymmetric adversaries, then there is a jarring aspect to descriptive words and phrases such as 'whole-heartedly', 'annihilation', 'grand-slam impact', 'get-it-over-with', and 'swiftly and absolutely'. Too much violence is often employed in efforts to try and 'win' too quickly. And nouns such as 'differentness' and 'distance' foster, as in Iraq today, an inability to engage with local populations. The sunglasses and the layers of armour pump prime accusations that 'The combat ethos of American troops . . . casts them, in the eyes of local civilians, as haughty conquerors.'[110] If we accept that one of the aims when conducting effective counter-insurgency and, indeed, counter-terrorist campaigns is to separate the insurgent or terrorist from his or her support base, then applying traditional American approaches will mean tactical performances that can have deleterious strategic consequences. In such *asymmetric encounters* conflict *is* a 'wrestling match'. David Grange describes well the quandary:

> We Americans look at conflict through a winner's eyes . . . and if our quick fix for the conflict at hand derails, due to unintended consequences, we usually overreact and are unable to deal with reality. Our standard approach to adversary actions means that we have trouble adapting to what we actually find on the ground. Past high tech, standoff warfare is largely ineffective against these fourth generation adversaries. We continue to play American football on a European soccer field.[111]

There are two specific results of this culture. The first is that there will tend to be an approach to tackling the asymmetric adversary which, as Grange says, will conform to a 'standard'. And when firm standards are set, alternative solutions are not sought. The standard way becomes *the* way. Thus, when options are considered, they are considered within parameters defined often by culture and not set by a so-called rational actor. For in any human endeavour culture will define rationality. Even introducing greater human input into military action against asymmetric adversaries or, indeed, any other, will always result in thinking that runs along certain cultural lines. Thus, even if you give leaders the ability to use their initiative and to apply their own 'thinking', that thinking will still be bounded by cultural preferences. Such preferences, as we have seen, may not suit the task at hand.

The second result is that culture acts as a further drag on change. There is not suddenly going to appear a 'new' way of warfare that is better suited to operations at the lower end of the conflict spectrum. The US military is not suddenly going to copy the tactics of the British or anyone else. Cultures can be overcome, of course, but it usually takes a radical learning (or 'unlearning') experience,[112] which in the case of military organizations is usually taken to mean defeat. However, there is the sense that even if the US military were forced to leave Iraq and Afghanistan, then no great driver for change would result. These are not the right 'wars' to lose. We had glimpses of the same mentality at work back in Vietnam. That conflict, despite being a major war, did not generate any push for change. And as the one-time Deputy to the Commander of US Military Forces in Vietnam put it: 'We didn't want to restructure or re-equip our combat forces to optimize their capabilities for Vietnam because we regarded Vietnam as a temporary diversion from their more normal [i.e. 'big war'] mission . . . it would have been so distorting to the preferred force structure, tactics and doctrine.'[113] During and after Vietnam, the US armed forces did not introduce any changes better to conduct low-intensity warfare. This type of warfare did not suit the military's preferred 'way'. Everything was against it: the structures, the bureaucracy, the technology, the doctrine and, above all, the mind-set. It is the same today.[114] Again, all the above are not suddenly going to change to deal with the asymmetric adversary, no matter how current and how threatening.

But there should be *some* changes made. The current asymmetric conflicts do not have the same background as did the Vietnam War. US troops could withdraw from South East Asia and say, 'OK, we lost that one but it was only really a sideshow in the great Cold War imbroglio.' Now there isn't another game in town – at least, not on the horizon. The insurgency operations in Iraq and Afghanistan and all the other expeditionary operations are now what powerful militaries have to do. Moreover, they are missions that require the formation of coalitions for them to be conducted with some measure of legitimacy. And when American operations are conducted in a way that coalition partners either find reprehensible or which appear adversely to affect mission accomplishment then they will be drawn away from supporting their ally. Fractured coalitions can be the harbingers of strategic failure. The most high-profile problems over contrasting approaches came in Kosovo, but there are issues today in Iraq that have caused fault lines in the Coalition. Strained relations have developed between the US and, for instance, its Italian and even British allies.[115]

Perhaps what is most noteworthy here is that asymmetric opponents will be mindful of the opportunity opened to them. They will be turning American cultural proclivities to their own particular advantage. Often they will encourage US military overreaction and sit back and wait for the operational and strategic consequences that can result. What is a great strength – the ability to win 'normal', conventional wars quickly – here can become a distinct weakness. As Lind sees it, 'As is so often the case in the Fourth Generation, what seems weak is strong and what seems strong is weak.'[116]

Conclusion

The major problem for the US military in shaping responses to asymmetric/4G adversaries is that it so desperately wants to be the 'sheaf of thunderbolts'. The main default setting seems to be the desire to conduct warfare as if it was of the 2G or 3G variety. And the US military, of course, conducts 2GW and 3GW very well. The temptation of course, because there is such proficiency at the high end of the conflict spectrum, is to then try and employ the same skill-sets at the low end. But the formula, as Hammes quite rightly indicates, is not that simple. The preference for technology and for displays of overwhelming force to produce 'shock and awe' is, in fact, often operationally and strategically debilitating against 4G/asymmetric adversaries.

Change is needed. There are many within the US military establishment who agree. But change is difficult. Having a large, technically sophisticated and, on the surface, very successful military organization – backed up as it is by a huge bureaucracy and by vested interests – militates against change – or at least, change to better conduct 4G/asymmetric warfare. For the irony is that the US military *is* changing. But the 'new' military as envisioned in the RMA and Transformation is decidedly not one geared to conducting the 'new' form of warfare. The drive for spectacular effect at the high end of the conflict spectrum has the concomitant that it can produce a military qualitatively less effective at the low end.

This is not to say that the B-2 should be thrown out with the bathwater. High-tech assets and machinery that can develop inordinate amounts of firepower will always be useful on any battlefield. And even if the adversaries are asymmetric, then yes, on occasion, there will be a requirement for some thunderbolts. But, as Admiral Cebrowski put it, the US armed forces need to become a more flexible instrument of foreign policy, not just one capable of tossing thunderbolts around. To create such flexibility, the most vital element, and one that has been widely recognized as vital when faced with the asymmetric opponent, is human input. Intellect has to be brought more into the loop, while technology should be increasingly marginalized.

Having greater human input begins, of course, with having more humans in the military. Tackling the asymmetric adversary/4G warrior in any battle space calls for the commitment of more troops than does 'normal' warfare. Technology cannot do what 'boots on the ground' can do in conflicts in complex terrain or in counter-insurgency campaigns. Force numbers are vital. Making the military bigger by adding more soldiers and Marines is, naturally enough, a move that lacks cheerleaders. However, there are other avenues that can be explored, in terms of creating in the actual personnel who are already in the military more nuanced – subtle – ways of approaching 4G/asymmetric warfare. Troops need to be better trained and more culturally aware, so that they can play a more refined role in attempts to achieve strategic successes.[117] For good tactics are vital in asymmetric warfare. US troops involved in counter-terrorist and counter-insurgency operations have to attract indigenous populations to them. This is especially important in Muslim lands where, for the most part, 'hearts and minds' have already been lost at the strategic level. They can only be won back, and mission accomplishment facilitated, by correct behaviour at the tactical level. Bad tactics that involve the use of unfocused violence will, of course, hamper the gathering of intelligence and possibly add recruits to the numbers of the asymmetric enemy. Leaders at the tactical level should also be allowed greater freedom of response, so that flexibility becomes built into the overall command philosophy. There must also be a means of generating the capacity to have forces operating comfortably down at the level of their asymmetric opponents – at least to some degree. For part of the formula for success in the fight against the asymmetric warrior is, in essence, to be more like them. Staying aloof and trying to let firepower from afar solve *all* situations will not prove strategically effective in the long run.

While trying to introduce the above changes has proved difficult, there is evidence of a positive drive in certain quarters. The USMC has clearly been thinking along these lines. It has very recently been looking at ways to make its organizational structures more adaptable. Included here are ideas such as having fighting units that are smaller (down to eight-man teams) and which rely on stealth, precision firepower and knowledge, rather than sheer mass. When necessary, they could call on greater firepower from higher formations.[118] On the whole, though, such changes are rare, and it remains to be seen how they will be put into effective practice. For such responses as these to the asymmetric adversary, characterized as they are by flexibility and by subtlety, run counter to a military culture that is deeply entrenched. The cultural preference to conduct warfare at all levels as if 'shock and awe' were fundamental combat prerequisites is one that will not change any time soon.

Again, though, there will always be those who say that this philosophy is one that should be nurtured, not nullified. They will say that the US military should not be making changes to respond to the asymmetric adversary; that it must hold firmly to the strategies, structures and mind-sets that are configured to conduct some future unspecified major war. Is there mileage, they say, in devoting great effort to the 'small wars' when perhaps skills need to be maintained and honed for the 'big war'? True, but it bears repeating that future major wars will contain elements of asymmetric approaches that, when they appear on the battlefield and when they appear after the 'normal' battlefield has been cleared, have to be dealt with. Possible big war adversaries down the line – the Chinas and the Irans – will adopt asymmetric tactics and techniques during conventional operations, and they will ensure that any big war will end up eventually dissolving into an insurgency, where the main centre of gravity is the support of the people. What is more, the opponents that face the US military today – the asymmetric ones in Iraq and Afghanistan – are likely to linger for a while yet. Indeed, many potential opponents of the US around the world will be watching and learning from the discomfiture exhibited by US forces in such regions and will store away details of the types of asymmetric warfare that cause the most problems. Experience will be gained, and opponents will adapt. So, likewise, must the US military. It will. The question remains, though, as to whether it will ever adapt enough.

8 CONCLUSION

Asymmetric warfare is a broad church. Its exponents range from individual computer hackers, through terrorist and insurgent groups, criminal gangs, all the way up to states themselves. It can be practised in land, sea and air battle spaces. The tools used by the asymmetric warrior can include everything from box cutters to submarines, from Trojan horses to jammers, and from dummy tanks to satellite-destroyers.

Asymmetric warfare is a type of warfare that is receiving much attention. And it will continue to receive attention for the foreseeable future. It is receiving such attention for two particular reasons. First, those who oppose Western, especially American, cultural and military might have no option, if they want to produce impact, but to adopt asymmetric techniques. The second reason is that individuals, groups and states are now having opened to them a Pandora's box of opportunities and capabilities with which to threaten, undermine, destabilize or perhaps even, in a military sense, defeat the strong Western liberal democracies.

It has been the actions of today's terrorists which have brought the idea of asymmetric warfare into the mainstream. The terrorists are the archetypically weak players intent on creating great impact out of what few assets they have to hand. We have seen how Islamist and other terrorist groups are now far more capable than the terrorists of the past of generating devastating consequences. They now have an increased fervour, which when allied to their greater access to a variety of weapons systems – including WMD – can strike fear into the hearts of many people and cause their governments immense concern.

We have seen too how asymmetric adversaries, including terror-ists, have opportunities to create impact given the fact that we now live in an 'information world'. Many a small player has made use of new, unfettered access to information sources and to the information system to communicate, plan and organize. The asymmetric adversary can now generate profound strategic effect through the utilization of such everyday items as mini-cams and laptops in conjunction with new media outlets and Internet sites.

Individuals, groups and organizations, whether bent on mischief or malfeasance, can make use of the fact that there is such reliance today, in many spheres of Western life, on the Internet to smooth everything from the passage of messages to the running of economies. And this reliance is on a system that is in large measure open to attack. The West's militaries have also looked to the quantity and quality of information passage as a huge force multiplier. But they have placed an inordinate amount of reliance on systems that can be interfered with (jamming) or fooled (deception). The vulnerabilities are there, and they will be exploited.

Asymmetric approaches are also now very evident in the military realm beyond the information battle space. For we are in an era in which our militaries are increasingly 'out there' on operational com-mitments, and are coming across weaker adversaries with a hitherto unknown frequency. Such opponents are now possessed of a zeal that was lacking in many a terrorist, guerrilla or insurgent of the past. And what is more, our Western forces are having to face such zeal amid a general self-imposed nervousness over casualties. This is not just a question, indeed, of casualties among our own troops but also of those among civilians and even the enemy. War, in the post-Cold War era from which the liberal democracies emerged so triumphant, was supposed to be bloodless. It is difficult to apply the levels of force that were built up so enthusiastically by Western forces during the Cold War.

We have seen how the powerful military organizations of the West, and in particular of the United States, have been victims of their own success. No state protagonist with an ounce of intelligence would try and take on the Western militaries on *their* level playing field. Such opponents, and non-state actors as well, will move down the conflict spectrum. This is new. History taught us previously that arms races always meant one thing: one side trying to outdo the other in a linear progression of increasingly sophisticated military technology. Nowadays the model has been turned on its head. If the powerful introduce a better technology, weaker opponents will not try and match it; rather, they will try to devise ways of negating its effect. Build a better tank, and opponents will build a better anti-tank weapon. Build a better ship, and opponents will build a better mine. Build a better aircraft, and opponents will build a better anti-aircraft missile. Build a better sensor, and opponents will find better means of deceiving it. Build a better remotely piloted vehicle, and opponents will build better jammers. For every step forward that technology takes, the human mind will find a counter. There is no escaping Newton and the laws of physics: for every action there will always be an equal and *opposite* reaction. Or put in a more military way, as one US Marine Corps general expressed it, 'Our very dominance of certain forms of warfare has driven the enemy into historic forms of warfare that we have not mastered.'[1] Al Qaeda, indeed, as we have seen, 'went back to primitive methods that we Americans cannot adapt to'.[2]

Some measure of adaptation is called for. It is this problem of response to the asymmetric adversary that has informed much of this book. The threat is new, and new measures, techniques, tactics and strategies are required. The Cold War period now appears as one characterized by 'comfortable' certainties. There was the known quantity of the threats from both terrorist and state adversaries. And while there was, ultimately, the dramatic threat of nuclear holocaust, it always appeared conveniently distant. Nowadays the threat from asymmetric actors seems to be far more immediate. Domestic populations are more conscious of the threat from terrorism, and our governments react to every new outrage with yet more draconian measures. But care is needed. To maintain their strength, liberal democracies must act in accordance with the very principles that make them liberal democracies. Once certain boundaries are crossed, they become like Rubicons; harsh measures come to be accepted as the norm, and harsh measures always have their innocent victims – often, indeed, actually creating those they seek to quell.

The West has to respond and ensure better protection for its information sources and its information passage. With such protection it must be accepted that defensive measures mean that information will flow less quickly. It must also be accepted that a huge amount of expense is involved. This is particularly the case with military organizations. There has to be redundancy built in, a Plan B: the ability to use another system, another technology, another way, if one particular system is corrupted, jammed, deceived or 'hacked' into.

Western military organizations will have to face and deal with a host of asymmetric adversaries on many different battlefields. The main problem lies in trying to respond to 'historic forms of warfare' and 'primitive methods'. These organizations need to make changes that can seem to take them backwards, to being less sophisticated. This makes such changes difficult to entertain. There are various reasons for this, including the arrogance of power, the strength of bureaucracies, and the influence of culture.

As Lord Acton reminded us, 'Power corrupts and absolute power corrupts absolutely.'[3] Those who stand ascendant in the power stakes rarely take time to navel-gaze and ponder where their weaknesses lie. They trust to the fact that the possession of power and the attrition it can provide leads to natural conclusions. It no longer seems be so clear-cut, however. Power today seems only to be the ability to persuade those that look like you to do something. If they do not, then raw military power in its attritive nakedness is not enough; power has to be used in more nuanced ways when the opponent is weak and is using asymmetric techniques.

Overall, Western militaries must slough off the tag that they are 'ponderous, clumsy and slow'. If the West's enemies are characterized by a fleetness of foot and a speed of thought, and are able to do the radically different, then the capacity has to be there for Western forces to move at a similar pace and to deal with the different and 'all forms of conflict where the other guy refuses to stand up and fight fair'.[4] The agility, flexibility, responsiveness, creativity and initiative of the smaller, nimble opponent must be matched to some degree. Human input – 'intellect' – here is vital. It is only human input that can generate adequate and timely responses. And this human input must be allowed to express itself, because often there will be little time to take effective action. Responses must not be stymied by layers of bureaucracy and command, by sheaths of doctrinal strictures, and by cultural preferences. In the case of the US military, huge bureaucracies have been built up which depend on warfare staying like it is. The general sense is that 'we can do 3GW if we must, but we like 2GW best of all'. Too much has been invested by too many people over too long a period for radical change to occur in terms of either equipment or the way in which conflict is managed by leaders. Change may come with time: learning curves will have their effect, and cultural boundaries will be stretched. It seems, though, that any movement may be glacial.

Western militaries and security organizations must increase their understanding of the opponents they face. They need to understand what motivates them, and why they have developed the zeal that they have. Through understanding, strategies can be deployed that will enable both defensive and offensive measures to be more effective.

More human intelligence will be needed, from as wide an array of sources as possible. And people who understand the enemy need to be tasked: from cultural specialists and linguists to 'white-hat hackers'.

Minds must also be geared to the quality of patience: 'One of the key problems is the Western tendency to try to accomplish in weeks or months key activities that require years of patient and consistent effort.'[5] Wars against asymmetric opponents will be long. In such wars there will be battles won and battles lost. The temptation should always be avoided, though, to try and shorten these wars by out-of-place displays of 'shock and awe'. They have their place, but then so does the quality of restraint.

Sometimes, though, Western militaries and security services are too restrained. The asymmetric adversaries realize that Western advantages – such as in technology – in order to be truly effective against them, can only be used in many instances when accompanied by a certain degree of will. In many ways the West has become too soft. We dislike the thought of sacrifice, since sacrifice is only ever accommodated easily when threat is most pronounced. Nowadays, the level of threat is much less than it was during the World Wars and the Cold War of the last century. We dislike the thought not only of losing the lives of our service personnel, but also of losing, given the size and sophistication of some modern military assets, our ships, planes and tanks. We can go one way, and protect and husband our people and their equipment through the use of unmanned technologies. But such measures will reduce operational effectiveness and make operations drag on longer. We could go the other way; we could say that to operate efficiently, we must accept that losses are inevitable and harden our hearts to the human sacrifice and develop cheaper technologies whose loss can be countenanced. We must match the will, at least to some degree, of those who would oppose us. We must accept that the successful completion of the mission is the most important factor, not protecting the people involved in the prosecution of that mission. Ships and their crews need to be risked in littorals; aircraft and their crews need to be risked in close air support missions; and troops have to be risked in complex terrain. If such will is not displayed, then the asymmetric adversary may have not just levelled the battlefield, but possibly actually taken it over.

On the flip side, of course, if we start trying to match the sense of will of asymmetric opponents, then we lose because domestic support will invariably be lost. It is not what the West does. Again, we come back to the view that violence should be limited, not only because of domestic sensibilities but also because of the desire to engineer successful end states. Violence has to be geared towards such ends, and never merely to obtaining tactical objectives. Violence has to be used with subtlety, as part of a flexible package of responses to asymmetric opponents. Thunderbolts must be to hand, of course, but also a lightness of touch. And flexibility of mind must be matched by flexibility of equipment. Aircraft, ships and armoured vehicles must be fielded with the asymmetric opponent in mind. If they are not, and if they too remain ponderous, clumsy and slow, then the battle spaces of the twenty-first century will often end up being controlled by the asymmetric enemy.

The September 11 hijackers used box cutters. What they lacked in weaponry, they made up for in tremendous will and intelligence. Will and intelligence will always prove effective qualities when taking on the powerful, especially when the powerful lack both these qualities. Sometimes the weak can avoid doing what they must, and the powerful cannot always do what they will.

Notes

Chapter 1   What is Asymmetric Warfare?

1 'For an example of asymmetry at work we need look no further than the September 11 World Trade Center attack': Christopher Coker, 'Asymmetric Warfare: Ends or Means?', in Olsen (ed.), *Asymmetric Warfare*, p. 320.
2 See Brian Whitaker, 'Al-Qaida is Bleeding US to Bankruptcy, Bin Laden Claims', *The Guardian*, 3 Nov. 2004, p. 3.
3 Osama bin Laden has estimated that every dollar spent by Al Qaeda results in a cost to the US of some $1 m. Figure of $700 bn based on an expenditure of $500 bn by 2004 (source: a British think tank) and by subsequent budgetary requests from President George Bush. See 'Bin Laden's Target: US Wallet' on CBS NEWS website, 2 Nov. 2004, online at <http://uttm.com.stories/2004>, accessed 23 May 2005. Also 'Bush Requests Another $72.4 bn for War on Terror', 17 Feb. 2006, online at <http://usgovinfo.about.com/>, accessed 17 Jan. 2006. See also Jackson, *Writing the War on Terrorism*, p. 15.
4 Quoted in Sandy Goodman, 'Air Force Dodges Sept 11 Flak', *Los Angeles Times*, 17 Jul. 2002, p. 8.
5 Sun Tzu, *The Art of War*, trans. Lionel Giles, online at <http://classics. mit.edu/Tzu/artwar>, accessed 20 Dec. 2004.
6 Sun Bin, *Lost Art of War*, quoted in Grange, 'Asymmetric Warfare', p. 1, online at <www.nationalstrategy.com/nsr/v10n2Winter00>, accessed 15 Jan. 2005.
7 Machiavelli, *The Prince*, ix. 3, p. 35.
8 See Delbruck, 'The Battle in the Teutoburger Forest', in *The Barbarian Invasions*, ch. 3, pp. 69–96. Goulding, 'Back to the Future with Asymmetric Warfare'.

9 See Paul Hitchin, 'The Bowman and the Bow', in Curry (ed.), *Agincourt, 1415*, pp. 37–52.
10 See Legro, *Cooperation under Fire*.
11 See e.g. Skelton, 'America's Frontier Wars'.
12 It is from this campaign that we get both the words *guerrilla* and *insurgé*. Read, *War in the Peninsular*, pp. 169–81.
13 Kenneth McKenzie, *Revenge of the Melians*, McNair Paper no. 69, online at <www.ndu.edu/inss/mcnair>, accessed 9 Mar. 2005.
14 Byford, 'The Wrong War'.
15 Hill, *War at Sea in the Ironclad Age*, p. 65.
16 National Defense University, *1998 Strategic Assessment: Engaging Power for Peace*, online at <www.ndu.edu/inssStrategic%20Assessments/sa98/sa98ch11.html>, accessed 20 Nov. 2004.
17 Bellamy, 'The Shifted Conflict Paradigm', p. 152.
18 Barnett, *Asymmetric Warfare*, p. 15.
19 Goulding, 'Back to the Future', p. 21; Richard Norton-Taylor, 'Asymmetric Warfare', *The Guardian*, 3 Oct. 2001, p. 3.
20 Tucker, 'Asymmetric Warfare'.
21 Quoted in Center for Defense Information, 'Military Domination or Constructive Leadership?', *Defense Monitor*, 27/3 (1998), p. 8.
22 Kaplan, 'How We Would Fight China'.
23 See O'Meara et al. (eds), *Globalization and the Challenges of a New Century*; Mackinlay, *Globalization and Insurgency*.
24 Cohen, 'History and the Hyperpower', p. 58.
25 Hiro, *War Without End*, pp. 154–5.
26 Gunaratna, 'An Examination of Al Qaeda and its Methods'.
27 B. Hoffman, 'The Changing Face of Al Qaeda and the Global War on Terrorism'.
28 There is some dispute as to whether Al Qaeda was indeed responsible for the bombing at Dharan, since it was perceived that the Saudi authorities wanted to blame external sources and not indigenous ones such as Al Qaeda. It seems actually to have been an Al Qaeda operation: James Dunnigan, 'What Really Happened When Al Qaeda Attacked', 23 Sept. 2003, online at <www.strategypage.com/dls/articles/20030903.asp>, accessed 24 May 2005. Also Schwartz, *The Two Faces of Islam*, pp. 278–9. The bomb at Khobar Towers in Dharan, Saudi Arabia, killed nineteen airmen. The bombings at the embassies in Nairobi, Kenya, and Dar es Salaam, Tanzania, killed 224, of whom twelve were Americans.
29 'US Pulls Out of Saudi Arabia', BBC News Online, 29 Apr. 2003, online at <http://:news.bbc.co.uk/1/hi/world/middle_east/2984547.stm>, accessed 10 Feb. 2006.
30 In current parlance the adjective 'Islamic' is seen as relating to a correct interpretation of the Koran. 'Islamist' implies that there is a deviation from true Koranic beliefs to interpret the holy book in a manner that suits extremists and excuses their violent acts.

31 See e.g. Bodansky, *Bin Laden*, p. 89.

32 Fukuyama, 'The End of History'.

33 See e.g. Luttwak, 'A Post-Heroic Military Policy'.

34 Thomas Weiss, 'Collective Spinelessness: UN Actions in the Former Yugoslavia', in Ullman (ed.), *The World and Yugoslavia's Wars*, p. 91.

35 See Bowen, 'Deterrence and Asymmetry'.

36 See Bowden, *Black Hawk Down*; Larson and Savych, *American Public Support for US Military Operations from Mogadishu to Baghdad*, p. 30.

37 Quoted in Michael Portillo, 'We All Sat Back and Let Londonistan Rise Against Us', *The Sunday Times*, 24 July 2005, p. 19.

38 See e.g. Hiro, *Desert Shield to Desert Storm*, pp. 164–5; Michael Clarke, 'The Diplomacy that Led to War in Iraq', in Cornish (ed.), *The Conflict in Iraq, 2005*, pp. 31–2.

39 Foreman, 'The Casualty Myth', p. 20.

40 Record, 'Collapsed Countries'.

41 Maj. Robert Barr, 'Can "Airpower" Counter the Asymmetric Threat?', unpublished Research Report (Maxwell Air Force Base, Ala.: Air Command and Staff College, Air University, 2001), p. 26.

42 This chariness came from both political and military figures. The USA took 'the absurd decision to fight a Kosovo War without a ground component': Ivo Daalder, quoted in John Hendren, 'High-Tech Strategy Guides Pentagon Plan', *Los Angeles Times*, 13 Jul. 2002, p. 2. See also Lambeth, 'Lessons from the Kosovo War', p. 17. Also Clark, *Waging Modern War*, p. 206; Judah, *Kosovo*, pp. 269–70.

43 Kutler, 'US Military Fatalities in Iraq', p. 540.

44 See Carl Conetta, 'Disappearing the Dead: Iraq, Afghanistan and the Idea of a "New Warfare"', *Project on Defense Alternatives*, Feb. 2004, online at <www.comw.org/pda/0402rm9/html>, accessed 26 July 2004; Record, 'Force-Protection Fetishism', online at <www.airpower. maxwell.af.mil/airchronicle>, accessed 9 Mar. 2005.

45 Christopher Marquis, 'US Intensifies Protest Against Arab TV Reports', *International Herald Tribune*, 30 Apr. 2004, p. 6.

46 'Photos of Military Coffins', online at <www.thememoryhole.org/war/ coffin_photos/dover>, accessed 9 Mar. 2005.

47 'Toll of British Wounded in Iraq War Reaches 800', 18 Jan. 2005, online at <www.timesonline.co.uk/article/0,,7374–1441320>, accessed 9 Mar. 2005. The Prime Minister has not visited any military hospital, and the then Defence Secretary only did so for the first time some 3 years after the end of the war. 'Reid to Visit Soldiers Wounded in Iraq', *The Herald*, 16 Jan. 2006, online at <http://www.theherald.co.uk/news/54292.html>, accessed 17 Feb. 2006.

48 B. Hoffman, 'Rethinking Terrorism and Counterterrorism since 9/11', p. 307.

49 See 'Philippines Start Iraq Pullout', online at <www.news.bbc.co.uk/2/ hi/middle_east>, accessed 10 May 2005.

50 Al Marashi, 'Iraq's Hostage Crisis'.
51 Pfaltzgraff and Stephen Wright, 'The Spectrum of Conflict: Symmetrical or Asymmetrical Challenge?', in Schultz and Pfaltzgraff (eds), *The Role of Naval Forces in 21ˢᵗ Century Operations*, p. 13.
52 Cols Liang and Xiangsui, *Unrestricted Warfare*.
53 CBRN (Chemical, Biological, Radiological, Nuclear) is the more formal security services/military designation.
54 See Spinzak, 'The Great Superterrorism Scare'; Bodansky, *Bin Laden*, pp. 326–7, 329–30.
55 Lumpe (ed.), *Running Guns*.
56 Edward Hanlon, 'Taking the Long View: Littoral Warfare Challenges', in Schultz and Pfaltzgraff (eds), *Role of Naval Forces*, p. 159.
57 'Worldwide holdings of tanks, artillery, jet fighters, warships and other so-called heavy conventional weapons were reduced by one quarter between 1985 and 2002': Richard Renner, 'Security Redefined', in *State of the World: Global Security 2005* (London: Earthscan, 2005), p. 17.
58 Barnett, *Asymmetric Warfare*, p. 15.
59 See e.g. Howard et al. (eds), *The Laws of War*.
60 Ibid., pp. 2–3. Walzer, *Just and Unjust Wars*.
61 See Yoram Dinstein, 'Collateral Damage and the Principle of Proportionality', in Wippman and Evangelista (eds), *New Wars, New Laws?*, pp. 211–24.
62 Ibid., pp. 220–1.
63 Delpech, 'The Imbalance of Terror', p. 34.
64 See ch. 2 below; Gray, *International Law and the Use of Armed Force*.
65 In UN Charter, Article 39, Chapter VII, online at <www.un.org/aboutun/charter/chapter7>, accessed 10 May 2005.
66 Torsten Stein, 'Coalition Warfare and Differing Legal Obligations of Coalition Members under International Humanitarian Law', in Wall (ed.), *Legal and Ethical Implications of NATO's Kosovo Campaign*, p. 326.
67 'Western democracies are becoming more interested in legitimacy than in strict legality': Coker, 'Asymmetric Warfare', p. 328.
68 Ibid., p. 329.
69 'Italian Press Shock at Iraq Killing', online at <http://news.bbc.co.uk/1/hi/world/europe/3628807.stm>, accessed 19 Oct. 2005; 'Spanish Withdraw Troops', <www.cnn.com/2004/WORLD//04/19/>, accessed 17 Oct. 2005.
70 Nils Naastad, 'Prologue', in Olsen (ed.), *Asymmetric Warfare*, p. 15.
71 Grange, 'Asymmetric Warfare', p. 1.
72 *Joint Warfare of the Armed Forces of the United States* (Washington, DC: Government Printing Office, 10 Jan. 1995), IV-10 and IV-11.
73 Barr, 'Can "Airpower"', p. 5.
74 *Joint Strategy Review* (Washington, DC: CJCS, 1999), p. 2.
75 See Metz, 'Strategic Asymmetry'.
76 *British Defence Doctrine, JWP0-01* (London: HMSO, 1996), p. 2.12.

77 'Security Priorities in a Changing World', in *Strategic Defence Review* (London: HMSO, 1998), ch. 2, para. 34.

78 Metz and Johnson, *Asymmetry and US Military Strategy*, p. 5.

79 For a useful discussion of the definition see Blank, 'Rethinking the Concept of Asymmetric Threats in US Strategy'.

80 Grange, 'Asymmetric Warfare', p. 1.

81 See<http://www.wellesley.edu/ClassicalStudies/CLCV102/Thucydides–MelianDialogue>, accessed 23 May 2005.

Chapter 2   The Terrorist Asymmetric Adversary

1 As Barnett puts it, 'terrorism provides an excellent example' of asymmetric warfare: Barnett, *Asymmetric Warfare*, p. 16. For a discussion of the definition of terrorism see Lutz and Lutz, *Global Terrorism?*, ch. 2. What constitutes a 'terrorist' is subjective. The mantra normally used in this regard is 'one man's terrorist is another man's freedom fighter'. Conscious of this aspect, the news agency Reuters, e.g., when using the words 'terrorist' or 'terrorism', always uses inverted commas. After the London bombings of 7 July 2005, the BBC also did not refer to the perpetrators as terrorists: Tom Leonard, 'BBC Edits Out The Word Terrorist', *Daily Telegraph*, 12 July 2005, p. 1.

2 Al Qaeda was formed in 1988 and is presumed now to have affiliates in seventy countries with, theoretically, some 20,000 volunteers to call on. Most of these were trained in Afghanistan when the country was under Taliban rule in the late 1990s. Al Qaeda first attacked US interests in 1992 in Yemen when a hotel where US service personnel were staying was bombed: Katzman, 'Al Qaeda Threat Retains its Potency under Pressure'.

3 For a thorough discussion of 'old' and 'new' terrorism, see Laqueur, *No End to War*.

4 Jenkins, *Will Terrorists Go Nuclear?*, p. 4.

5 Laqueur, *No End to War*, p. 14.

6 See e.g. Laqueur, *The New Terrorism*; Mackinlay, *Globalisation and Insurgency*, p. 80.

7 Stephen Sloane, 'Terrorism and Asymmetry', in Matthews (ed.), *Challenging the US Symmetrically and Asymmetrically*, pp. 180–1.

8 Millenarian terrorist groups are concerned with ending the world as we know it, in order that they can take it over and 'start again'. Aum Shinrikyo in Japan is an example of a millenarian sect.

9 B. Hoffman, *"Holy Terror"*, p. 5.

10 Gurr and Cole, *The New Face of Terrorism*, p. 26. The followers of Al Qaeda who flooded into Afghanistan in the 1990s had no real political motivation. They wanted merely to 'realise their dreams of violent action against the West': Burke, *Al Qaeda*, p. 5.

11 See Sookhdeo, *Understanding Islamic Terrorism*, ch. 6; also Schwartz, *Two Faces of Islam*, pp. 266–7.
12 Laqueur, *No End to War*, p. 14.
13 Fisk, *The Great War for Civilization*, p. 176.
14 See Manji, *The Trouble with Islam*; also Laqueur, *No End to War*, chs 2, 3.
15 Combs, *Terrorism in the Twenty-First Century*, p. 66.
16 Laqueur, *No End to War*, pp. 15–8.
17 Rogers, *Losing Control*, pp. 86–7.
18 See Burke, *Al Qaeda*; Ali, *The Clash of Fundamentalisms*; Rubin and Rubin, *Anti-American Terrorism and the Middle East*.
19 Doran, 'Somebody Else's Civil War'.
20 A Gallup poll in Feb. 2002 in nine Muslim countries found that 74 per cent refused to believe that Arabs had been responsible for September 11: Hiro, *War Without End*, p. 417.
21 B. Hoffman, 'Rethinking Terrorism and Counterterrorism since September 11', p. 314.
22 Schwartz, *Two Faces of Islam*, pp. 134, 198. Also Laqueur, *No End to War*, ch. 4, and Schanzer, *Al Qaeda's Armies*.
23 Laqueur, *No End to War*, p. 22.
24 Ibid., pp. 209–31.
25 See Sookhdeo, *Understanding Islamic Terrorism*, pp. 172–5.
26 See Lifton, *Destroying the World in Order to Save It*.
27 In April 1995 two men with a grudge against the federal government drove a truck bomb to a federal building in Oklahoma City. The bomb killed 168.
28 B. Hoffman, *Inside Terrorism*, p. 155.
29 Townend, *Guarding Europe*, p. 3, online at <http://www.cer.org.uk/pdf.wp440_borders.pdf>, accessed 17 Jan. 2006.
30 Laqueur, *No End to War*, p. 17.
31 Arquilla et al., 'Networks, Netwar and Information-Age Terrorism', in Lesser et al., *Countering the New Terrorism*, p. 60.
32 Conway, 'Nitro to the Net'.
33 See White, *Terrorism*, ch. 3.
34 Arquilla et al., 'Networks', p. 57.
35 Thom Shanker, 'Rumsfeld's Search for a Way to Fight a New Type of Foe', *The New York Times*, 4 Sept. 2002, p. 4.
36 In a speech in March 2001. Dan Verton, 'Terror and Info Tech: New Thinking Needed to Counter New Realities', *Homeland Security*, 1/1 (Jan. 2004) p. 29.
37 Ibid.
38 The London bombers of both 7 and 21 July 2005 mixed such everyday items as nail varnish to produce the explosive, triacetone triperoxide. While this explosive has 80 per cent of the power of TNT, it is very unstable, and the mixing has to be correct. The 7 July bombers got it

right, those of 21 July did not: 'Schott's Almanac, 2006', supplement to *The Guardian*, 19 Dec. 2005, p. 13.

39 Such as the alleged 'mastermind' behind the London bombings of 2005: <http://abcnews.go.com/GMA/LondonBlasts/story?id=941406>, accessed 6 Feb. 2006.

40 MANPADS (SA-7, or *Strela*) made in Slovakia were used in an attempt to shoot down an Israeli airliner in Kenya in Nov. 2002. A Russian army helicopter was shot down in Chechnya with a missile actually sold to the Chechen rebels by some Russian troops: Jiri Kominek, 'Bush–Putin Summit Sees a Meeting of Minds if not Hearts', *Jane's Homeland Security and Resilience Monitor*, 4/3 (Apr. 2005), pp. 17–19. In Nov. 2003 a DHL cargo plane leaving Baghdad airport was hit by a missile and forced to return to the airport. A month later the same occurred with a C-17: <http://www.freerepublic.com>, accessed 2 May 2005. An RAF Hercules transport plane was brought down by a missile in Iraq in Jan. 2005: 'Hercules Hit by Terrorists', <http://www.thisislondon.co.uk/news/articles/16268660?source=Evening+Standard>, accessed 9 Feb. 2006.

41 To stop Iraq using WMD in the First Gulf War, the USA made it clear to Saddam that American forces would retaliate with nuclear weapons: Hiro, *From Desert Shield to Desert Storm*, p. 370.

42 The Soviets, as a major power, did use chemical weapons in Afghanistan (1979–89) in response to Mujahideen attacks. This was in a different era, however, and conducted by a state which was not a liberal democracy. It was also in secret away from the world's prying eyes. See McMichael, *Stumbling Bear*, p. 183.

43 In contrast, the Hamas leader, Abu Shannab, has said that it is against Islamic teachings to use poisons: Parachini, 'Putting WMD Terrorism into Perspective'.

44 For a review of the past use by terrorists of WMD, see Tucker (ed.), *Toxic Terror*.

45 Manningham-Buller, 'Countering Terrorism', p. 10.

46 For the arguments presented here see Laqueur, *New Terrorism*, chs 2 and 11; Gurr and Cole, *New Face of Terrorism*; Cordesman, *The Challenge of Biological Terrorism*.

47 See Croddy and Wirtz (eds), *Weapons of Mass Destruction*, Vol. 1 pp. 256, 279, 266.

48 'The Facts about Biological and Chemical Weapons', *Intersec*, 15/12 (Feb. 2005), pp. 49–50.

49 The sarin was sprayed from a truck near an apartment block. The deaths at the time were not linked to Aum: A. Oppenheimer, 'Aum Shinrikyo: Lessons to be Learnt', *Jane's Terrorism and Security Monitor*, Mar. 2004, pp. 3–4.

50 Parachini, 'Putting WMD Terrorism into Perspective'.

51 Gurr and Cole, *New Face of Terrorism*, p. 63.

52 Christine Gosden, 'The 1988 Chemical Weapons Attack on Halabja, Iraq', in Alexander and Hoenig (eds), *Superterrorism*, pp. 7–11.

53 Crody and Wirtz (eds), *Weapons of Mass Destruction*, pp. 317–19.

54 'The Facts about Biological and Chemical Weapons'.

55 Gurr and Cole, *New Face of Terrorism*, p. 9.

56 'Risks of Chemical Terrorism', *Jane's Intelligence Digest*, 10 Sept. 2004.

57 See Croddy and Wirtz (eds), *Weapons of Mass Destruction*, pp. 261–65.

58 A. Venter, 'Smallpox: The Most Immediate Threat', *Jane's Terrorism and Security Monitor*, (Jan. 2003), pp. 5–6.

59 There are such things as man-made toxins, but the true definition of toxin refers only to substances produced by living material. Croddy and Wirtz (eds), *Weapons of Mass Destruction*, p. 287.

60 Combs, *Terrorism in the Twenty-First Century*, p. 262.

61 'The Facts about Biological and Chemical Weapons'. Also Mangold and Goldberg, *Plague Wars*, p. 262.

62 Croddy and Wirtz (eds), *Weapons of Mass Destruction*, p. 255.

63 Joseph Pilat, 'The Bioterrorism Threat: Technological and Political Considerations', in Alexander and Hoenig (eds), *Superterrorism*, pp. 63–6.

64 Croddy and Wirtz (eds), *Weapons of Mass Destruction*, pp. 97–9.

65 Libicki, 'Rethinking War', p. 34.

66 Combs, *Terrorism in the Twenty-First Century*, pp. 263–5.

67 Libicki, 'Rethinking War', p. 35.

68 Ibid. Also 'Nuclear Threats in 2005', *Jane's Intelligence Digest*, 15 Jan. 2005.

69 See Cole, *The Anthrax Letters*.

70 Venter, 'Smallpox'.

71 Rumours abound that smallpox is held in other labs, notably in North Korea: Osterholm and Schwartz, *Living Terror*, p. 107.

72 Tucker (ed.), *Toxic Terror*, pp. 153–6.

73 In 1990 Aum attacked three US bases in Japan by spraying botulinum toxin mist from three trucks. No effects were noted. Three years later the same was tried in Tokyo city centre, again with no casualties. Also in 1993 Aum tried to spray anthrax over the city from a tower block, but merely created a foul odour: Mangold and Goldberg, *Plague Wars*, pp. 341–5.

74 See e.g. Loeppky, ' "Biomania" and US Foreign Policy'; Chyba, 'Toward Biological Security'; Ostfield, 'Bioterrorism as a Foreign Policy Issue'.

75 Ed Blanche, 'Radioactive Material and Terrorism', *Jane's Terrorism and Security Monitor*, Feb. 2005, pp. 2–4.

76 'Nuclear Terrorism: A Real Risk?', *Jane's Intelligence Digest*, 24 Sept. 2004, pp. 1–2.

77 Kamien, 'What Keeps Port Security Directors Up at Night', p. 14.

78 'WMD Terrorism: How Real is the Threat?', *Military Technology*, 8 (2002), pp. 8–12; Reuters Report: 'Sydney Nuclear Reactor Terror Plot Target – Police', 14 Nov. 2005, online at <http://uk.news.yahoo.com/14112005/325/>, accessed 20 Dec. 2005.

79 Schaper, 'Dirty Weapons', pp. 18–19.

80 Russian nuclear plant security, though, is seen as quite lax, and material has gone missing. See 'Bratislava Enhances East–West Ties', *Jane's Terrorist and Security Monitor*, Mar. 2005, pp. 11–13.

81 These bombs, intended for use by Soviet Spetsnatz troops, weigh some 30 kg. They are coded against use by unauthorized actors: A. Oppenheimer, 'The Nuke that Fits in a Suitcase', *Jane's Terrorism and Security Monitor*, July 2005, pp. 3–4.

82 'Nuclear Terrorism: A Real Risk?'.

83 Laqueur, *No End to War*, p. 9; *idem*, *New Terrorism*, ch. 11.

84 US Secretary of Defense, Donald Rumsfeld, quoted in Shanker, 'Rumsfeld's Search'.

85 Gould and Spinney, 'Fourth-Generation Warfare is Here'.

86 Laqueur, *No End to War*, p. 23.

87 See Moloney, *A Secret History of the IRA*, pp. 481–9; Wardlaw, *Political Terrorism*, pp. 154–7.

88 Delpech, 'Imbalance of Terror', p. 40.

89 *Countering Terrorism: The UK Approach to the Military Contribution* (Shrivenham: Joint Doctrine and Concepts Centre, 2004), p. 16.

90 Gray, 'Combating Terrorism', p. 20.

91 Concerned by the fact that villagers in northern Kenya still supported Al Qaeda operatives after the East African embassy bombings in 1998, the US military sent special Army 'community outreach' teams to the area. They were supposed to create good will in terms of building schools, providing health care and inoculating cattle, etc. But they were treated with widespread suspicion, and riots resulted: Marc Lacey, 'Why a Village Is a Weapon in the War on Terror', *New York Times*, 30 Apr. 2004, p. 6.

92 David Wedgwood Benn, 'Hearts and Minds', *The World Today*, Dec. 2004, pp. 8–9.

93 *Countering Terrorism*, p. 16.

94 See Hamill, *Pig in the Middle*.

95 Parachini, 'Putting WMD Terrorism in Perspective'.

96 See Carter, 'How to Counter WMD'.

97 See Cole, Anthrax Letters, ch. 1.

98 *Jane's Sentinel Security Assessment* – North America, online at <www.janes.co.uk> accessed 16 Jan. 2004.

99 Hospitals should have only 80 per cent occupancy rates to allow scope for emergency situations. At present, though, the figure in British hospitals is much higher: Report by Tim Brimelow, 'Breakfast', BBC Radio 5, 14 July 2004.

100 Manningham-Buller, 'Countering Terrorism', p. 9.
101 Central Intelligence Agency, Federal Bureau of Investigation, National Security Agency, Defense Intelligence Agency.
102 See Laqueur, *No End to War*, ch. 6.
103 Ibid., p. 139.
104 Manningham-Buller, 'Countering Terrorism', p. 9.
105 See Hiro, *War without End*, ch. 5.
106 Laqueur, *No End to War*, p. 126.
107 Quoted in Robert Fisk, 'With Runners and Whispers, Al Qa'ida Outfoxes US Forces', *The Independent*, 6 Dec. 2002, p. 6.
108 Pilat, 'Bioterrorism Threat'.
109 See Tomas Biersteker, 'Targeting Terrorist Finances: The New Challenges of Financial Market Globalization', in Booth and Dunne (eds), *Worlds in Collision*, ch. 6.
110 Rammell, 'The Financial War Against Terrorism'.
111 Patrick Buckley and Michael Meese, 'The Financial Front in the Global War on Terrorism', in Howard Russell and Reid Sawyer (eds), *Defeating Terrorism: Shaping the New Security Environment* (Guilford, Conn.: McGraw-Hill, 2002), ch. 3.
112 Nail varnish contains acetone, which is the raw material to make cordite. Olive oil is a thickening agent to develop more explosive potential: Tim Radford, 'Blondes or Bomb Shells?', *The Guardian*, 17 Nov. 2001, p. 3.
113 See e.g. Burke, *Al Qaeda*, pp. 151–5.
114 In this system no money actually moves in the official channels. If a group or individual in country A wants to give money to a group or individual in country B, then a person in B is asked to give money to that group or individual on the promise that someone known to that person in country B will receive the same amount and they can collect it from them: Hiro, *War without End*, p. 278.
115 After cash seizures in 1998, Al Qaeda began to move assets around in the form of gemstones: Mawson, 'Waging War on Terror Funds'.
116 Tamara Makarenko, 'The Ethics of Counterterrorism', *Jane's Intelligence Review*, 15/9 (Sept. 2003), p. 55.
117 Kennedy-Pipe, *The Origins of the Present Troubles in Northern Ireland*, p. 59.
118 *Customary* law applies here, because Article 51 of the UN Charter does not define exactly what 'self-defence' can include. See Michael Byers, 'Terror and the Future of International Law', in Booth and Dunne (eds), *Worlds in Collision*, p. 119. Customary international law is 'an informal, unwritten body of rules derived from the practice and opinions of states': ibid. Customary law pre-dates and forms the underpinnings of today's international law as set down by the UN and other bodies.
119 The principles that make a war 'just' are seen as legal authority, right intention, probability of success, proportionality and last resort. For a

useful review of these principles see Mohammed Taghi Karoubi, *Just or Unjust War?*.

120 Mary Ellen O'Connell, 'Lawful and Unlawful Wars Against Terrorism', in Nanda (ed.), *Law in the War on International Terrorism*, ch. 4.

121 As is the International Court of Justice: ibid., p. 81.

122 Elshtain, *Just War Against Terror*, pp. 182–92.

123 In 1967 the Israelis struck first against Egyptian forces, as it was generally felt that these forces were on the point of invading Israel. In 1981 Israeli aircraft bombed the Osiraq nuclear power plant to prevent Iraq from possibly producing nuclear weapons – even though it was nowhere near doing so. See Gray, *International Law and the Use of Armed Force*, pp. 7, 133.

124 Bowen, 'Deterrence and Asymmetry'.

125 Laid out in *The National Security Strategy of the USA*, online at <http://whitehouse.gov/nsc/nss.html>, accessed 10 June 2005. See also Harry Conley, 'Not with Impunity: Assessing US Policy for Retaliating to a Chemical or Biological Attack', in Schneider and Davis (eds), *The War Next Time*, p. 79.

126 See Steinberg, 'Preventive Force in US National Security Strategy'.

127 Ibid., p. 58.

128 As Michael McGinty points out, 'Great Britain has, to all intents and purposes, followed suit' in adopting the doctrine of anticipatory self-defence: Michael McGinty, 'That Was the War that Was', p. 24.

129 Byers, 'Terror and the Future of International Law', p. 124; Barnett, *Asymmetric Warfare*, p. 58; Whitman, 'Humanitarian Intervention in an Era of Pre-Emptive Self-Defence'. The British government, though, seems conscious of certain obligations: 'Where the use of force is justified,' says one government publication, 'it is important that the conduct of military action is in accordance with obligations under international humanitarian law': *The Strategic Defence Review: A New Chapter: Supporting Information and Essays* (London: MoD, 2002), p. 19.

130 Slocombe, 'Force, Pre-emption and Legitimacy', p. 124.

131 Nabati, 'Anticipatory Self-Defense'.

132 Krauss and Lacey, 'Utilitarian vs. Humanitarian'.

133 Gray, 'Thinking Asymmetrically in Times of Terror', p. 8.

134 Hirsch, 'On Dinosaurs and Hornets'.

135 McKenzie, *The Revenge of the Melians*, p. 49. For a general review of this whole issue see Rosenthal, 'New Rules for War'.

136 Paul Murphy, 'Markets Bounce Back', *The Guardian*, 9 July 2005, p. 30: quotation from Spanish newspaper reflecting the lack of comprehension in Spain as to Londoners' stoicism. Spaniards behaved very differently after the Madrid bombs: Giles Tremett, 'Spanish Reaction: Admiration Mingled with Astonishment over Calm Response', *The Guardian*, 12 July 2005, p. 3.

137 The professionally delivered London bombings of 7 July 2005 were fol-
    lowed a couple of weeks later by some 'copy-cat' attacks that were very
    amateurish in nature.
138 Mike O'Brien, 'Morality in Asymmetric War and Intervention Opera-
    tions', *RUSI Journal*, 147/5 (Oct. 2002), pp. 40–5.
139 Ian Lesser, 'Implications for Strategy', in Lesser et al., *Countering the
    New Terrorism*, p. 126.
140 Hence the titles of recent books on terrorism such as *War Without End*
    (Hiro, 2002) and *No End to War* (Laqueur, 2003).

Chapter 3   Asymmetry and Information Warfare

1 From the US Department of Defense, as quoted in Andrew
  Krepinevich, 'Cavalry to Computer: The Pattern of Military Revolu-
  tions', *National Interest*, Fall 1994, pp. 30–7.
2 Eliot Cohen, 'A Revolution in Warfare'. Jones et al., *Global Information
  Warfare*, p. 608.
3 Anthony Cordesman, 'A Lesson in Transforming Warfare', *Financial
  Times*, 17 Feb. 2005.
4 Almost every weapon in the US inventory depends on GPS to some
  degree (as do all ships, aircraft, vehicles and, indeed, almost all soldiers
  in US ground forces): Hancock and Pettit, 'Global Positioning System
  – Our Achilles' Heel?'.
5 Or Uninhabited Aerial Vehicle. This was the term used during the
  'politically correct' period in the US under President Bill Clinton. The
  term 'uninhabited' was later dropped, however, because no one actually
  'lived' in the vehicles.
6 Bruce Berkowitz, 'Warfare in the Information Age', in Arquilla and
  Ronfeldt (eds), *In Athena's Camp*, pp. 141–74.
7 Matt Bishop and Emily Goldman, 'The Strategy and Tactics of Information Warfare', in Goldman (ed.), *National Security in the Information
  Age*, p. 118.
8 Libicki, 'Rethinking War', p. 30.
9 John Rothrock, 'Information Warfare: Time for Some Constructive
  Skepticism?', in Arquilla and Ronfeldt (eds), *In Athena's Camp*, p. 220.
10 'Information Operations', in *Canadian Forces Operations Manual*, ch. 32,
   online at <www.dnd.ca/dcds/jointDoc/docs>, accessed 9 Jan. 2005.
11 Jones et al., *Global Information Warfare*, p. 21.
12 Ibid., p. 5. To illustrate the confusion that can arise over the term IW,
   we can point to the example of the differing US and UK approaches to
   the idea of 'media ops'. In American parlance, operations involving the
   media *are* a subset of IW. See Dunnigan, *The Next War Zone*, pp. 115–
   30. In UK thinking, however, media ops are not IW, since any information given to the media must always be the unalloyed truth, and therefore

cannot involve misinformation and cannot be a form of warfare. Thus, as the British put it, 'Media Ops are not a subordinate subset of Information Operations [the UK name for IW] but are closely related activity [*sic*]' and are 'separate and distinct'. The UK definition of media ops is 'That line of activity developed to ensure timely, accurate, and effective provision of Public Information and implementation of Public Relations policy within the operational environment whilst maintaining operational security': in Joint Warfare Publication, 3-45, *Media Operations* (Shrivenham: JDCC, 2001), pp. 1-1, 1-2.

13 Based roughly on the typology of O'Brien and Nusbaum, 'Intelligence Gathering on Asymmetric Threats – Part One'.

14 Dunnigan, *Next War Zone*, p. 20.

15 Arquilla and Ronfeldt, 'Cyber War is Coming!'; *idem*, 'The Advent of Netwar: Analytical Background', in O'Day (ed.), *Cyberterrorism*, p. 166.

16 Bishop and Goldman, 'Strategy and Tactics', p. 117.

17 Trojan horses are alien programmes masquerading as other, legitimate ones. They can destroy data on computers. A zombie programme is a type of Trojan horse, but it can, once placed by a hacker, communicate back to the hacker. It can seize control of the computer. Trojan horses evolved into viruses. Viruses will spread, causing damage elsewhere in other computers. Worms are viruses that do not attach themselves to programmes. They will begin to work when the right conditions are met. Logic bombs are worms planted to go off and cause disruption as and when required. See Dunnigan, *Next War Zone*, pp. 8–10.

18 'Commission to Assess the Threats to the United States from Electromagnetic Pulse Attack' created by Congress in 2000. See Michael Sirak, 'US Vulnerable to EMP Attack', *Jane's Defence Weekly*, 28 July 2004, p. 6.

19 Jones et al., *Global Information Warfare*, p. 603.

20 Dunnigan, *Next War Zone*, p. 3.

21 O'Brien and Nusbaum, 'Intelligence Gathering on Asymmetric Threats – Part One', p. 53.

22 Rathmell, 'Information Operations'.

23 Jones et al., *Global Information Warfare*, p. 151.

24 Kevin Poulson, 'Satellites at Risk of Hacks', *Security Forces On-line*, 3 Oct. 2002, <http://online.securityfocus.com/news/942>, accessed 10 Jan. 2005.

25 See Berkowitz, 'Warfare in the Information Age'.

26 Glasstone and Dolan, *The Effects of Nuclear Weapons*, ch. 11.

27 O'Brien and Nusbaum, 'Intelligence Gathering . . . Part One', p. 54; Denning, *Information Warfare and Security*, p. 198.

28 'City Surrenders to £400 Million Gangs', *Sunday Times*, 2 June 1996, p. 4, and 'Secret DTI Inquiry into Cyber Terror', *Sunday Times*, 9 June 2001, p. 12. Also Denning, *Information Warfare and Security*, p. 199.

29 Dunnigan, *Next War Zone*, p. 43.
30 Jones et al., *Global Information Warfare*, p. 602.
31 The cost of repairing the damage he caused was $700,000: Owen Bowcott, '"Biggest Hacker" Fights Extradition', *The Guardian*, 9 June 2005, p. 1.
32 Dunnigan, *Next War Zone*, p. 6. Even as far back as 1995, for instance, it was estimated that the US Department of Defense was being attacked 250,000 times a year. Of these attacks, 66 per cent were considered to be successful. The most alarming fact, however, is that it was estimated that only 4 per cent of the attacks were actually detected: 'Computer Attacks at Department of Defense Pose Increasing Risks', US GAO, May 1996, online at <www.pbs.org/wgbh/pages/frontline/shows/hackers/risks>, accessed 9 Jan. 2005.
33 One Australian set up a rival computer-controlled sewage system in the back of his van and was able to release effluent from a local sewage works at random. He then applied for the contract to clean up the mess: Barton Gellman, 'Cyber-Attacks by Al Qaeda Feared', *Washington Post*, 27 June 2002, p. A01.
34 Erbschloe, *Information Warfare*, p. 260.
35 Dunnigan, *Next War Zone*, p. 15.
36 O'Brien and Nusbaum, 'Intelligence Gathering . . . Part One'.
37 Erbschloe, *Information Warfare*, p. 250.
38 Giles Trendle, 'E-Jihad against Western Business', on IT-Director.com, 5 Apr. 2002, p. 3, online at <www.it-director.com/article.php?id=2744>, accessed 17 May 2005.
39 <www.ummah.net/unity>, accessed 10 Dec. 2004.
40 See Verton, *Black Ice*.
41 Gellman, 'Cyber-Attacks', p. A01.
42 O'Brien and Nusbaum, 'Intelligence Gathering . . . Part One'.
43 Frank Vizard, 'A Hacker Attack against NATO Spawns a War in Cyberspace', *Popular Science*, 17 Sept. 1999.
44 Thomas, 'NATO and the Current Myth of Information Superiority'.
45 Posen, 'The War for Kosovo'.
46 Jones et al., *Global Information Warfare*, p. 232.
47 Liang and Xiangsui, *Unrestricted Warfare*.
48 Kaplan, 'How We Would Fight China', p. 55.
49 Jones et al., *Global Information Warfare*, p. 233.
50 O'Brien and Nusbaum, 'Intelligence Gathering . . . Part One', p. 52.
51 Berkowitz, 'Warfare in the Information Age', p. 63.
52 Bill Gertz, 'Pentagon Study Finds China Preparing for War with US', *Washington Post*, 2 Feb. 2000, p. A04.
53 Feigenbaum, *China's Techno-Warriors*.
54 Jones et al., *Global Information Warfare*, p. 145.
55 Erbschloe, *Information Warfare*, p. 238.

56 Dunnigan, *Next War Zone*, p. 14.
57 Ibid., pp. 83, 87–8.
58 Libicki, 'Rethinking War', p. 35.
59 Lt. Gen. Mi Zhenyu, Vice Commandant, Academy of Military Sciences, Beijing, quoted in 1996: Jones et al., Global Information Warfare, p. 233.
60 O'Brien and Nusbaum, 'Intelligence Gathering . . . Part Two'.
61 Swetman, 'High Tech and Low Cunning'.
62 Ibid., p. 83.
63 See Berkowitz, 'Warfare in the Information Age'.
64 O'Brien and Nusbaum, 'Information Gathering . . . Part Two'.
65 See e.g. Thomas, 'NATO and the Current Myth'.
66 Gooch and Perlmutter (eds), *Military Deception and Strategic Surprise*, p. 1.
67 Sun Tzu, *The Art of War*, trans. Samuel Griffith, p. 133.
68 Clausewitz, *On War*, p. 203.
69 See Latimer, *Deception in War*.
70 Betts, *Surprise Attack*, p. 109.
71 Thomas, 'NATO and the Current Myth'.
72 Sun Tzu, *Art of War*.
73 Latimer, *Deception in War*, ch. 1.
74 Q-Ships were merchant ships with hidden guns which would be exposed when German U-boats surfaced to take the surrender of what they thought was an easy prize.
75 R. James Woolsey, quoted on dust cover of Holt, *The Deceivers*.
76 Hastings, *Overlord*, p. 24.
77 Maskelyne established a pattern of lights in empty desert and encouraged German night-bomber pilots to 'bomb' the lights and not the real blacked-out city of Alexandria several kilometres away. He also, among other 'japes', built full-size inflatable submarines and an inflatable battleship, hid part of the Suez Canal, and used mirrors to make one tank into thirty-six!: Farago, *The Game of the Foxes*, p. 278.
78 See, for a thorough review of such examples, Latimer and Michael Dewar, *The Art of Deception in Warfare* (Newton Abbot: Sterling Publishers, 1989).
79 Michael Handel, 'Intelligence and Deception', in Gooch and Perlmutter (eds), *Military Deception*, p. 124.
80 Latimer, *Deception in Warfare*, p. 305.
81 Hastings, *Overlord*, p. 72.
82 It appeared to work to great effect in Serbia's struggle against NATO. See Thomas, 'NATO and the Current Myth'.
83 See <http://www.wellesley.edu/ClassicalStudies/CLCV102/Thucydides–MelianDialogue>, accessed 23 May 2005.
84 Quoted in Latimer, *Deception in Warfare*, p. 304.

85 The one notable recent use of deception by the strong powers was the 'feint' to conduct amphibious landings in the First Gulf War in 1991. See Friedman, *Desert Victory*, p. 216.
86 Libicki, *What is Information Warfare?*, p. 27.
87 Denning, *Information Warfare and Security*, p. 195.
88 Latimer, *Deception in Warfare*, pp. 194–6.
89 See Browne and Thurbon, *Electronic Warfare*.
90 Libicki, *What is Information Warfare?*, p. 35.
91 Shafritz et al., *The Facts on File Dictionary of Military Science*, p. 371. The British define psyops as 'planned psychological activities designed to influence attitudes and behaviour affecting the achievement of political and military objectives': *Joint Warfare Publication, 3–45* (London: HMSO, 2000), p. 1.3.
92 Janos Radvanyi, 'Introduction to Psyops', in Radvanyi (ed.), *Psychological Operations*, p. 1.
93 Linebarger, *Psychological Warfare*.
94 Kenneth McKenzie, 'The Rise of Asymmetric Threats: Priorities for Defense Planning', in *QDR 2001: Strategy Driven Choices for America's Security*, online at <http://www.ndu.edu/inss/press/QDR_2001/sdcasch03.html>, accessed 9 Jan. 2005.
95 For a useful review of psyops in general see Denning, *Information Warfare and Security*, ch. 5.
96 Quoted in Tony Karon, 'Al Qaeda Today: Not Winning, But Not Losing Either', *Time Magazine*, 10 Sept. 2003, online at <www.time.com/time/world/article>, accessed 16 Mar. 2005.
97 Blood, *The Tet Offensive*.
98 Mils Hills and Rachel Holloway, 'Competing for Media Control in an Age of Asymmetric Warfare', Jane's International Security Website, 23 Apr. 2002, p. 1, online at <www.janes.com/security/international_security/news/jir/jr020423>, accessed 19 May 2005.
99 Ibid.
100 Thomas, 'NATO and the Current Myth'.
101 Jones et al., *Global Information Warfare*, p. 287.
102 Miles, *Al Jazeera*.
103 Zayani (ed.), *The Al Jazeera Phenomenon*.
104 Christopher Marquis, 'US Intensifies Protest Against Arab TV Reports', *International Herald Tribune*, 30 Apr. 2004, p. 6.
105 Ibid.
106 Tatham, 'Al Jazeera'.
107 Marquis, 'US Intensifies Protest'.
108 Ibid.
109 Brian Knowlton, 'Anti-US Anger Spreading in Islamic States, Survey Finds', *International Herald Tribune*, 19 May 2005, p. 17.
110 Matt Bivens, 'Fallujah's Untold Story: Civilian Casualties', *The Moscow Times*, 19 Apr. 2004, p. 8.

111 Ibid.
112 Cordesman, *Lessons of Afghanistan*, p. 137.
113 Cohen, 'History and the Hyperpower', p. 58.
114 Libicki, 'Rethinking War'.

Chapter 4   Asymmetry and Air Power

 1 President Ronald Reagan's despatch of aircraft to bomb Libya in Oper-
    ation *El Dorado Canyon* in 1982 is such an example.
 2 See Budiansky, *Air Power*.
 3 McInnes, 'Fatal Attraction?', p. 34.
 4 John Warden, 'Afterword: Challenges and Opportunities', in Hallion
    (ed.), *Air Power Confronts an Unstable World*, p. 235.
 5 Clark, *Waging Modern War*, p. 434; Byman and Waxman, 'Kosovo and
    the Great Air Power Debate'.
 6 'US Kills Al Qaeda Suspects in Yemen', *USA Today*, 5 Nov. 2002, online
    at   <www.usatoday.com/news/world/2002-11-04-yemen-side-usat>,
    accessed 5 May 2005.
 7 In the First Gulf War, most Iraqi military aircraft were flown out of
    harm's way to Iran or covered in sand in the desert: Cordesman and
    Wagner, *The Lessons of Modern War*, Vol. 4, p. 424. The Serbs tended
    to hide their aircraft in woods: Posen, 'The War for Kosovo'.
 8 These are radar-guided, and therefore once their radar ground stations
    are destroyed, the missiles themselves become useless. The latest Russia
    systems, the S-300 and S-400, are more effective, but have not yet been
    launched against Western aircraft.
 9 See O'Halloran, *A Kill is a Kill*, ch. 4.
10 Landauer, 'The Threat from MANPADS', pp. 12–13.
11 Alon Ben-David, 'Israel Seeks to Block Sale of Iglas to Syria', *Jane's
    Defence Weekly*, 42/3 (19 Jan. 2005), p. 4.
12 Budiansky, *Air Power*, p. 412.
13 Both Tornados and US F-16s were forced from low up to medium alti-
    tudes. See Budiansky, *Air Power*, p. 424, and 'Air Operations during
    Operation Granby – An Overview', at <www.raf.mod.uk/bob1940/
    operations.html>, accessed 5 May 2005.
14 John Snider, 'The War in Bosnia: The Evolution of the United Nations
    and Air Power in Peace Operations' at <www.globalsecurity.org/
    military/library/report/1997/Snider.html>, accessed 5 May 2005.
15 Glosson, *War with Iraq*, p. 139.
16 The Apache was designed to operate on Cold War battlefields. Its
    mission was to use its missiles to engage tanks several kilometres away.
    But it would do this only when hovering above friendly territory where
    it could not be engaged by ground fire. Helicopters are very vulnerable,
    and were never designed to operate above hostile territory. See Clark,

Waging Modern War, p. 248; Hunter, 'Making the Tough Tougher', *Jane's* p. 25.

17 Wilson et al., 'An Alternative Future Force', p. 25.

18 Naylor, *Not a Good Day to Die*, p. 312.

19 Wilson et al., 'An Alternative Future Force', p. 27.

20 Nick Paton Walsh, 'Chechen who Killed 127 Russians Jailed', *The Guardian*, 30 Apr. 2004, p. 8.

21 Hunter, 'Making the Tough Tougher', p. 25.

22 Such weapons have become so concerning to the US Air Force and US Navy that both will, in future, only conduct air strike and ground support operations from altitudes above 10,000 feet. Wilson et al., 'An Alternative Future Force', p. 25.

23 McInnes, 'Fatal Attraction?', p. 34; Clark, *Waging Modern War*, p. 343.

24 'US Trying to Perfect Scud Hunting' at <www.cnn.com/2003/WORLD/meast/01/15/sproject.irq.scud.hunting>, accessed 5 May 2005. The Scud is a medium range missile (600–900 km) that can be transported on a truck-trailer.

25 Freedman and Karsh, *The Gulf Conflict, 1990/91*, pp. 308–9.

26 Apparently, four out of nine *dummy* Scuds were hit: Rip and Hasik, *The Precision Revolution*, p. 311 and 421. Also Cordesman, *Lessons of Afghanistan*, p. 106. Coalition aircraft and SF claimed that a total of eighty-nine Scuds were destroyed during the war. Yet the Iraqis began the war with only 30! See Cordesman and Wagner, *Lessons of Modern War*, vol. 4 p. 331.

27 Rip and Hasik, *Precision Revolution*, p. 405.

28 US House of Representatives, *Intelligence Successes and Failures in Operations Desert Shield/Desert Storm*, Committee on Armed Services, 103rd Congress – 1st Session. Supplement to the House Armed Services Committee's 1992 'Defense for a New Era: Lessons of the Persian Gulf War' (Washington, DC: US GPO, 1993), p. 45.

29 Cordesman, *Lessons of Afghanistan*, p. 114.

30 Ibid.

31 Simmons, 'Air Operations over Bosnia'.

32 Richardson, *No Escape Zone*.

33 Only European NATO countries had such aircraft, the US having phased out theirs: Tim Ripley, 'Balkan Picture', *Flight International*, 6–12 July 1994, pp. 26–7.

34 Cohen, 'The Mystique of US Air Power', p. 119.

35 Byman and Waxman, 'Kosovo'.

36 Lambeth, 'Lessons from the Kosovo War', p. 13.

37 Department of Defense, *Report to Congress: Kosovo After-Action Report* (Washington, DC: Department of Defense, 2000), pp. 10–11.

38 The fear of losing the large AC-130 (Hercules) gunships in Afghanistan and Iraq means that they are used only at night: Naylor, *Not a Good Day to Die*, p. 199.

39 Ben-David, 'Israel Seeks to Block Sale', p. 4.

40 See, e.g. Byman and Waxman, 'Kosovo'.

41 Cordesman, *Lessons of Afghanistan*, p. 106.

42 Hasken, *A Historical Look at Close Air Support*.

43 See Page, *Lions, Donkeys and Dinosaurs*, pp. 118–20.

44 'Peacekeeping: Perils and Prospects: "The Big Ten" Lessons Learned from Recent Operations in Somalia, Rwanda, Haiti and Bosnia', Report of BENS-Sponsored Symposia, Jan. 1996, <http://www.bens.org/pubs_0196.html> accessed 27 Sept. 2005.

45 Cordesman, *The Lessons and Non-Lessons of the Air and Missile Campaign in Kosovo*, p. 320.

46 Lambeth, 'Lessons', p. 16.

47 Richard Hallion, 'Precision Air Attack in the Modern Era', in Hallion (ed.), *Airpower Confronts an Unstable World*, pp. 117–19.

48 Hancock and Pettit, 'Global Positioning System'.

49 'Integrated INS/GPS Takes Off in the US', *International Defense Review*, 26/2 (Feb. 2003), pp. 172–4.

50 Rip and Hasik, *Precision Revolution*, p. 278.

51 Hancock and Pettit, 'Global Positioning System'.

52 This Russian firm reported that one of its best customers was the US Department of Defense, which wanted to test how good the jammers actually were: 'Russian Firm Reiterates Denial of Selling Jamming Systems to Iraq', ITAR–TASS News Agency, quoted on BBC Monitoring 25 Mar. 2003. Denning has the Russian system costing $4,000: *Information Warfare and Security*, p. 195. Hancock and Pettit, 'Global Positioning System', have it costing $40,000.

53 Sheila Melvin, 'Why Chinese Can Believe Worst about US Bombing', *USA Today*, 12 May 1999, p. 15A.

54 'Military Wipes Out Iraqi GPS Jammers', *Fox News*, 25 Mar. 2003, online at <http://www.foxnews.com/story/0,2933,82018,00html>, accessed 10 Feb. 2006.

55 'The Global Positioning System: Charting the Future', in *Report of the National Academy of Public Administration and the National Research Council to the US Congress and Department of Defense*, May 1995, quoted in Rip and Hasik, *Precision Revolution*, p. 276.

56 'US Forces Destroy Iraqi GPS Jammers', *United Press International*, 25 Mar. 2003, online at <http://www.upi.com/inc/view.php?StoryID=20030325>, accessed 10 Feb. 2006.

57 Browne and Thurbon, *Electronic Warfare*, ch. 15.

58 Cordesman, *Lessons and Non-Lessons*, pp. 291–5.

59 Hancock and Pettit, 'Global Positioning System'.

60 Ibid.

61 Rip and Hasik, *Precision Revolution*, p. 406; Dunnigan, *Next War Zone*, p. 73.

62 Rip and Hasik, *Precision Revolution*, p. 402.

63 See Daalder and O'Hanlon, *Winning Ugly*, pp. 120–4.
64 See Latimer, *Deception in Warfare*.
65 See e.g., Hastings, *Overlord*.
66 John Gresham, 'A New Generation Emerges: Precision Guided Munitions', <www.aviation100.com/web04/yid/precision/html>, accessed 12 June 2004.
67 See Arkin, 'Smart Bombs, Dumb Targeting?'; also Mandel, 'The Wartime Utility of Precision Versus Brute Force in Weaponry'.
68 Col. Fred Wieners, quoted in Lisa Burgess, 'Afghanistan War Showing Air Force the Importance of "Eyes on the Ground"', *European Stars and Stripes*, 15 Aug. 2002.
69 For an example of the lack of training time shared by pilots and SF, see e.g., Richardson, *No Escape Zone*, ch. 4.
70 Cordesman, *Lessons and Non-Lessons*, p. 206.
71 Ibid., p. 345.
72 See Clark, *Waging Modern War*, pp. 279–81; McInnes, 'Fatal Attraction?', p. 36.
73 Peter Gray, 'The Balkans: An Air Power Basket Case?', in Cox and Gray, *Air Power History*, p. 335; Roy Thomas, 'Bombing in the Service of Peace: Sarajevo and Gorazde, Spring 1994', *Air and Space Power Chronicles*, online at <http://wvvw.airpower.maxwell.af.mil/airchronicles/cc/thomasrev.html>, accessed 10 Feb. 2006.
74 Rip and Hasik, *Precision Revolution*, p. 406.
75 Byman and Waxman, *The Dynamics of Coercion*, pp. 146–7.
76 Yenne, *Attack of the Drones*, p. 12.
77 Budiansky, *Air Power*, p. 405.
78 Thomas Ricks, 'Beaming the Battlefield: Live Video of Afghan Fighting had Questionable Effect', *Washington Post*, 26 Mar. 2002, p. A04.
79 Yenne, *Attack of the Drones*, p. 8.
80 Ibid., p. 66.
81 Some forty UAVs (US, French, German and British) were lost over Kosovo in *Operation Allied Force*. The British lost all fourteen of their Phoenix machines. See also Budiansky, *Air Power*, p. 411.
82 Ricks, 'Beaming the Battlefield', p. A04.
83 Nathan Hodge, 'CIA's Predatory Behaviour is Cause for Concern', <www.newsday.com/news/opinion/ny-vphod062734170jun06.story>, accessed 5 Apr. 2005.
84 Hammes, 'War Isn't a Rational Business'.
85 Hirst, *War and Power in the 21st Century*, p. 92.
86 Libicki, *What is Information Warfare?*, pp. 27–33.
87 See e.g., Werrell, *Chasing the Silver Bullet*.
88 Gordon and Trainor, *The Generals' War* (Boston: Little, Brown and Co., 1995), p. 271.
89 Denning, *Information Warfare and Security*, pp. 198–9.

90 Michael Krepon, Christopher Clary, Space Assurance or Space Dominance? The Case Against Weaponising Space, <www.stimson. org/pubs.cfm?ID=81>, accessed 11 Jan. 2005.

91 Ibid.

92 Berkowitz, 'Warfare in the Information Age'.

93 Quoted in interview with Jay Davis, then Director of the US Defense Reduction Agency, *Jane's Defence Weekly*, 33/7 (16 Feb. 2000), p. 56.

94 Hancock and Pettit, 'Global Positioning System'.

95 CIA Report, 'Global Trends 2015: A Dialog about the Future with Nongovernment Experts', p. 34, <www.cia.gov/cia/publications>, accessed 14 May 2004.

96 *Report of the Commission to Assess US National Security Space Management and Organisation* at <www.defenselink.mil/pubs/space2001>, accessed 12 July 2004.

97 Wilson et al., 'An Alternative Future Force', p. 23. See also Peter Wilson, 'Asymmetric Threats', in Binnendijk (ed.), *Strategic Assessment 1998*, pp. 171–2; and Larabee et al., *The Changing Global Security Environment*, pp. 202–4.

98 'Commission to Assess the Threats to the United States from Electromagnetic Pulse Attack', created by Congress in 2000. Michael Sirak, 'US Vulnerable to EMP Attack', *Jane's Defence Weekly*, 8 July 2004, p. 6.

99 Fogleman, 'Advantage USA: Air Power and Asymmetric Force Strategy'.

100 One such example would be the targeting during *Operation Allied Force* of assets belonging to Slobodan Milošević and his backers: Lambeth, 'Lessons', p. 17.

101 Ibid.

102 Ibid.

103 Ibid.

Chapter 5   Asymmetry and Sea Power

1 Shepherd, *Sea Power in Ancient History*.

2 Hill, *War at Sea in the Ironclad Age*, pp. 63–5.

3 Walden, *The Short Victorious War*.

4 Spector, *At War, At Sea*, p. 6.

5 Ibid.

6 As one US admiral put it in the 1970s, 'the main mission for carriers is to assist in carrying out the navy's prime mission, control of the sea. Supporting the land battle is strictly a secondary and collateral task': Vice-Admiral Malcolm Cagle, quoted in Spector, *At War, At Sea*, p. 374. See also Baer, *The US Navy, 1890–1990*, pp. 412–13.

7 Technically, the littoral also covers that area a few miles *inland* from the coast.
8 Rear-Admiral James Burnell-Nugent, quoted in Ballantyne, *Strike from the Sea*, p. 164.
9 Kaplan, 'How We Would Fight China', p. 50.
10 See O'Meara et al. (eds), *Globalization and the Challenges of a New Century*, esp. pp. 310–12.
11 Kaplan, 'The Coming Anarchy'.
12 Griffin, *Joint Operations*, ch. 8.
13 Edward Hanlon, 'Taking the Long View: Littoral Warfare Challenges', in Schultz and Pfaltzgraff (eds), *Role of Naval Forces*, p. 156.
14 Greco, 'New Trends in Peacekeeping'.
15 Friedman, 'The Role of Aircraft Carriers'.
16 See Hanlon, 'Taking the Long View', and Charles Dunlap, 'Asymmetrical Warfare and the Western Mind-Set', in Schultz and Pfaltzgraff (eds), *Role of Naval Forces*, pp. 73–83; Corless, 'Hunting Goliath in the Age of Asymmetric Warfare'.
17 Quoted in Pack, *Sea Power in the Mediterranean*, p. 160.
18 Thalassocrates, 'Anti-Ship Missiles Tactics for Littoral Warfare Scenarios'.
19 Ibid.
20 For the effect of clutter on radar, see Wagner et al. (eds), *Naval Operational Analysis*, pp. 123–36.
21 Thalassocrates, 'Anti-Ship Missiles'.
22 Kaplan, 'How We Would Fight China', p. 55.
23 Ibid.
24 Spector, *At War, At Sea*, pp. 387–90.
25 The Silkworm, aimed at the USS *Missouri*, was engaged first by a Phalanx gun fired from a US ship. This did not destroy the missile, but some of the Phalanx rounds did actually hit the *Missouri*. It was HMS *Gloucester* whose Sea Dart missile brought the Silkworm down: Ballantyne, *Strike from the Sea*, pp. 121–2.
26 Ibid., p. 117; Till, *Seapower*, p. 129.
27 Pengelley, 'The Call for Fire Returns'.
28 Kaplan, 'How We Would Fight China', p. 58.
29 These can be seen 'as a frigate in all but name': E. R. Hooton, 'The Move Towards Corvettes and Frigates', *Armada International*, 6 (Dec.–Jan. 2005), p. 16.
30 Scott, 'Anti-Ship Weapons Updated to Target the Shore'.
31 Solomon, 'Lethal in the Littoral'.
32 Truver, 'Transformation'.
33 Kaplan, 'How We Would Fight China'; Kimura, 'A Gunboat Navy for the 21st Century'.
34 Corless, 'Hunting Goliath'.
35 Foxwell, 'Sub Proliferation Sends Navies Diving for Cover'.

36 Ibid.
37 Preston, 'Submarine Technology'.
38 Loren, 'Close-in Naval Dominance'.
39 Hewish, 'Wanted: A Quiet Walk on the Beach'.
40 Koburger, *Sea Power in the Twenty-First Century*, p. 77.
41 Foxwell, 'Sub Proliferation'.
42 Kaplan, 'How We Would Fight China', p. 55.
43 Solomon, 'Lethal in the Littoral'.
44 Corless, 'Hunting Goliath'.
45 Pengelley and Scott, 'Lower Frequencies Ping the Littoral ASW Threat'.
46 Friedman, 'Littoral Anti-Submarine Warfare', p. 53.
47 Ibid.
48 Scott, 'Lightweight Torpedoes Take a Shallow Dive'; *idem*, 'Heavy-weight Contenders Shape up for the Littoral'.
49 Rear-Admiral Mark Edwards, Director, Surface Warfare, USN, quoted in Truver, 'Mix and Match', p. 24.
50 Ibid.
51 Hill, *War at Sea*, p. 65.
52 Spector, *At War, At Sea*, pp. 22–3.
53 Pack, *Sea Power*, p. 160.
54 Spector, *At War, At sea*, p. 226.
55 Wagner et al., *Naval Operational Analysis*, p. 235.
56 As Rear-Admiral Allan Smith, the commander of the Amphibious Task Force at the time put it, 'We have lost control of the seas to a nation without a navy, using pre-World War I weapons, laid by vessels that were utilized at the time of the birth of Christ:' quoted in Moser Melia, 'Damn the Torpedoes', p. 89.
57 Loren, 'Close-in Naval Dominance'. The others were from air attack (two) and terrorist action (one).
58 Mine sweeping is carried out by vessels which trail a wire that snags the mines, cuts their mooring cables, and exposes them for demolition (this relates to the 'dumb iron' variety of mine). Minehunters seek out (usually through sonar) and neutralize mines that lie on the bottom (such as influence mines).
59 In the 1980s, the US had only six Korean War-vintage minesweepers: Koburger, *Sea Power*, p. 81.
60 Loren, 'Close-in Naval Dominance'.
61 Annati, 'Mine Hunting and Mine Clearance Revisited'.
62 Ballantyne, *Strike from the Sea*, p. 155.
63 Ibid., p. 113.
64 Koburger, *Sea Power*, p. 80.
65 Before such operations as the D-Day landings there was very little mine clearance. The casualties that would result from the mines were considered a price that must be paid. If attempts had been made to clear the

mines, then surprise would have been lost. In today's operations, the casualties that would result from mines cannot be contemplated. They have to be cleared, and so surprise will always be lost.

66 Koburger, *Sea Power*, p. 74.
67 Pokrant, *Desert Shield at Sea*, pp. 231–44.
68 Annati, 'Mine Hunting'.
69 Loren, 'Close-in Naval Dominance'.
70 Ibid.
71 Legally, mines should automatically make themselves safe after 6 months, but the settings can be altered.
72 Hewish, 'Wanted'.
73 Wagner et al., *Naval Operational Analysis*, p. 237.
74 Till, *Sea Power*, p. 128.
75 Ibid.
76 Rear Admiral John Ryan, quoted in Truver, 'US Navy in Review', p. 81.
77 J. R. Wilson, 'Undersea Dominance: New Threats, Missions, Shape Future Sub Fleets', *Armed Forces Journal*, Oct. 2003, pp. 62–3. Brown, 'Not Just a Remote Possibility'.
78 Vego, 'Future MCM Systems'.
79 Babcock, 'Just Mines Please!'.
80 Ibid., p. 49.
81 Some of the Tigers' FIACs were used on suicide missions. B. Hoffman, 'A Nasty Business'.
82 Spector, *At War, At Sea*, p. 389.
83 Thalassocrates, 'Anti-ship Missiles'.
84 Where the Harpoon is concerned, as with other anti-ship missiles, there is a drive now to make them more sophisticated and discriminating: Scott, 'Anti-Ship Weapons Updated'.
85 Scott, 'Close-In Firepower Aims at Asymmetric Threats'.
86 Joris Janssen Lok, 'Countering Asymmetrical Threats', *Jane's International Defense Review*, 36 (Nov. 2003), p. 5.
87 Scott, 'Anti-Ship Weapons Updated'.
88 'Pentagon: Cole Not Irreparably Damaged', online at <http://www.edition.cnn.com/2000/US/11/01/uss.cole>, accessed 10 Oct. 2005.
89 In August 2005, the amphibious warfare ship the USS *Kearsage* came under rocket fire from terrorists when alongside the harbour in Aqaba, Jordan: Shafika Mattar, 'Jordan Hunts for Suspects in US Attack', *Washington Post*, 19 Aug. 2005, p. A04. Royal Navy vessels have orders to be surrounded by containers when in certain ports as a defence against truck bombs. Plans have been thwarted to attack some US ships in port in the Philippines and UK ships in Gibraltar. Several Saudi nationals were arrested in 2002 in Morocco for plotting to bomb British ships in Gibraltar harbour. 'Navy on Suicide Bomber Alert', *The Sunday Times*, 19 Oct. 2002, p. 5.

90 See Gourley, 'Naval Force Protection in an Asymmetric World', p. 10.
91 Hoffman, 'Nasty Business'.
92 Gourley, 'Naval Force Protection'.
93 Ibid, p. 14.
94 As one ex-RN officer put it, 'The British taxpayer is forking out immense sums to run warships whose only real use is as venues for diplomatic cocktail parties': Page, 'Wasted Warships', p. 28.
95 Nick Brown, 'Sails of the Unexpected. UK Trains for Asymmetric Threat', *Jane's Navy International*, 110/10 (Dec. 2005), pp. 20–4.
96 See e.g. Ian Storey and You Ji, 'China's Aircraft Carrier Ambitions', online at <www.globalsecurity.org/military/library/report/2004>, accessed 10 Oct. 2005.
97 Kaplan, 'How We Would Fight China'.
98 Truver, 'Mix and Match', p. 24.
99 Page, 'Wasted Warships', pp. 24, 29.
100 Kimura, 'Gunboat Navy'.
101 Gourley, 'Naval Force Protection'. p. 11.

Chapter 6   Asymmetry and Land Power

1 Clausewitz, *On War*, p. 94.
2 Peters, *Fighting for the Future*, p. 94.
3 See Wright, *Tank*.
4 See Murray and Scales, *The Iraq War*.
5 Sun Tzu, *The Art of War*, trans. Samuel Griffith, p. 78.
6 Lt.-Gen. Edwin Smith, 'Challenges of Urban Combat as We Transform', *Army*, 52/9 (Sept. 2002), pp. 14–15.
7 For reasons why these cannot be used in urban battlegrounds, see Hills, *Future War in Cities*, ch. 3.
8 Hirsch, 'On Dinosaurs and Hornets'.
9 Grau, 'Urban Combat'.
10 Hills, *Future War in Cities*, ch. 8.
11 Hammes, *The Sling and the Stone*, p. 231.
12 Alex Renton, 'The Lessons of Somalia', *Evening Standard*, 12 June 2000, p. 61.
13 An RPG-7 round will penetrate 450 mm of amour – not enough to go through the most protected parts of a tank, but enough to cause sufficient damage in certain areas and disable it: Huntiller, 'Asymmetric Warfare'.
14 'US Armour in Combat: The Iraqi Lessons', *Military Technology*, 27/11 (Nov. 2003), pp. 54–61.
15 While such systems as infra-red sensors will detect people in buildings, there is no way of knowing, in an urban situation, if they are fighters or innocent occupants.

16 Peters, *Fighting for the Future*, p. 94.
17 Peters, 'Our Soldiers, their Cities', p. 47.
18 Scott Peters, 'Iraq Prepares for Urban Warfare', *Christian Science Monitor*, 4 Oct. 2002, p. 11.
19 Eric Schmitt and Tom Shanker, 'US Refines Plan for War in Cities', *New York Times*, 22 Oct. 2002, p. 5.
20 See e.g. Beevor, *Stalingrad*.
21 'The Challenge of Urban Warfare', *Military Technology*, 27/8–9 (Aug.–Sept. 2003), pp. 85–90.
22 Hills, 'Can We Fight in Cities?', p. 10.
23 Schmitt and Shanker, 'US Refines Plan'.
24 Peters, 'Our Soldiers, their Cities', p. 45.
25 See Avant, 'Are the Reluctant Warriors Out of Control?'.
26 Peterson, *Me Against My Brother*, p. 61.
27 Bowden, *Black Hawk Down*, p. 342.
28 Helicopters flying too low were engaged by RPG rockets (these are anti-*tank* weapons). They were effective in the anti-air role when the rocket fuse was altered so that it exploded at a given time after being fired, and not when it hit something. When pointed at a helicopter's vulnerable rear rotor assembly, any proximity blast proved very effective. This method was first used in Afghanistan against Soviet helicopters. See Al Ahmad Jalali and Grau, *The Other Side of the Mountain*, p. 29. See also Hunter, 'Making the Tough Tougher', p. 25. The Israelis had long recognized the problems with using helicopters over urban areas. See Hills, *Future War in Cities*, pp. 77–9.
29 Bowden, *Black Hawk Down*, p. 341.
30 Ibid., p. 334.
31 See e.g. Alagiah, *A Passage to Africa*, p. 118. See also Dallaire, *Shake Hands with the Devil*; Dauber, 'Image as Argument'.
32 The actual raid was conducted by 160 US troops. This should only have required at most a major to be in command. However, there were present on the ground one lieutenant-colonel, at least one major, and at least two captains. In helicopters above were two captains and two lieutenant-colonels. Watching on video in Mogadishu were two major-generals. And these were just the Army ranks involved. Air Force officers were also present. The rescue convoy of about 200 men somehow needed a brigadier and a lieutenant-colonel to command it. See Bowden, *Black Hawk Down*.
33 Cordesman, *Lessons of Afghanistan*, p. 104.
34 See e.g. Moore, *We Were Soldiers Once*; Komer, *Bureaucracy at War*.
35 Martin Libicki, 'Adapting Forces', in *Strategic Assessment 1998* (Washington, DC: National Defense University, 1998), p. 232.
36 Pilloni, 'Burning Corpses in the Street', p. 40.

37 One analyst gives the figures for ratios (Russian first): troops, 0.5:1; tanks, 1.6:1; APCs, 2:1; artillery, 1.8:1: Raevsky, 'Russian Military Performance in Chechnya', p. 683.

38 Pilloni 'Burning Corpses', p. 51.

39 Van Dyke, 'Kabul to Grozny', p. 690.

40 Thomas, 'The Caucasus Conflict and Russian Security'.

41 Schmitt and Shanker, 'US Refines Plan'.

42 Maj. Jeffrey Voight et al., *V Corps Battle Damage Assessment (BDA) Outbrief* (Fort Leavenworth, Kan.: US Army Acquisition Corps, 28 Apr. 2003).

43 Kim Sengupta, 'Rumsfeld "Ignored Fallujah Warnings"', *The Times*, 26 Oct. 2004, p. 8. US land forces were conscious of the need not to let any Iraqi city become another Grozny: Fontenot et al., *On Point*, p. 49.

44 Sengupta, 'Rumsfeld "Ignored Fallujah Warnings"'.

45 Col. Randy Gangle, quoted in Julian Borger, 'Violent US Gamble on Election Success', *The Guardian*, 9 Nov. 2004, p. 2.

46 Richard Beeston and Roland Watson, 'Battle for Fallujah', *The Times*, 10 Nov. 2004, p. 9.

47 'Arab World Deplores "Barbaric" Offensive', *The Times*, 10 Nov. 2004, p. 9. US Marine, Gen. Anthony Zinni, was right before the war when he said that the images of destruction of cities 'on Al Jazeera wouldn't help us at all': Schmitt and Shanker, 'US Refines Plan'. The attack 'drove 300,000 Sunnis from their homes and completely devastated the city': Hendrickson and Tucker, 'Revisions in Need of Revising,' p. 21.

48 Robert Worth, 'Challenge in Falluja: Restoring Confidence', *International Herald Tribune*, 2 Dec. 2004, p. 2.

49 Gregory Stanford, 'Powell a Voice of Reason', *Milwaukee Journal Sentinel*, 7 Oct. 2001, <http://www.jsonline.computers/news/editorials>, accessed 10 Mar. 2005.

50 Avant, 'Are the Reluctant Warriors Out of Control?', pp. 78–9.

51 See e.g. Record, 'Ready for What and Modernized against Whom?'.

52 In Bosnia in 1993, e.g., Danish UN Centurion tanks were to move into Bosnia to act as a deterrent to the Serbs. But they could not enter Bosnia from the West because of a number of bridges that could not take their weight. Permission then had to be asked of the Serbs to let these tanks drive into Bosnia through Serb territory. This was granted, the tanks moved in, parked themselves on Tuzla airfield, and were soon shelling Serb positions around Tuzla! See Rod Thornton, 'A Conflict of Views: The Press and the Soldier in Bosnia', *South Slav Journal*, 15/3–4 (Autumn–Winter 1992), p. 16.

53 Duncan, 'Operating in Bosnia'.

54 Jungle can produce the same problems as thick woods.

55 Cordesman, *Lessons of Afghanistan*, p. 73. Also McMichael, *Stumbling Bear*, pp. 101–3; Grau, *The Bear Went Over the Mountains*.

56 See Stewart, *Broken Lives*.

57 Hirsch, 'On Dinosaurs and Hornets'.

58 Cordesman, *Lessons of Afghanistan*, p. 66.

59 Russian General Staff, *The Soviet–Afghan War*, p. 210.

60 Cordesman, *Lessons of Afghanistan*, pp. 66–8.

61 Ibid., p. 105.

62 Ibid., p. 110. One particular consequence of slow decision making was apparent at Tora Bora in Afghanistan in 2002. Coalition forces chased Al Qaeda suspects, including, it was thought, Osama bin Laden, to the cave complex at Tora Bora. British SAS troops who had cornered them were asked to withdraw to allow US troops to finish off the job. Once the SAS had gone, the attack was not pushed through immediately because US forces had a slow operational tempo brought about by the fact that commanders were constantly having to refer back to headquarters in both Tampa and Washington in order to discuss the risks involved and what air cover was needed. The delay allowed the Al Qaeda fighters to escape: Richard Norton-Taylor, 'Scores Killed by SAS in Afghanistan', *The Guardian*, 5 July 2002, p. 12. See also Barton Gellman and Thomas Ricks, 'US Concludes Bin Laden Escaped at Tora Bora Fight; Failure to Send Troops in Pursuit Termed Major Error', *Washington Post*, 17 Apr. 2002, p. 1.

63 Peters, 'Our Soldiers, their Cities'.

64 David, 'Facing a Future without Front Lines'.

65 Quoted in Heyman, *The Armed Forces of the United Kingdom*, p. 178.

66 Ibid.

67 Fontenot et al., *On Point*, p. 390.

68 Schmitt and Shanker, 'US Refines Plan'.

69 MacGregor, 'XVIII Airborne Corps', p. 4.

70 David, 'Facing a Future'.

71 The Israelis have much experience of tailoring armoured vehicles to the needs of the urban battle space: Partridge, 'Deployable versus Survivable'.

72 Appliqué armour consists of extra slabs of armour attached to the sides of any vehicle. Reactive armour (first used by the Israelis in 1982) can also be added as extra slabs. These slabs have the characteristic that they will explode when an anti-tank rocket or missile hits them. The energy of the round is thus pushed away from the side of the vehicle.

73 Huntiller, 'Asymmetric Warfare'.

74 An RPG round works by firing a jet of molten metal through armour. If the round does not explode against the side of a vehicle, the jet loses its penetrative potency.

75 Barzilay, *The British Army in Ulster*, vol. 1, p. 20.

76 Rip and Hasik, *Precision Revolution*, p. 25.
77 Joshua Kucera, 'FCS Ground Vehicles Delayed', *Jane's Defence Weekly*, 28 July 2004, p. 4.
78 'US Armour in Combat'.
79 Kucera, 'FCS Ground Vehicles Delayed'.
80 The back-blast from weapons such as RPGs means that if the firer operates the weapon from inside a building, the blast has nowhere to go and may actually injure the operator.
81 Mounting heavy calibre weapons in turrets on light vehicles (e.g. Humvees) serves little purpose. While guns with a calibre of 0.5 might fire out to long range, RPG threats will appear at short range. Unwieldy weapons like 0.5 Brownings also take too long to bring to bear on targets.
82 'The RPG-7 Syndrome and its Significance', *Military Technology*, 27/11 (Nov. 2003), p. 59.
83 As the US Marine analyst William Lind puts it, 'The British approach of getting helmets off as soon as possible may actually be saving lives': Lind, 'Understanding Fourth Generation Warfare', p. 15.
84 Norimitsu Onishi, 'Dutch Soldiers Find Smiles are a More Effective Protection', *New York Times*, 24 Oct. 2004.
85 Byman and Waxman, *Dynamics of Coercion*, p. 191.
86 MacGregor, 'XVIII Airborne Corps', p. 2.
87 Wilson et al., 'An Alternative Future Force'. UAVs are being used more and more in Iraq, and there is a greater demand for them to carry ordnance: Joshua Kucera, 'UAV Missions in Iraq Set to Rise', *Jane's Defence Weekly*, 42/3 (19 Jan. 2005), p. 11.
88 See e.g. Scales, 'Culture-Centric Warfare'.
89 Fontenot et al., *On Point*, p. 390.
90 Cordesman, *Lessons of Afghanistan*, p. 111.
91 David Buchbinder, 'In Afghanistan, A New Robosoldier Goes to War', *Christian Science Monitor*, 31 Jul. 2002, p. 6.
92 Hammes, *Sling and Stone*, pp. 226–7.
93 Chuck Spinney, Donald Vandergriff and John Sayen, 'Why it is Time to Adapt to Changing Conditions', in Vandergriff (ed.), *Spirit, Blood and Treasure*, ch. 4.
94 Peters, 'Our Soldiers, their Cities', p. 45.
95 Hills, 'Can We Fight in Cities?'.
96 Peters, 'Our Soldiers, their Cities', p. 43.
97 Scales, 'Culture-Centric Warfare'.
98 Lieven, *Chechnya*, p. 114.
99 MacGregor, 'XVIII Airborne Corps'. p. 2.
100 'Reforging the Sword: US Forces for a 21st-century Security Strategy', *Center for Defense Information*, 5 Oct. 2001, p. 72, at <www.cdi.org/mrp>, accessed 10 May 2004.
101 Peters, 'Our Soldiers, their Cities', p. 44.

Chapter 7   The US Military and its Response to the Asymmetric Opponent

1 See Record, 'Ready for What?'; Lambeth, 'Lessons from the Kosovo War'; Cordesman, *The Iraq War; idem, Lessons of Afghanistan.*
2 Buzzanco, *Vietnam and the Transformation of American Life*, p. 82. See also Ambrose, *The Military and American Society*, p. 8; Lewy, *America in Vietnam*, pp. 59, 72.
3 Lewy, *America in Vietnam*, p. 138, and Robert O'Neill, 'US and Allied Leadership and Command in the Korean and Vietnam Wars', in Sheffield (ed.), *Leadership and Command*, p. 187.
4 Colin Powell (with Joseph Persico), *My American Journey* (London: Hutchinson, 1995), p. 434.
5 Adkins, *Urgent Fury*, p. 339.
6 J. Wallace, 'Manoeuvre Theory in Operations Other Than War', in Holden-Reid (ed.), *Military Power*, p. 220. Donnelly et al., *Operation Just Cause*, p. 17.
7 Bildt, *Peace Journey*, p. 175.
8 Robert Patman, 'Beyond the "Mogadishu Line": Some Australian Lessons for Managing Intra-State Conflicts', *Small Wars and Insurgencies*, 12/1 (Spring 2001), p. 68.
9 Bowden, *Black Hawk Down*, p. 343.
10 Sloan, *The Revolution in Military Affairs*, p. 36.
11 Dexter Filkins, 'Flaws in US Air War Left Hundreds of Civilians Dead', *New York Times*, 22 July 2002, p. 1; Jill Treanor, 'US Raids "Killed 800 Afghan Civilians"', *The Guardian*, 22 July 2002, p. 11.
12 According to a survey, US forces in Iraq are killing four times as many innocent civilians as the insurgents are themselves. According to two research groups, Oxford Research Centre and Iraq Body Count, the total of civilian casualties in Iraq from March 2003 to March 2005 was 24,865. Of these (apparently) 9,144 were killed by US forces, 86 by British, 23 by Italians, and 13 by Ukrainians. Anti-occupation forces (insurgents) killed 2,353, and the rest were killed by criminal violence. Quoted in Jonathan Steele and Richard Norton-Taylor, '25,000 Iraqi Civilians Killed Since Invasion', *The Guardian*, 20 July 2005, p. 12.
13 Adm. Arthur Cebrowski, 'Transformation and the Changing Character of War', in *Office of Force Transformation* (Washington, DC: June 2004), p. 4. <www.cia.gov/nic/PDF_GIF_2020>, accessed 10 Oct. 2005.
14 There are many articles in the US Army's main periodical, *Parameters*, that question the Army's ability adequately to conduct the types of operation that are currently in vogue.
15 See Weigley, *The American Way of War.*
16 The debate began with the publication of an article in the *Marine Corps Gazette* which spurred several subsequent articles. See Lind et al., 'The Changing Face of Warfare'. See also Hammes, *Sling and Stone.*

17 Lind et al., 'Changing Face of Warfare', p. 25.
18 Ibid., p. 23.
19 Peters, 'In Praise of Attrition'.
20 Col. Daniel Smith (retd), Marcus Corbin and Christopher Hellman, 'Reforging the Sword: US Forces for a 21st-Century Security Strategy', Center for Defense Information, <www.cdi.org/mrp/reforging-full.pdf>, accessed 10 May 2004, p. 37. See also Weigley, *American Way of War*.
21 See Hammes, 'War Evolves into the Fourth Generation'.
22 Hammes, *Sling and Stone*, p. 2.
23 See William Lind, 'Tactics of the Crescent Moon', <http://www.lewrockwell.com/lind/lind47.html>, accessed 19 Nov. 2004; and Hammes, *Sling and Stone*.
24 Donald Vandergriff, quoted in Vernon Loeb, ' "Up or Out" System Should Go, Army Author Writes in New Book', *Washington Post*, 18 June 2002, p. A17.
25 F. Hoffman, 'Small Wars Revisited'.
26 Scales, 'Culture-Centric Warfare', p. 33.
27 Parsons, 'British Air Control'.
28 Henry Kissinger, 'What Vietnam Teaches us about Pulling out of Iraq', *The Guardian*, 15 Aug. 2005, p. 18.
29 Murray and Scales, *Iraq War*, pp. 154–5.
30 This seeming need to find a leadership and target that as a centre of gravity has been seen as a US weakness by the two Chinese colonels quoted earlier. See Cassman and Lai, 'Football vs Soccer'.
31 Lind, 'Tactics of the Crescent Moon'.
32 Quoted in Buzzanco, *Vietnam*, p. 81.
33 Daryl Press and Benjamin Valentino, 'A Victory, But Little Is Gained', *New York Times*, 17 Nov. 2004, p. 3.
34 There has always been some doubt as to what these terms actually mean. See Douglas MacGregor, 'Transformation and the Illusion of Change', in Vandergriff (ed.), *Spirit, Blood and Treasure*, p. 281. See also Cohen, 'Change and Transformation in Military Affairs'; Scales, 'Culture-Centric Warfare'.
35 Hammes, *Sling and Stone*, p. 225.
36 Scales, 'Culture-Centric Warfare', p. 33.
37 See 'Misdirected Defense Dollars' (editorial), *New York Times*, 16 Jan. 2002, p. 10.
38 Cordesman, 'A Lesson in Transforming Warfare'.
39 Hammes, *Sling and Stone*, p. 261.
40 Sloan, *Revolution in Military Affairs*, p. 54.
41 Hammes, *Sling and Stone*, p. 226.
42 Spinney et al., 'Why it is Time to Adapt to Changing Conditions'. Also Hammes, *Sling and Stone,* pp. 225–7.
43 Gregory Wilcox, 'Manoeuvre Warfare and Attrition', in Vandergriff (ed.), *Spirit, Blood and Treasure*, p. 157.

44 For a general review of this aspect see Avant, *Political Institutions and Military Change.*

45 See e.g. Mahnken and Fitzsimonds, 'Tread-Heads or Technophiles?'; MacGregor, 'XVIII Airborne Corps'.

46 See e.g. Allison, *Essence of Decision.*

47 See e.g. Scott, *Organizations*; Mahnken and Fitzsimonds, 'Tread-Heads or Technophiles?'.

48 Lind, 'Tactics of the Crescent Moon'.

49 Brownlee and Schoomaker, 'Serving a Nation at War'.

50 Thom Shanker, 'Rumsfeld's Search for a Way to Fight a New Type of Foe', *New York Times*, 4 Sept. 2002, p. 4. See also Rumsfeld, 'Transforming the Military'.

51 Vernon Loeb, 'Rumsfeld Mulls Missile to Replace Crusader', *Washington Post*, 23 June 2002, p. A06.

52 Bryan Bender, interview with Gen. Denis Reimer, *Jane's Defence Weekly*, 27/7 (19 Feb. 1997); Sullivan and Twomey, 'The Challenges of Peace'. On Shinseki see Ben Greenman, 'Battle Pieces', *New Yorker*, 1 July 2002.

53 Cohen, 'History and the Hyperpower', p. 53.

54 See Stephen Biddle, 'Toppling Saddam; Iraq and American Military Transformation', Strategic Studies Institute Report for Department of the Army, p. 39, online at <www.fas.org/mcn/eprint/biddle>, accessed 10 Oct. 2005. Also 'A Talk with the Chief', interview with Gen. Gordon Sullivan, *Army*, June 1995, p. 16.

55 Cohen, 'Change and Transformation', p. 401.

56 Esther Schrader, 'General Draws Fire for Saying "It's Fun to Shoot" the Enemy', *Los Angeles Times*, 4 Feb. 2005, p. 2.

57 Scales, 'Culture-Centric Warfare', p. 33.

58 Adams, 'Future Warfare and the Decline of Human Decisionmaking'.

59 US forces made many mistakes in Afghanistan with their use of airpower against what were supposed to be Al Qaeda or Taliban villages. This was because the information they were given to this effect was from local warlords giving false intelligence in order to see rival villages punished. US actions in this regard created a legacy of bitterness that reached as far as the president, Mohammed Karzai. In Afghanistan in general, 'the most common factor in the civilian deaths was the American reliance on incomplete information to decide on targets': Filkins, 'Flaws in US Air War', p. 1.

60 See Mao Tse Tung, *On Guerrilla Warfare*, trans. Samuel Griffiths (London: Cassell, 1962).

61 Kitson, *Bunch of Five,* p. 282.

62 Cordesman, 'Lesson'.

63 Robert Killebrew, 'Land Power and Future American Defense Policy', *The Strategic Review*, 25/3 (Summer 1997), p. 41.

64 Smith et al., 'Reforging the Sword', p. 72.

65 Foot patrolling is not an inherently dangerous enterprise if done correctly. Mutually supporting foot patrols with vehicle and helicopter back-up prevent the possibility of ambush. Indeed, in many ways foot patrolling is safer than vehicle patrols, in that troops can go anywhere; they are not tied to obvious routes – i.e. roads – and therefore do not really set patterns. For vehicles it is different; they have to use roads and will employ obvious routes. IEDs can then be planted in advance to catch them. Moreover, any IED used against a vehicle promises to kill several personnel. Any IED used against a foot patrol will kill only an individual, since troops will always be spread out (each man 25–50 yards apart, depending on the terrain, is a norm).

66 Onishi, 'Dutch Soldiers Find Smiles are a More Effective Protection'.

67 Hammes, *Sling and Stone*, p. 233.

68 See Maj. Robert Leonhard, 'The Death of Mission Tactics', *Army*, 44/7 (July 1994), pp. 15–18; John Nelson, ' "Auftragstaktik": A Case for Decentralized Battle', *Parameters*, 17/3 (Sept. 1987), pp. 21–34; Capt. Robert Bateman, 'Force XXI and the Death of "Auftragstaktik"', *Armor*, 105/1 (Jan.–Feb. 1996), pp. 13–15; Maj. Donald Vandergriff, 'Creating the Officer Corps of the Future to Execute Force XXI Blitzkrieg', *Armor*, 106/2 (Mar.–Apr. 1997), pp. 25–31; David Keithly and Stephen Ferris, 'Auftragstaktik, or Directive Control, in Joint and Combined Operations', *Parameters*, 19/3 (Autumn 1999), pp. 118–33.

69 Scott, *Organizations*.

70 Van Crefeld, *The Transformation of War*, p. 13.

71 Correlli Barnett, 'The Education of Military Elites', in Rupert Wilkinson (ed.), *Governing Elites: Studies in Training and Selection* (New York: Oxford University Press, 1969), p. 189.

72 Keegan, *The Iraq War*, p. 132. Keegan was contrasting such officers with the US Army's Lt.-Gen. David McKiernan, who was decidedly *not* one of them.

73 Col. Tim Collins, 'Watch Out, Black Watch', *The Sunday Times*, 24 Oct. 2004, News Review, p. 3.

74 Lt.-Col. Douglas Scalard, 'People of Whom We Know Nothing: When Doctrine Isn't Enough', *Military Review*, 77/4 (July–Aug. 1997), pp.4–8.

75 Ancker and Burke, 'Doctrine for Asymmetric Warfare', p. 22.

76 See Brownlee and Schoomaker, 'Serving a Nation at War', p. 20. See also Hooker, 'The Mythology Surrounding Manoeuvre Warfare'; Johnston, 'Doctrine Is Not Enough'.

77 Smith et al., 'Reforging the Sword', pp. 10, 11, 72.

78 Scott, *Organizations*, p. 311.

79 Nicholas Rengger, 'Culture, Society and Order in World Politics', in John Baylis and Nicholas Rengger (eds), *Dilemmas in World Politics* (Oxford: Oxford University Press, 1992), p. 85.

80 Ken Booth, 'US Conceptions of Soviet Threat: Prudence and Paranoia', in Carl Jacobsen (ed.), *Strategic Power: USA/USSR* (London: St Martin's Press, 1990), p. 58.

81 There is a 'revisionist' view now as to whether the conduct of the counter-insurgency campaign in the Philippines was actually a great success. See e.g. Deady, 'Lessons from a Successful Counterinsurgency'. Cassidy in the same vein sees it as a 'relatively bloodless' campaign: Cassidy, 'Back to the Street without Joy', p. 80. Other works see the campaign in a less benign light: e.g. Boot, *The Savage Wars of Peace*, ch. 5. Linn saw it as 'very harsh warfare indeed': Linn, *The Philippine War, 1899–1902*, p. 328. Feuer has it that '1 million Filipinos died while resisting the Americans': A. B. Feuer, *America at War: The Philippines, 1898–1913* (Westport, Conn.: Praeger, 2002).

82 Avant, *Political Institutions*, p. 34.

83 See Ambrose, *Duty, Honor, Country*; Huntington, *The Soldier and the State*; van Aller, *The Culture of Defense*.

84 William Pfaff, 'Needed, a New Military Mind-Set for the World's Kosovo's', *International Herald Tribune*, 8 Mar. 2001, p. 15.

85 See Murphey, 'American Philosophy', in Luther Luedtke (ed.), *Making America*.

86 Gorer, *The American People*, p. 246.

87 See Madsen, *American Exceptionalism*.

88 Lawrence, *Modernity and War*, p. 164.

89 See e.g. Lipset, *American Exceptionalism*.

90 Deborah Millikan, 'US Foreign Policy in the Post-Cold War World: Options and Constraints', in Petrie (ed.), *Essays on Strategy*, p. 78.

91 See Fischer, *Albion's Seed*.

92 Buzan and Segal, 'The Rise of "Lite" Powers', p. 5.

93 Van Aller, *Culture of Defense*, p. 24. See also Downey and Metz, 'The American Political Culture and Strategic Planning', p. 36.

94 Huntington, *Soldier and State*, p. 151.

95 William Kincade, 'American National Style and Strategic Culture', in Jacobsen (ed.), *Strategic Power*, p. 13.

96 Daniel Snowman, *Kissing Cousins: An Interpretation of British and American Culture, 1945–1975* (London: Temple Smith, 1977), p. 142.

97 Ken Booth, 'US Perceptions of Soviet Threat: Prudence and Paranoia', in Jacobsen (ed.), *Strategic Power*, p. 64.

98 Hoffman, *Gulliver's Troubles*, p. 47.

99 Richard Payne, *The Clash with Distant Cultures: Values, Interests, and Force in American Foreign Policy* (Albany, NY: SUNY Press, 1995), p. 85.

100 Ibid., p. 62.

101 Waltz, *Foreign Policy and Democratic Politics*, p. 71.

102 Payne, *Clash with Distant Cultures*, pp. xv, 34.

103 Ken Booth, 'American Strategy: The Myth Revisited', in Booth and Wright (eds), *American Thinking about Peace and War*, p. 29.

104 Fawcett and Thomas, *America, Americans*, p. 7.
105 Booth, 'American Strategy', p. 9.
106 Wilkinson, *American Tough*, p. 17.
107 Freedman, *Evolution of Nuclear Strategy*, p. 48.
108 Weigley, *American Way of War*, p. xxii.
109 Vertzberger, *The World in their Minds*, p. 260.
110 Joseph Fitchett, 'British Make Impression on US Tactics', *International Herald Tribune*, 9 Apr. 2003, p. 3.
111 Grange, 'Asymmetric Warfare', p. 6.
112 When an organization is faced with new situations that threaten its 'equilibrium', it has to come to a level of understanding with the consequences of such scenarios. 'Understanding', as March and Olsen relate, 'involves both learning new knowledge and discarding obsolete and misleading knowledge. The discarding activity – unlearning – is as important a part of understanding as is adding new knowledge': March and Olsen, *Ambiguity and Choice in Organisations*, p. 54.
113 Komer, *Bureaucracy at War*, p. 73.
114 Daalder and Lindsay, *America Unbound*, p. 80.
115 John Hooper, 'Berlusconi to Pull out Troops from Iraq', *The Guardian*, 16 Mar. 2005, p. 8. The head of the British Army, Gen. Mike Jackson, saw that in Iraq and elsewhere his soldiers 'must be able to fight with the Americans. That does not mean we must be able to fight as the Americans': Richard Norton-Taylor, 'Serious Implications as Chessboard Changes', *The Guardian*, 19 Oct. 2004, p. 13.
116 William Lind, 'The Sling and the Stone', <http://www.lewrockwell.com/limd/lind45.html>, accessed 7 Nov. 2004.
117 Meigs, 'Unorthodox Thoughts about Asymmetric Warfare'.
118 Andrew Koch, 'Marines Opt for Smaller Units to Get Bigger Results', *Jane's Defence Weekly*, 41/18 (5 May 2004), p. 8.

Chapter 8 Conclusion

1 Schrader, 'General Draws Fire', p. 1.
2 Fisk, 'With Runners and Whispers'.
3 Lord Acton (1834–1902), in Anthony Jay (ed.), *Oxford Dictionary of Political Quotations* (Oxford: Oxford University Press, 1996), p. 1.
4 Article on the Internet by Chester Richards in *Defense and the National Interest*, quoted by Gould and Spinney, 'Fourth-Generation Warfare', p. 4.
5 Cordesman, *Lessons of Afghanistan*, p. 51.

SELECT BIBLIOGRAPHY

Books

Adkins, Mark, *Urgent Fury: The Battle for Grenada* (London: Leo Cooper, 1989).

Alagiah, George, *A Passage to Africa* (London: Little, Brown, 2001).

Al Ahmad Jalali, and Lester Grau, *The Other Side of the Mountain: Mujahideen Tactics in the Soviet–Afghan War* (Quantico, Va.: USMC, 1995).

Alexander, Yonah, and Milton Hoenig, *Superterrorism: Biological, Chemical and Nuclear* (Ardsley, NY: Transnational, 2001).

Ali, Tariq, *The Clash of Fundamentalisms: Crusades, Jihad and Modernity* (London: Verso, 2002).

Allison, Graham, *Essence of Decision: Explaining the Cuban Missile Crisis* (Boston: Little, Brown, 1971).

Ambrose, Stephen, *The Military and American Society* (New York: Free Press, 1972).

Ambrose, Stephen, *Duty, Honor, Country: A History of West Point* (Baltimore: Johns Hopkins University Press, 1999).

Arquilla, John, and David Ronfeldt (eds), *In Athena's Camp: Preparing for Conflict in the Information Age* (Santa Monica, Calif.: RAND, 1997).

Avant, Deborah, *Political Institutions and Military Change: Lessons from Peripheral Wars* (Ithaca, NY: Cornell University Press, 1994).

Baer, George, *The US Navy, 1890–1990* (Stanford, Calif.: Stanford University Press, 1994).

Ballantyne, Iain, *Strike from the Sea* (Barnsley: Pen and Sword, 2004).

Barnett, Roger, *Asymmetric Warfare: Today's Challenges to US Military Power* (Washington, DC: Brassey's, 2002).

Barzilay, David, *The British Army in Ulster*, Vol. 1 (Belfast: Century, 1973).

Beevor, Anthony, *Stalingrad* (London: Penguin, 1999).

Betts, Richard, *Surprise Attack* (Washington, DC: Brookings, 1982).

Biddle, Stephen, *Afghanistan and the Future of Warfare: Implications for Army and Defense Policy* (Carlisle, Pa.: US Army War College Strategic Studies Institute, 2002).

Bildt, Carl, *Peace Journey: The Struggle for Peace in Bosnia* (London: Weidenfeld & Nicolson, 1998).

Binnendijk, Hans (ed.), *Strategic Assessment 1998: Engaging Power for Peace* (Washington, DC: National Defense University Press, 1998).

Blood, Jake, *The Tet Offensive: Intelligence and the Public Perception of War* (London: Routledge, 2005).

Bodansky, Yossef, *Bin Laden: The Man Who Declared War on America* (Roseville, Calif.: Prima, 2001).

Boot, Max, *The Savage Wars of Peace: Small Wars and the Rise of American Power* (New York: Basic Books, 2002).

Booth, Kenneth, and Moorhead Wright (eds), *American Thinking about Peace and War* (New York: Harper and Row, 1978).

Booth, Ken, and Tim Dunne (eds), *Worlds in Collision: Terror and the Future of Global Order* (Basingstoke: Palgrave Macmillan, 2002).

Bowden, Mark, *Black Hawk Down* (New York: Atlantic Monthly Press, 1999).

Browne, J., and M. Thurbon, *Electronic Warfare* (London: Brassey's, 1998).

Budiansky, Stephen, *Air Power* (London: Penguin, 2003).

Burke, Jason, *Al Qaeda: The True Story of Radical Islam* (London: Penguin, 2004).

Buzzanco, Robert, *Vietnam and the Transformation of American Life* (Malden, Mass.: Blackwell, 1999).

Byman, Daniel, and Matthew Waxman, *The Dynamics of Coercion: American Foreign Policy and the Limits of Military Might* (New York: Cambridge University Press, 2002).

Clark, Wesley, *Waging Modern War* (Oxford: Public Affairs, 2003).

Clausewitz, Carl von, *On War*, (ed. and trans. Michael Howard and Peter Paret) (Princeton: Princeton University Press, 1976).

Cole, Leonard, *The Anthrax Letters: A Medical Detective Story* (Washington, DC: Joseph Henny, 2003).

Combs, Cindy, *Terrorism in the Twenty-First Century* (Upper Saddle River, NJ: Prentice-Hall, 2003).

Cordesman, Anthony, *The Lessons and Non-Lessons of the Air and Missile Campaign in Kosovo* (Westport, Conn.: Praeger, 2001).

Cordesman, Anthony, *The Lessons of Afghanistan* (Washington, DC: CSIS Press, 2002).

Cordesman, Anthony, *The Iraq War: Strategy, Tactics, and Military Lessons* (Washington, DC: CSIS, 2003).

Cordesman, Anthony, *The Challenge of Biological Terrorism* (Washington, DC: CSIS, 2005).

Cordesman, Anthony, and Abraham Wagner, *The Lessons of Modern War*, Vol. 4 (Boulder, Colo.: Westview Press, 1996).

Cornish, Paul (ed.), *The Conflict in Iraq, 2003* (London: Palgrave, 2004).

Cox, Sebastian, and Peter Gray, *Air Power History* (London: Frank Cass, 2002).

Croddy, Eric, and James Wirtz (eds), *Weapons of Mass Destruction*, Vol. 1 (Santa Barbara, Calif.: ABC-Clio, 2005).

Curry, Anne (ed.), *Agincourt, 1415* (Stroud: Tempus, 2000).

Daalder, Ivo, and James Lindsay, *America Unbound: The Bush Revolution in Foreign Policy* (Washington, DC: Brookings Institution Press, 2003).

Daalder, Ivo, and Michael O'Hanlon, *Winning Ugly* (Washington, DC: Brookings Institution, 2000).

Dallaire, Lt.-Gen. Roméo, *Shake Hands with the Devil: The Failure of Humanity in Rwanda* (London: Arrow, 2004).

Delbruck, Hans, *The Barbarian Invasions* (Lincoln, Nebr.: University of Nebraska Press, 1990).

Denning, Dorothy, *Information Warfare and Security* (Upper Saddle River, NJ: Pearson, 1999).

Dewar, Michael, *The Art of Deception in Warfare* (Newton Abbot: Sterling Publishers, 1989).

Donnelly, Thomas, Margaret Roth and Caleb Baker, *Operation Just Cause: The Storming of Panama* (New York: Lexington Books, 1991).

Doubler, Michael, *Closing with the Enemy: How GIs Fought the War in Europe, 1944–45* (Lawrence, Kan.: University of Kansas Press, 1994).

Duncan, Col. Alistair,'Operating in Bosnia', *Defence and International Security* (June 1994).

Dunnigan, James, *The Next War Zone: Confronting the Global Threat of Cyberterrorism* (New York: Citadel Press, 2002).

Elshtain, Jean Bethke, *Just War Against Terror* (Cambridge, Mass.: Basic Books, 2003).

Erbschloe, Michael, *Information Warfare: How to Survive Cyber Attacks* (Berkeley: McGraw-Hill, 2001).

Farago, Ladislas, *The Game of the Foxes* (London: Hodder & Stoughton, 1971).

Fawcett, Edmund, and Tony Thomas, *America, Americans* (London: Collins, 1983).

Feigenbaum, Evan, *China's Techno-Warriors: National Security and Strategic Competition from the Nuclear Age to the Information Age* (Stanford, Calif.: Stanford University Press, 2003).

Feuer, A. B., *America at War: The Philippines, 1898–1913* (Westport, Conn.: Praeger, 2002).

Fischer, David, *Albion's Seed: Four British Folkways in America* (New York: Oxford University Press, 1989).

Fisk, Robert, *The Great War for Civilization: The Conquest of the Middle East* (London: Fourth Estate, 2005).

Fontenot, Gregory, E. J. Degan and David Tohn, *On Point: The US Army in Operation Iraqi Freedom* (Fort Leavenworth, Kan.: Combat Studies Institute Press, 2004).

Freedman, Lawrence, *The Evolution of Nuclear Strategy* (London: Macmillan, 1981).

Freedman, Lawrence, and Efraim Karsh, *The Gulf Conflict, 1990/91* (London: Faber, 1993).

Friedman, Norman, *Desert Victory* (Annapolis, Md.: Naval Institute Press, 1991).

Glasstone, Samuel, and Philip Dolan, *The Effects of Nuclear Weapons* (Washington, DC: Department of Defense, 1977).

Glosson, Gen. Buster, *War with Iraq: Critical Lessons* (Charlotte, NC: Glosson Family Foundation, 2003).

Goldman, Emily (ed.), *National Security in the Information Age* (London: Taylor and Francis, 2004).

Gooch, John, and Amos Perlmutter (eds), *Military Deception and Strategic Surprise* (London: Frank Cass, 1982).

Gordon, Michael, and Bernard Trainor, *The Generals' War* (Boston: Little, Brown and Co., 1995).

Gorer, Geoffrey, *The American People: A Study in National Character* (New York: Norton, 1948).

Grau, Lester, *The Bear Went Over the Mountains: Soviet Tactics and Tactical Lessons Learned during their War in Afghanistan* (Washington, DC: National Defense University, 1996).

Gray, Christine, *International Law and the Use of Armed Force* (Oxford: Oxford University Press, 2004).

Griffin, Stuart, *Joint Operations: A Short History* (Shrivenham: JDCC, 2005).

Gurr, Nadine, and Benjamin Cole, *The New Face of Terrorism: Threats from Weapons of Mass Destruction* (New York: IB Tauris, 2000).

Haldane, Lt.-Gen. Sir Aylmer, *The Insurrection in Mesopotamia, 1920* (London: William Blackwood & Sons, 1922).

Hallion, Richard (ed.), *Airpower Confronts an Unstable World* (London: Brassey's, 1997).

Hamill, Desmond, *Pig in the Middle: The British Army in Northern Ireland, 1969–1984* (London: Methuen, 1985).

Hammes, Col. Thomas, *The Sling and the Stone* (St Paul, Minn.: Zenith Books, 2004).

Hasken, Scott, *A Historical Look at Close Air Support* (Fort Leavenworth, Kan.: Army Command and Staff College, 2003).

Hastings, Max, *Overlord: D-Day and the Battle for Normandy* (London: Pan, 1984).

Heyman, Charles, *The Armed Forces of the United Kingdom, 2004–05* (Barnsley: Pen and Sword, 2003).

Hill, Richard, *War at Sea in the Ironclad Age* (London: Cassell, 2000).

Hills, Alice, *Future War in Cities* (London: Frank Cass, 2004).

Hiro, Dilip, *From Desert Shield to Desert Storm* (London: HarperCollins, 1992).

Hiro, Dilip, *War Without End: The Rise of Islamist Terrorism and Global Response* (London: Routledge, 2002).

Hirst, Paul, *War and Power in the 21ˢᵗ Century* (Cambridge: Polity, 2001).

Hoffman, Bruce, '*Holy Terror': The Implications of Terrorism Motivated by a Religious Imperative* (Santa Monica, Calif.: RAND, 1993).

Hoffman, Bruce, *Inside Terrorism* (New York: Columbia University Press, 1998).

Hoffman, Stanley, *Gulliver's Troubles: The Setting of American Foreign Policy* (New York: McGraw-Hill, 1968).

Holden-Reid, Brian (ed.), *Military Power: Land Warfare in Theory and Practice* (London: Frank Cass, 1997).

Holt, Thaddeus, *The Deceivers: Allied Military Deception in the Second World War* (London: Weidenfeld & Nicolson, 2004).

Howard, Michael, George Andreopoulos and Mark Shulman (eds), *The Laws of War: Constraints on Warfare in the Western World* (New Haven, Conn.: Yale University Press, 1994).

Huntington, Samuel, *The Soldier and the State: The Theory and Politics of Civil–Military Relations* (New York: Vintage Books, 1964).

Inbar, Efraim, *Democracies and Small Wars* (London: Frank Cass, 2003).

Jackson, Richard, *Writing the War on Terrorism* (Manchester: Manchester University Press, 2005).

Jenkins, Brian, *Will Terrorists Go Nuclear?* (Santa Monica, Calif.: RAND, 1975).

Jones, A., G. Kovacich, and P. Luzwick, *Global Information Warfare* (Boca Raton, Fla.: Auerbach, 2002).

Judah, Tim, *Kosovo: War and Revenge* (New Haven, Conn.: Yale University Press, 2000).

Keaney, Thomas, and Eliot Cohen, *Gulf War Air Power Survey Summary Report* (Washington, DC: USGPO, 1993).

Keegan, John, *The Iraq War* (London: Hutchinson, 2003).

Kennedy-Pipe, Caroline, *The Origins of the Present Troubles in Northern Ireland* (London: Longman, 1997).

Kitfield, James, *Prodigal Soldiers: How the Generation of Officers Born of Vietnam Revolutionized the American Style of Warfare* (New York: Simon & Schuster, 1995).

Kitson, Frank, *Bunch of Five* (London: Faber & Faber, 1977).

Koburger, Charles, *Sea Power in the Twenty-First Century* (Westport, Conn.: Praeger, 1997).

Komer, Robert, *Bureaucracy at War: US Performance in the Vietnam Conflict* (Boulder, Colo.: Westview Press, 1986).

Laqueur, Walter, *The New Terrorism: Fanaticism and the Arms of Mass Destruction* (New York: Continuum, 1999).

Laqueur, Walter, *No End to War: Terrorism in the Twenty-First Century* (New York: Continuum, 2003).

Larabee, Stephen, et al., *The Changing Global Security Environment: New Opportunities and Challenges* (Santa Monica, Calif.: RAND, 2003).

Larson, Eric, and Bogdan Savych, *American Public Support for US Military Operations from Mogadishu to Baghdad* (Santa Monica, Calif.: RAND, 2005).

Latimer, Jon, *Deception in Warfare* (London: John Murray, 2003).

Lawrence, Philip, *Modernity and War: The Greed of Absolute Violence* (London: Macmillan, 1997).

Legro, Jeffrey, *Cooperation under Fire: Anglo-German Restraint during World War II* (Ithaca, NY: Cornell University Press, 1995).

Lesser, Ian, et al., *Countering the New Terrorism* (Santa Monica, Calif.: RAND, 1999).

Lewy, Guenter, *America in Vietnam* (New York: Oxford University Press, 1978).

Liang, Col. Qiao, and Col. Wang Xiangsui, *Unrestricted Warfare* (New York: Pan American Publishing Co., 2002).

Libicki, Martin, *What is Information Warfare?* (Washington, DC: National Defense University, 1995).

Lieven, Anatol, *Chechnya: Tombstone of Russian Power* (New Haven, Conn.: Yale University Press, 1998).

Lifton, Robert Jay, *Destroying the World in Order to Save It: Aum Shinrikyo, Apocalyptic Violence, and the New Global Terrorism* (New York: Metropolitan Books, 1999).

Linebarger, Paul, *Psychological Warfare* (Washington, DC: Combat Forces Press, 1954).

Linn, Brian McAllister, *The Philippine War, 1899–1902* (Lawrence, Kan.: University of Kansas Press, 2000).

Lipset, Seymour, *American Exceptionalism: A Double-Edged Sword* (New York: Norton, 1989).

Luedtke, Luther (ed.), *Making America: The Society and Culture of the United States* (Chapel Hill, NC: University of North Carolina Press, 1992).

Lumpe, Lora (ed.), *Running Guns: The Global Black Market in Small Arms* (London: Zed Books, 2000).

Lutz, James, and Brenda Lutz, *Global Terrorism?* (London: Routledge, 2003).

Machiavelli, Nicolo, *The Prince* (London: Penguin, 1961).

Mackinlay, John, *Globalization and Insurgency* (Oxford: Oxford University Press, 2002).

Madsen, Deborah, *American Exceptionalism* (Edinburgh: Edinburgh University Press, 1999).

Mangold, Tom, and Jeff Goldberg, *Plague Wars* (London: Pan, 2000).

Manji, Irshad, *The Trouble with Islam: A Wake-Up Call for Honesty and Change* (Toronto: Random Honse, 2003).

March, James, and Johan Olsen, *Ambiguity and Choice in Organisations* (Bergen: Aniversiteforslager, 1976).

Matthews, Lloyd (ed.), *Challenging the US Symmetrically and Asymmetrically: Can America be Defeated?* (Fort Leavenworth, Kan.: US Army War College, Strategic Studies Institute, 1998).

McKenzie, Kenneth, *The Revenge of the Melians: Asymmetric Threats and the Next QDR* (Washington, DC: National Defense University, 2000).

McMaster, H. R., *Dereliction of Duty* (New York: HarperCollins, 1997).

McMichael, Scott, *Stumbling Bear: Soviet Military Performance in Afghanistan* (London: Brassey's, 1991).

Metz, Steven, and Douglas Johnson, *Asymmetry and US Military Strategy* (Carlisle, Pa.: US Army Strategic Studies Institute, 2001).

Miles, Hugh, *Al Jazeera: The Inside Story of the Arab News Channel that Challenges the West* (New York: Grove, 2005).

Mockaitis, Thomas, *British Counter-Insurgency, 1919–1960* (London: Macmillan, 1990).

Moloney, Ed, *A Secret History of the IRA* (London: Penguin, 2002).

Moore, Lt.-Gen. Hal, *We Were Soldiers Once . . . and Young* (New York: HarperCollins, 1993).

Moser Melia, Tamara, *'Damn the Torpedoes': A Short History of US Naval Mine Countermeasures, 1777–1991* (Washington, DC: Naval Historical Center, 1991).

Murray, Williamson, and Robert Scales, *The Iraq War: A Military History* (Cambridge, Mass.: Harvard University Press, 2003).

Nanda, Ved (ed.), *Law in the War on International Terrorism* (Ardsley, NY: Transnational, 2005).

Naylor, Sean, *Not a Good Day to Die: The Untold Story of Operation Anaconda* (New York: Penguin, 2005).

O'Day, Alan (ed.), *Cyberterrorism* (Aldershot: Ashgate, 2004).

O'Halloran, Michael, *A Kill is a Kill: Asymmetrically Attacking United States Airpower* (Maxwell, Ala.: Air University Press, 2000).

Olsen, John Andreas (ed.), *Asymmetric Warfare* (Oslo: Royal Norwegian Air Force Academy, 2002).

O'Meara, Patrick, Howard Mehlinger, and Matthew Krain (eds), *Globalization and the Challenges of a New Century* (Bloomington, Ind.: Indiana University Press, 2000).

Osterholm, Michael, and John Schwartz, *Living Terror* (New York: Delacorte, 2000).

Pack, S. W. C., *Sea Power in the Mediterranean* (London: Arthur Baker, 1971).

Page, Lewis, *Lions, Donkeys and Dinosaurs: Waste and Blundering in the Armed Forces* (London: Heinemann, 2006).

Payne, Richard, *The Clash with Distant Cultures: Values, Interests, and Force in American Foreign Policy* (Albany, NY: SUNY Press, 1995).

Peters, Ralph, *Fighting for the Future: Will America Triumph?* (Mechanicsburg, Pa.: Stackpole Books, 1999).

Peterson, Scott, *Me Against My Brother: At War in Somalia, Sudan and Rwanda* (New York: Routledge, 2000).

Petrie, J. (ed.), *Essays on Strategy* (Washington, DC: National Defense University Press, 1994).

Pokrant, Marvin, *Desert Shield at Sea: What the Navy Really Did* (London: Greenwood Press, 1999).

Radvanyi, Janos (ed.), *Psychological Operations and Political Warfare in Long-Term Strategic Planning* (New York: Praeger, 1990).

Read, Jan, *War in the Peninsular* (London: Faber & Faber, 1977).

Richardson, Nick, *No Escape Zone* (London: Little, Brown and Co., 2000).

Rip, Michael, and James Hasik, *The Precision Revolution: GPS and the Future of Aerial Warfare* (Annapolis, Md.: Naval Institute Press, 2002).

Rogers, Paul, *Losing Control: Global Security in the Twenty-First Century* (London: Pluto, 2002).

Rubin, Barry, and Judith Colp Rubin, *Anti-American Terrorism and the Middle East: Understanding the Violence* (New York: Oxford University Press, 2002).

Russian General Staff, *The Soviet–Afghan War*, trans. and ed. Lester Grau and Michael Gress (Lawrence, Kan.: University of Kansas Press, 2002).

Schanzer, Jonathan, *Al Qaeda's Armies: Middle East Affiliate Groups and the Next Generation of Terror* (Washington, DC: SPI, 2005).

Schneider, Barry, and Jim Davis (eds), *The War Next Time: Countering Rogue States and Terrorists Armed with Chemical and Biological Weapons* (Maxwell, Ala.: USAF Counterproliferation Center, 2004).

Schultz, Richard, and Robert Pfaltzgraff (eds), *The Role of Naval Forces in 21st Century Operations* (Washington, DC: Brassey's, 2002).

Schwartz, Stephen, *The Two Faces of Islam: Sandi Fundamentalism and its Role in Terrorism* (New York: Anchor, 2003).

Scott, W. Richard, *Organizations: Rational, Natural and Open Systems* (Englewood Cliffs, NJ: Prentice-Hall, 1991).

Shafritz, Jay, et al., *The Facts on File Dictionary of Military Science* (New York: Facts on File, 1989).

Sheffield, Gary (ed.), *Leadership and Command* (London: Brassey's, 1997).

Shepherd, Arthur, *Sea Power in Ancient History* (Boston: Little, Brown and Co., 1924).

Sloan, Elinor, *The Revolution in Military Affairs* (Montreal: McGill–Queen's University Press, 2002).

Snowman, Daniel, *Kissing Cousins: An Interpretation of British and American Culture, 1945–1975* (London: Temple Smith, 1977).

Sookhdeo, Patrick, *Understanding Islamic Terrorism* (Pewsey: Isaac, 2004).

Spector, Ronald, *At War, At Sea: Naval Warfare in the Twentieth Century* (London: Allen Lane, 2001).

Stewart, Bob, *Broken Lives: A Personal View of the Bosnia Conflict* (London: HarperCollins, 1993).

Sun Tzu, *The Art of War*, trans. Samuel Griffith (New York: Oxford University Press, 1963).

Sun Tzu, *The Art of War*, trans. Thomas Cleary (Boston: Shambhala, 2000).

Taghi Karoubi, Mohammed, *Just or Unjust War?* (Burlington, Vt.: Ashgate, 2004).

Taheri, Amer, *Holy Terror – The Inside Story of Islamic Terrorism* (London: Century-Hutchinson, 1997).

Till, Geoffrey, *Seapower: A Guide for the Twenty-First Century* (London: Frank Cass, 2004).

Townend, Adam, *Guarding Europe*, Centre for European Reform Working Paper (May 2003).

Tucker, Jonathan (ed.), *Toxic Terror: Assessing Terrorist Use of Chemical and Biological Weapons* (Cambridge, Mass.: MIT Press, 2000).

Ullman, R. H. (ed.), *The World and Yugoslavia's Wars* (New York: The Council on Foreign Relations, 1991).

van Aller, Christopher, *The Culture of Defense* (Lanham, Md.: University of Lexington Press, 2001).

van Crefeld, Martin, *The Transformation of War* (New York: Free Press, 1991).

Vandergriff, Donald (ed.), *Spirit, Blood and Treasure: The American Cost of Battle in the 21st Century* (Novato, Calif.: Presidio, 2001).

Verton, Dan, *Black Ice: The Invisible Threat of Cyber-Terrorism* (Emeryville, Calif.: McGraw-Hill, 2003).

Vertzberger, Yacov, *The World in their Minds* (Stanford, Calif.: Stanford University Press, 1990).

Wagner, Daniel, Charles Mylander, and Thomas Sanders (eds), *Naval Operational Analysis* (Annapolis, Md.: Naval Institute Press, 1999).

Walden, David, *The Short Victorious War: The Russo–Japanese Conflict of 1904–05* (London: Hutchinson, 1973).

Wall, Andru (ed.), *Legal and Ethical Implications of NATO's Kosovo Campaign* (Newport, RI: Naval War College, 2002).

Waltz, Kenneth, *Foreign Policy and Democratic Politics: The American and British Experience* (London: Longmans, 1968).

Walzer, Michael, *Just and Unjust Wars* (London: Basic Books, 1992).

Wardlaw, Grant, *Political Terrorism* (Cambridge: Cambridge University Press, 1995).

Weigley, Russell, *The American Way of War: A History of US Strategy and Policy* (New York: Macmillan, 1973).

Wervell, Kenneth, *Chasing the Silver Bullet: US Air Force Weapons Development from Vietnam to Desert Storm* (Washington, DC: Smithsonian Books, 2003).

White, Jonathan, *Terrorism: An Introduction* (Belmont, Calif.: Wadsworth, 2002).

Wilkinson, Rupert, *American Tough* (Westport, Conn.: Greenwood Press, 1984).

Wippman, David, and Matthew Evangelista (eds), *New Wars, New Laws?: Applying the Laws of War in the 21st Century* (Ardsley, NY: Transnational, 2005).

Wright, Patrick, *Tank* (London: Faber & Faber, 2000).

Yenne, Bill, *Attack of the Drones* (St Paul, Minn.: Zenith Press, 2004).

Zayani, Mohammed (ed.), *The Al Jazeera Phenomenon: Critical Perspectives on New Arab Media* (London: Pluto Press, 2005).

Journal Articles

Adams, Thomas, 'Future Warfare and the Decline of Human Decisionmaking', *Parameters*, 31/4 (Winter 2001–2), pp. 57–71.

Al Marashi, Ibrahim, 'Iraq's Hostage Crisis: Kidnappings, Mass Media and the Iraqi Insurgency', *The Middle East Review of International Affairs*, 8/4 (Dec. 2004), pp. 1–13.

Ancker, Col. Clinton (rctd), and Lt.-Col. Michael Burke (retd), 'Doctrine for Asymmetric Warfare', *Military Review*, 83/4 (July–Aug. 2003), pp. 18–25.

Annati, Massimo, 'Mine Hunting and Mine Clearance Revisited', *Military Technology*, 8–9 (Aug.–Sept. 2003), pp. 48–58.

Arkin, William, 'Smart Bombs, Dumb Targeting?', *The Bulletin of Atomic Scientists*, 56 (May/June 2000), pp. 46–53.

Arquilla, John, and David Ronfeldt, 'Cyber War is Coming!', *Comparative Strategy*, 12 (1993), pp. 141–65.

Avant, Deborah, 'Are the Reluctant Warriors Out of Control?: Why the US Military is Averse to Responding to Post-Cold War Low-Level Threats', *Security Studies*, 6/2 (Winter 1996/7), pp. 51–90.

Babcock, John, 'Just Mines Please!', *Proceedings*, 131/7 (July 2005), pp. 47–9.

Band, Adm. Jonathan, 'Maritime Security and the Terrorist Threat', *RUSI Journal*, 147/6 (Dec. 2002), pp. 26–32.

Bellamy, Christopher, 'The Shifted Conflict Paradigm and Reduced Role of Conventional Military Power', *Cambridge Review of International Affairs*, 15/1 (Apr. 2002), pp. 147–58.

Blank, Stephen, 'Rethinking the Concept of Asymmetric Threats in US Strategy', *Comparative Strategy*, 23/4–5 (Oct.–Dec. 2004), pp. 343–67.

Bowen, Wyn, 'Deterrence and Asymmetry: Non-State Actors and Mass Casualty Terrorism', *Contemporary Security Policy*, 25/1 (Apr. 2004), pp. 54–70.

Brown, Nick, 'Not Just a Remote Possibility: USVs Enter the Fray', *Jane's Navy International*, 109/1 (Jan.–Feb. 2004), pp. 14–19.

Brown, Nick, 'Sails of the Unexpected – UK Trains for Asymmetric Threat', *Jane's Navy International*, 110/10 (Dec. 2005), pp. 20–4.

Brownlee, Les, and Peter Schoomaker, 'Serving a Nation at War: A Campaign Quality Army with Joint Expeditionary Capabilities', *Parameters*, 34/2 (Summer 2004), pp. 4–23.

Buzan, Barry, and George Segal, 'The Rise of "Lite" Powers', *World Policy Journal*, 13/2 (Fall 1996), pp. 1–10.

Byford, Grenville, 'The Wrong War', *Foreign Affairs*, 81/4 (July–Aug. 2002), pp. 34–43.

Byman, Daniel, and Matthew Waxman, 'Kosovo and the Great Air Power Debate', *International Security*, 24/4 (Spring 2000), pp. 5–38.

Carter, Ashton, 'How to Counter WMD', *Foreign Affairs*, 83/5 (Sept.–Oct. 2004), pp. 72–85.

Cassidy, Robert, 'Back to the Street without Joy: Counterinsurgency Lessons from Vietnam and Other Small Wars', *Parameters*, 34/2 (Summer 2004), pp. 73–83.

Cassman, Joel, and David Lai, 'Football vs Soccer: American Warfare in an Era of Unconventional Threats', *Armed Forces Journal*, Nov. 2003, pp. 49–54.

Chyba, Christopher, 'Toward Biological Security', *Foreign Affairs*, 81/3 (May–June 2002), pp. 122–36.

Cohen, Eliot, 'The Mystique of US Air Power', *Foreign Affairs*, 73/1 (1994), pp. 109–24.

Cohen, Eliot, 'A Revolution in Warfare', *Foreign Affairs*, 75/2 (Mar.–Apr. 1996), pp. 37–54.

Cohen, Eliot, 'History and the Hyperpower', *Foreign Affairs*, 83/4 (July–Aug. 2004), pp. 49–63.

Cohen, Eliot, 'Change and Transformation in Military Affairs', *Journal of Strategic Studies*, 27/3 (Sept. 2004), pp. 395–407.

Conway, Maura, 'Nitro to the Net', *The World Today*, Aug.–Sept. 2004, pp. 19–22.

Corless, Josh, 'Hunting Goliath in the Age of Asymmetric Warfare', *Jane's Navy International*, 104/10 (Dec. 1999), pp. 23–6.

Dauber, Cori, 'Image as Argument: The Impact of Mogadishu on US Military Intervention', *Armed Forces and Society*, 27/2 (Winter 2001), pp. 205–99.

David, G. John, 'Facing a Future without Front Lines', *Proceedings*, 129/11 (Nov. 2003), pp. 36–8.

Deady, Timothy, 'Lessons from a Successful Counterinsurgency: The Philippines, 1899–1902', *Parameters*, 35/1 (Spring 2005), pp. 53–68.

Delpech, Thérèse, 'The Imbalance of Terror', *The Washington Quarterly*, 25/1 (Winter 2002), pp. 31–40.

Doran, Michael, 'Somebody Else's Civil War', *Foreign Affairs*, 81/1 (Jan.–Feb. 2002), pp. 22–42.

Downey, Frederick, and Steven Metz, 'The American Political Culture and Strategic Planning', *Parameters*, 18/3, Sept. 1988, pp. 33–43.

Fogleman, Ronald, 'Advantage USA: Air Power and Asymmetric Force Strategy', *Air Power History*, 42/2 (Summer 1996), pp. 4–13.

Foreman, Jonathan, 'The Casualty Myth', *National Review*, 3 May 1999, pp. 13–20.

Foxwell, David, 'Sub Proliferation Sends Navies Diving for Cover', *Jane's International Defence Review*, 30/8 (Aug. 1997), pp. 30–9.

Friedman, Norman, 'Littoral Anti-Submarine Warfare: Not as Easy as it Sounds', *International Defense Review*, 28/6 (June 1995), pp. 53–8.

Friedman, Norman, 'The Role of Aircraft Carriers: Naval War in a Land-Locked Country', *Naval Forces*, 22/2 (2002), pp. 8–10.

Fukuyama, Francis, 'The End of History', *National Interest*, Summer 1989, pp. 10–18.

Goulding, Vincent, 'Back to the Future with Asymmetric Warfare', *Parameters*, 30/4 (Winter 2000–1), pp. 21–30.

Gourley, Scott, 'Naval Force Protection in an Asymmetric World', *Jane's Navy International*, 107/6 (July–Aug. 2002), pp. 10–17.

Grange, David, 'Asymmetric Warfare: Old Method, New Concern', *National Strategy Forum Review*, Winter 2000, pp. 1–7.

Grau, Lester, 'Urban Combat: Confronting the Spectre', *Military Review*, 79/4 (July–Aug. 1999), pp. 9–15.

Gray, Colin, 'Combating Terrorism', *Parameters*, 23/3 (Autumn 1993), pp. 17–23.

Gray, Colin, 'Thinking Asymmetrically in Times of Terror', *Parameters*, 32/1 (Spring 2002), pp. 5–14.

Greco, Ettore, 'New Trends in Peacekeeping: The Experience of Operation Alba', *Security Dialogue*, 29/2 (June 1998), pp. 201–12.

Gunaratna, Rohan, 'An Examination of Al Qaeda and its Methods', *Intersec*, 15/3 (Mar. 2005), pp. 85–7.

Hammes, Col. Thomas, 'War Isn't a Rational Business', *Proceedings*, 124/7 (July 1998), pp. 22–5.

Hammes, Col. Thomas, 'War Evolves into the Fourth Generation', *Contemporary Security Policy*, 26/2 (Aug. 2005), pp. 189–221.

Hancock, John, and Robin Pettit, 'Global Positioning System – Our Achilles' Heel?', *Proceedings*, 128/1 (Jan. 2002), pp. 85–7.

Hendrickson, David, and Robert Tucker, 'Revisions in Need of Revising: What Went Wrong in the Iraq War', *Survival*, 47/2 (Summer 2005), pp. 7–32.

Hewish, Mark, 'Wanted: A Quiet Walk on the Beach', *International Defense Review*, (Mar. 2003), pp. 70–8.

Hills, Alice, 'Can We Fight in Cities?', *RUSI Journal*, 146/5 (Oct. 2001), pp. 6–10.

Hirsch, Gal, 'On Dinosaurs and Hornets – A Critical View on Operational Moulds in Asymmetric Conflict', *RUSI Journal*, 148/4 (Aug. 2003), pp. 60–3.

Hoffman, Bruce, 'Rethinking Terrorism and Counterterrorism since 9/11', *Studies in Conflict and Terrorism*, 25/5 (Sept.–Oct. 2002), pp. 303–16.

Hoffman, Bruce, 'The Changing Face of Al Qaeda and the Global War on Terrorism', *Studies in Conflict and Terrorism*, 27/6 (Nov.–Dec. 2004), pp. 549–60.

Hoffman, Bruce, 'A Nasty Business', *Atlantic Monthly*, 289/1 (Jan. 2002), pp. 32–40.

Hoffman, Frank, 'Small Wars Revisited: The United States and Non-Traditional Wars', *Journal of Strategic Studies*, 28/6 (Dec. 2005), pp. 913–40.

Hooker, Richard, 'The Mythology Surrounding Manoeuvre Warfare', *Parameters*, 23/1 (Spring 1993), pp. 27–38.

Hunter, Jamie, 'Making the Tough Tougher', *Jane's Defence Weekly*, 41/17 (28 Apr. 2004), pp. 25–9.

Huntiller, Mark, 'Asymmetric Warfare – Armour', *Armada International*, 6 (Dec.–Jan. 2005), pp. 38–43.

Johnston, Paul, 'Doctrine Is Not Enough: The Effect of Doctrine on the Behaviour of Armies', *Parameters*, 30/3 (Autumn 2000), pp. 30–9.

Kamien, David, 'What Keeps Port Security Directors Up at Night', *Homeland Security*, 1/1 (Jan. 2004), pp. 10–15.

Kaplan, Robert, 'The Coming Anarchy', *Atlantic Monthly*, 273/2 (Feb. 1994), pp. 44–76.

Kaplan, Robert, 'How We Would Fight China', *Atlantic Monthly*, 295/5 (June 2005), pp. 28–35.

Katzman, Kenneth, 'Al Qaeda Threat Retains its Potency under Pressure', *RUSI/Jane's Homeland Security and Resilience Monitor*, 3/10 (Dec.–Jan. 2005), pp. 4–7.

Kimura, Eric, 'A Gunboat Navy for the 21st Century', *Proceedings*, 131/7 (July 2005), pp. 44–6.

Krauss, Eric, and Mike Lacey, 'Utilitarian vs. Humanitarian: The Battle Over the Law of War', *Parameters*, 32/2 (Summer 2002), pp. 73–85.

Kutler, Glenn, 'US Military Fatalities in Iraq: A Two-Year Retrospective', *Orbis*, 49/3 (Summer 2005), pp. 529–44.

Lambeth, Benjamin, 'Lessons from the Kosovo War', *Joint Force Quarterly*, 28 (Spring 2002), pp. 12–19.

Landauer, Martin, 'The Threat from MANPADS', *RUSI/Jane's Homeland Security and Resilience Monitor*, 2/7 (Oct. 2003), pp. 12–17.

Libicki, Martin, 'Rethinking War: The Mouse's New Roar?', *Foreign Policy*, 117 (Winter 1999), pp. 30–43.

Lind, William, 'Understanding Fourth Generation Warfare', *Military Review*, 84/5 (Sept.–Oct. 2004), pp. 12–16.

Lind, Col. William, Keith Nightengale, Capt. John Schmitt, Col. Joseph Sutton, and Lt. Col. Gary Wilson, 'The Changing Face of Warfare: Into the Fourth Generation', *Marine Corps Gazette*, Oct. 1989, pp. 22–6.

Loeppky, Rodney, ' "Biomania" and US Foreign Policy', *Millennium*, 34/1 (2005), pp. 85–113.

Loren, Donald, 'Close-in Naval Dominance', *Armed Forces Journal*, Sept. 2003, pp. 36–42.

Luttwak, Edward, 'A Post-Heroic Military Policy: The New Season of Bellicosity', *Foreign Affairs*, 75/4 (July–Aug. 1996), pp. 33–44.

MacGregor, Douglas, 'XVIII Airborne Corps: Spearhead of Military Transformation', *Defense Horizons*, 37 (Jan. 2004), pp. 1–6.

Mahnken, Thomas, and James Fitzsimonds, 'Tread-Heads or Technophiles? Army Officer Attitudes Toward Transformation', *Parameters*, 34/2 (Summer 2004), pp. 57–72.

Mandel, Robert, 'The Wartime Utility of Precision Versus Brute Force in Weaponry', *Armed Forces and Society*, 30/2 (Winter 2004), pp. 171–201.

Manningham-Buller, Eliza, 'Countering Terrorism', *RUSI Journal*, 148/4 (Aug. 2003), pp. 8–12.

Mawson, James, 'Waging War on Terror Funds', *RUSI/Jane's Homeland Security and Resilience Monitor*, 4/7 (Sept. 2004), pp. 12–15.

McGinty, Michael, 'That was the War that Was: International Law, Pre-emption, and the Invasion of Iraq', *RUSI Journal*, 148/3 (June 2003), pp. 20–6.

McInnes, Colin, 'Fatal Attraction? Air Power and the West', *Contemporary Security Policy*, 22/3 (Dec. 2001), pp. 28–51.

Meigs, Montgomery, 'Unorthodox Thoughts about Asymmetric Warfare', *Parameters*, 33/2 (Summer 2003), pp. 4–18.

Metz, Steven, 'Strategic Asymmetry', *Military Review*, 81/4 (July–Aug. 2001), pp. 22–31.

Nabati, Mikael, 'Anticipatory Self-Defense: The Terrorism Exception', *Current History*, 102/664 (May 2003), pp. 222–32.

O'Brien, Kevin, and Joseph Nusbaum, 'Intelligence Gathering on Asymmetric Threats – Part One', *Jane's Intelligence Review*, 12/10 (Oct. 2000), pp. 50–5.

O'Brien, Kevin, and Joseph Nusbaum, 'Intelligence Gathering on Asymmetric Threats – Part Two', *Jane's Intelligence Review*, 12/11 (Nov. 2000), pp. 45–50.

Ostfield, Marc, 'Bioterrorism as a Foreign Policy Issue', *SAIS Review*, 24/1 (2002), pp. 63–98.

Page, Lewis, 'Wasted Warships', *Prospect*, Feb. 2004, pp. 22–9.

Parachini, John, 'Putting WMD Terrorism into Perspective', *The Washington Quarterly*, 26/4 (Autumn 2002), pp. 37–50.

Parsons, David, 'British Air Control', *Aerospace Power Journal*, 8/2 (Summer 1994), pp. 28–39.

Partridge, Ira, 'Deployable versus Survivable', *Armor*, Mar.–Apr. 2001, pp. 12–14.

Pengelley, Rupert, 'The Call for Fire Returns', *Jane's Navy International*, 110/2 (Mar. 2005), pp. 18–23.

Pengelley, Rupert, and Richard Scott, 'Lower Frequencies Ping the Littoral ASW Threat', *Jane's Navy International*, 109/9 (Nov. 2004), pp. 31–7.

Peters, Ralph, 'Our Soldiers, their Cities', *Parameters*, 26/1 (Spring 1996), pp. 43–50.

Peters, Ralph, 'In Praise of Attrition', *Parameters*, 34/2 (Summer 2004), pp. 24–32.

Pilloni, John, 'Burning Corpses in the Street: Russia's Doctrinal Flaws in the 1995 Fight for Grozny', *Journal of Slavic Military Studies*, 13/2 (June 2000), pp. 39–66.

Posen, Barry, 'The War for Kosovo: Serbia's Political-Military Strategy', *International Security*, 24/4 (Spring 2000), pp. 39–84.

Preston, Antony, 'Submarine Technology: Evolution not Revolution', *Maritime Defence*, 22/2 (Mar. 1997), pp. 26–30.

Raevsky, Andrei, 'Russian Military Performance in Chechnya', *Journal of Slavic Military Studies*, 8/4 (Dec. 1995), pp. 675–89.

Rammell, Bill, 'The Financial War Against Terrorism: The Contribution of Islamic Banking', *RUSI Journal*, 148/3 (June 2003), pp. 72–5.

Rathmell, Andrew, 'Information Operations: Coming of Age?', *Jane's Intelligence Review*, 12/5 (May 2000), pp. 52–5.

Record, Jeffrey, 'Ready for What and Modernized against Whom? A Strategic Perspective on Readiness and Modernization', *Parameters*, 25/3 (Autumn 1995), pp. 20–30.

Record, Jeffrey, 'Force-Protection Fetishism: Sources, Consequences, and (?) Solutions', *Aerospace Power Journal*, 14/2 (Summer 2000), pp. 30–7.

Record, Jeffrey, 'Collapsed Countries, Casualty Dread, and the New American Way of War', *Parameters*, 32/2 (Summer 2002), pp. 4–23.

Rosenthal, Joel, 'New Rules for War', *Naval War College Review*, 57/3–4 (Summer–Autumn 2004), pp. 91–102.

Rumsfeld, Donald, 'Transforming the Military', *Foreign Affairs*, 81/3 (May–June 2002), pp. 20–32.

Scales, Robert, 'Culture-Centric Warfare', *Proceedings*, 130/10 (Oct. 2004), pp. 32–7.

Schaper, Annette, 'Dirty Weapons', *The World Today*, Jan. 2002, pp. 18–20.

Scott, Richard, 'Lightweight Torpedoes Take a Shallow Dive', *Jane's Navy International*, 109/5 (June 2004), pp. 27–32.

Scott, Richard, 'Heavyweight Contenders Shape up for the Littoral', *Jane's Navy International*, 110/5 (June 2005), pp. 12–19.

Scott, Richard, 'Anti-Ship Weapons Updated to Target the Shore', *Jane's Navy International*, 110/6 (July–Aug. 2005), pp. 20–6.

Scott, Richard, 'Close-In Firepower Aims at Asymmetric Threats', *Jane's Navy International*, 110/7 (Sept. 2005), pp. 16–29.

Seaquist, Larry, 'Community War', *Proceedings*, 126/8 (Aug. 2000), pp. 56–9.

Simmons, Dean, 'Air Operations over Bosnia', *Proceedings*, 123/5 (May 1997), pp. 58–63.

Skelton, Ike, 'America's Frontier Wars; Lessons for Asymmetric Conflict', *Military Review*, 81/5 (Sept.–Oct. 2001), pp. 22–7.

Slocombe, Walter, 'Force, Pre-emption and Legitimacy', *Survival*, 45/1 (Spring 2003), pp. 117–30.

Solomon, Jonathan, 'Lethal in the Littoral: A Smaller, Meaner LCS', *Proceedings*, 130/1 (Jan. 2004), pp. 36–9.

Spinzak, Ehud, 'The Great Superterrorism Scare', *Foreign Policy*, 112 (Fall 1998), pp. 110–24.

Steinberg, James, 'Preventive Force in US National Security Strategy', *Survival*, 47/4 (Winter 2005–6), pp. 55–72.

Swetman, Bill, 'High Tech and Low Cunning', *Jane's International Defence Review*, 36 (Mar. 2003), pp. 79–83.

Sullivan, Gen. Gordon, and Lt. Col. A. Twomey, 'The Challenges of Peace', *Parameters*, 24/3 (Autumn 1994), pp. 4–17.

Tatham, Steve, 'Al Jazeera: Get Used To It, It's Not Going Away', *Proceedings*, 131/8 (Aug. 2005), pp. 28–32.

Thalassocrates, Alcibiades, 'Anti-ship Missile Tactics for Littoral Warfare Scenarios', *Military Technology*, 27/9 (Sept. 2003), pp. 91–6.

Thomas, Timothy, 'The Caucasus Conflict and Russian Security: The Russian Armed Forces Confront Chechnya III. The Battle for Grozny, 1–26 January 1995', *Journal of Slavic Military Studies*, 10/1 (Mar. 1997), pp. 50–108.

Thomas, Timothy, 'NATO and the Current Myth of Information Superiority', *Parameters*, 30/1 (Spring 2000), pp. 13–29.

Truver, Scott, 'US Navy in Review', *Proceedings*, 130/5 (May 2004), pp. 80–90.

Truver, Scott, 'Transformation: A Bridge Too Far?', *Jane's Navy International*, 110/2 (Mar. 2005), pp. 24–31.

Tucker, Jonathan, 'Asymmetric Warfare', *Forum* (Summer 1999), pp. 32–8.

Van Dyke, Carl, 'Kabul to Grozny: A Critique of Soviet (Russian) Counter-Insurgency Doctrine', *Journal of Slavic Military Studies*, 9/4 (Dec. 1996), pp. 689–705.

Vego, Milan, 'Future MCM Systems: Organic or Dedicated, Manned or Unmanned?', *Naval Forces*, 26/4 (2005), pp. 8–18.

Vest, Jason, 'Fourth-Generation Warfare', *Atlantic Monthly*, 288/5 (Dec. 2001), pp. 48–50.

Whitman, Jim, 'Humanitarian Intervention in an Era of Pre-Emptive Self-Defence', *Security Dialogue*, 36/3 (Sept. 2005), pp. 259–74.

Wilson, Peter, John Gordon, and David Johnson, 'An Alternative Future Force: Building a Better Army', *Parameters*, 33/4 (Winter 2003–4), pp. 19–38.

INDEX